LAND OF THE LONG DAY

LAND OF THE LONG DAY

DOUG WILKINSON

CLARKE, IRWIN & COMPANY LIMITED

Toronto, Vancouver

LAND OF THE LONG DAY

GLOSSARY

(of Eskimo terms used in this book)

Aglos: Openings under the snow in which young seals are raised. Also breathing holes of seals.

Aluk: Dish to be eaten with a spoon. Also a special dish made of caribou fat.

Angakok: Eskimo wizard.

Avatuk: Sealskin float.

Igloo: Eskimo house.

Iglooviuk: Snow house.

Ilningwah: In the likeness of a son.

Inoongwah: In the likeness of the Eskimo.

Iyonamut: It can't be helped.

Kingmik: Dog; Eskimo name for Doug Wilkinson.

Kudlik: Seal-oil lamp and stove.

-miut: People of—, e.g. Aulatseevikmiut: People of Aulatseevik.

Muktuk: Thick outer skin of the narwhal.

Nanook: Polar bear.

Netiak: Baby seal.

Netiavenik: That which was a baby seal before; a young seal that has lost its baby fur.

Nixee: A small gaff.

Ookeeakshuk: Eskimo season corresponding to our October and November.

Ootook: Seal asleep on the ice.

Teeguk: Old male seal.

2

CHAPTER
1

THE SMALL pup shivered violently and came awake to the bitter cold. Stiffly he clambered to his feet shaking the loose snow from his heavy, matted coat. This done he sat down and let his gaze wander over the sleeping camp. All was silent. From the vent holes of the little houses thin plumes of steam rose lazily straight up into the moonlit sky. The camp lay bathed in the cold clear light of the January moon, four little houses almost buried in deep drifts of wind-blown snow, facing out to the ice-covered bay, dwarfed by the immensity of the walls of snow-covered rock that rose steeply to the sky at their back.

Aulatseevik in mid-winter. Snow blanketed the land and sea, reflecting the light of the three-quarter moon as it climbed higher and higher in the afternoon sky. For two months the sun had been lost below the horizon to the south, its presence almost forgotten. The only sign that it still circled in the heavens was a slight lightening of the horizon to the south each day at noon, providing there were no clouds about. On overcast days there was no light at all; darkness hung over the land for time without end.

Under the light of the moon the land stood out sharp and clear. On the hills across the bay, light and shadow interplayed across the rugged terrain. To the right the dark mass of sheer rock cliffs rose up out of the flat white floor that was the surface of the sea, the face of the cliff broken here and there by long ghostly tendrils of glistening white, snow-filled crevices in the rock face. The snow on the sea ice sparkled with a fairy-like radiance as if sprinkled over with tiny pinpoints of light that danced and shifted in the still night air. The air itself was luminous; shafts of moonlight reflecting back from thousands of tiny ice crystals through the night.

On the gently shelving beach the houses no longer stood up on the rough gravel. Storms had swept snow out of the north, piling it against the houses until each one squatted deep in a bed of feathery white. The rough sod walls disappeared behind an exterior trim of white snow that reached up to and almost over the roof. On the front of each house the round porches, made of blocks of hard-packed snow, reflected the glow of light from the tiny windows set high in the front wall, four pinpricks of soft yellow flickering flame, ghost candles over the sea.

The pup saw nothing of this for he was cold and lonely. He lifted one paw clear of the snow and whimpered softly to himself. Then he tilted back his head and began to howl. He did not have much voice for he was still too young, but it was enough. The thin reedy sound caused other heads to rise from the snow, stronger voices to join in the chorus. Soon more than sixty heads were tilted back, sixty snouts pointed up to the impassive face of the moon, while from sixty throats poured the long-drawn howl of the Eskimo husky dog: "Ow-ow-oooooooooooooh, ow-ow-oooooooooooooh", the lament of the Arctic snows. The sound rose and fell, gained in crescendo, and then fell off only to swell in chorus again and again. Slowly it died, ending in a single long-drawn note. The camp was silent once more.

Inside the little house, lying on the sleeping platform snuggled into the warmth of my sleeping bag, I came slowly awake, for the sound of the dogs had penetrated the thick walls of sod and snow. I rolled over and let my gaze wander over the sleeping house, my Arctic home. The house was small, about twelve feet by nine feet, and a bare six feet from floor to peak. The walls were covered with pages from magazines, *Time* and *Saturday Night* mostly, stuck on with paste made from flour and water, spread with a ptarmigan's wing. In the corners of the house the paper was damp with frost and, along the bottom of the door, a thick wedge of ice had formed overnight sealing the door to its frame. The sleeping platform, raised about a foot above the level of the floor, covered the rear half of the house from wall to wall.

I lay on the extreme left side of the sleeping platform, head towards the front of the house. Immediately in front of me, on the platform along the side of the house, Leah slept soundly, invisible under a heavy quilt of patchwork design. To get away from the cold she had pulled the cover up over her head and slept peacefully, wrapped in a multi-coloured cocoon. To my right along the sleeping platform lay the other members of my family, Paneeluk beside me, then Mosesee, Pauloosee and Noahkudluk. Next came Idlouk and beside him against the far wall, Kidlak with her little daughter Ruthee snuggled tight to her breast.

Only I was awake. The others still slept, heads tucked under the robes of skin or the woollen blankets, their warm breath curling lazily up into the cold air. In front of Kidlak the seal-oil lamp that provided light and heat for our home was almost out, after having burned steadily throughout the night. Near the door was another lamp, smaller than the first; this one had long since been out, the wick of cotton grass now only a charred mass along the straight leading edge of the half-moon-shaped lamp.

At the far end of the sleeping platform, a figure stirred, reluctantly at first, for it was cosy and warm inside the robes. A brown arm pushed out into the frosty air, followed quickly by a head. Slanted brown eyes squinted and blinked sleepily in the yellow light. Another head appeared until only Leah slept on. Someone muttered, "Ikee, it is cold." Kidlak rose to her knees and, still wrapped in her fur robe, began patiently to build up the flame of the low-burning lamp.

Kidlak, my Eskimo mother; thirty-eight years of age, mother of nine children. Jet black hair pulled back tightly from a wide brow, slightly slanted brown eyes, high cheek bones and dark skin all combined to give her appearance

5

an Oriental cast. Here, you would say, was true Eskimo, descended in unbroken strain for the past ten thousand years, whose ancestors once roamed the Asiatic mainland before pushing westward into America, always keeping close by the edge of the Arctic sea. But you would be wrong. For Kidlak's grandfather was a white man, a crew member on a whaling ship that once prowled these far north waters.

By now Idlouk was fully awake and the children were starting to play, naked despite the chill. They would not dress until they had had a piece of bannock and a mug of steaming hot tea. Idlouk rolled and lit a cigarette. Slowly he drew in the smoke resting his chin on cupped hands.

The kettle boiled over the kudlik; Kidlak reached out and tossed in a handful of tea, and lined nine white enamel mugs in a row. The tea boiled for a few minutes making it strong and black, then it was poured into the waiting cups. It was hot, far too hot; Mosesee scrambled over to the ice bucket and dropped a small sliver of ice in each mug. There was no sugar or milk; milk was never put in tea, and we had been out of sugar for two weeks past and would be until Kadluk went in to the store next week to trade. Kidlak cut up a thin bannock and passed a piece to each one of us, even little Ruthee, the smallest of the children at one year old, getting her share. Silence descended on the house as we ate the bannock and sipped the tea.

One by one, we dressed in leisurely fashion while sitting in the sleeping bags and robes. My clothes were much the same as I would put on for a winter's day in southern Canada; heavy underwear, shirt and trousers. But my footwear was quite different. First I donned a pair of long caribou skin stockings that reached well above my knees. The fur on these stockings was short and turned inside next to my skin. Over these went another pair of stockings, with the fur on the outside, reaching to just below the knee. A woven tie pulled tight held them in place. On my feet went slippers of sealskin on the bottom of which had been sewn extra soles made of the heavy skin of a polar bear.

6

I would need all this footwear for today Idlouk and I were going off on a hunting trip over the ice of Eclipse Sound. We expected to be gone for five days, hunting seals at new cracks in the ice, travelling about a hundred miles over the sea. We would travel largely by the light of the moon, hoping no clouds came our way. If all went well we would return with fresh seal meat and fat for the camp, and perhaps a fine sealskin or two.

While we dressed, Kidlak put fish on to boil, two Arctic char each about ten pounds in weight, brought into the house the night before to thaw. Cut into sections, they were put in a pot to boil on the kerosene-burning primus stove. Idlouk and I would be leaving shortly and the kudlik would be too slow to boil fish. This was too bad for there is nothing so tasty as a fine fish boiled over the gentle flame of the seal-oil lamp. In the old days time would not have mattered, for what was a day or so as long as you were well fed. But today, time means money, and money the Eskimo must have.

By then Leah was up and dressed. She brought our outer clothes in from the snow porch. The outer clothes were made of caribou skins, three garments in all: inner parka with fur on the inside, outer parka with fur on the outside, and trousers that reached just below the knee. The fur on my parka hood was matted with frost, for yesterday Idlouk and I had been for eighteen hours on a circuit of the traps set close by the camp. Leah beat the frost and ice from the hood with a heavy wooden stick especially made for this purpose. She then put the parkas on a cross slat near the ceiling of the house so that the fur would dry before we left. There is nothing worse than wet fur on your face when the temperature is at thirty or forty below.

While the fish boiled, Idlouk and I put on our duffel cloth parkas and went outside to harness the dogs and load the sleigh. Idlouk has three sleds, the largest over twenty feet long, costing over one hundred dollars to build. Each runner is a single plank of oak, two inches thick and ten inches high, tapering slightly upward at each end, rising

7

to a high point in front. Between the runners cross slats of hardwood are lashed by sealskin thongs. Lashing instead of nailing makes the sled loose so that it can "work" when going through rough ice, thus taking the hard going with a minimum of strain. Sealskin lashings are better than white man's cord bought from the store, but if the dogs are hungry they will eat them. On one of our hunting trips we awoke one morning to find the sled reduced to scattered pieces of wood lying in disarray on the snow. The dogs had eaten all the lashings in the night.

For our trip we took the smallest of Idlouk's sleds. The ten-foot long runners were shod with strips of heavy whalebone worn smooth with constant use. The whalebone had belonged to Idlouk's father and to his father before him, passed on from father to son. In the extreme cold of the Arctic winter these runners would drag heavily, as if the sled were running over sand instead of snow. They must be coated with a thin film of ice that would provide an almost frictionless surface to the snow. Dipping a small piece of bearskin into a tin of warm water, Idlouk painted each runner with layers of quick-freezing water. In the cold weather of January and February this coating of ice lasts all day, but in the spring it soon wears off and has to be renewed every four hours. The driver must protect the ice coating from rocks or gravel that would soon scrape it off; from warm dog droppings that, if run over, would stick to the ice causing the runners to drag; from slamming the sled into rough broken ice that would crack the thin film and cause it to fall off. Sometimes the Eskimos pack a heavy layer of water-soaked snow on the runner before putting on the smooth ice finish; this lasts longer than the layer of ice itself. Or they will paint the runner with the blood of a newly killed ptarmigan or rabbit and then add the ice surface on top.

If the sleds have no whalebone runners, a shoeing of frozen "mud" is built up along the length of the wood. This "mud" is really decomposed vegetable matter gathered in certain locations in the fall before the ground freezes.

8

It is kept in the house and, mixed with water, applied to the runners while warm, moulded into a shoeing about one inch thick. Trimmed smooth with a carpenter's plane, it can be coated with a film of ice in the same manner as the whalebone runner. It must be treated with great care; heavy blows of the sled pounding on rough ice will crack it off. On mild days "mud" is useless as it melts and drags on the snow. On trips overland when "mud" runners damage easily, many items can be used for patching, flour and water or rolled oats and water being two of the most commonly used.

On our hunting trip we took twelve dogs and three pups. The pups were too small to pull with the team, but they ran with their mothers, learning the life that faced them in their far north land. While Idlouk iced the runners, I carried the traces down to the edge of the sea ice, calling the dogs to me as I went.

"Huh, huh, huh, huh, huh, huh, huh, Nikpee, Magneeah, huh, huh, huh."

Reluctantly the dogs rose to their feet, shaking snow from matted coats. Slowly they gathered around Nikpee, the leader, then with a few snarls and woofs, but never a bark, all ran down the beach to where I stood. They milled about, playfully nipping at the fur of my mitts, or pressing wet muzzles against my leg, eager for a pat on the head.

"Woah, woah, woah, Nikpee, woah, woah, oonah pate-eoaluk,* woah, woah."

I scolded them softly and they began to lie down. Each harness, made of sealskin strips sewn with narwhal sinew thread, had the name of the dog to whom it belonged printed in syllabic character writing on the short strap across the back. This was not much use in winter, even in the light of the brilliant moon, but long practice had made me familiar with every dog and its gear. In fifteen minutes all the dogs were harnessed and the traces cleared to the sled. The sled, loaded with the usual minimum of gear, stood ready to depart.

* You are a bad one.

In the house the fish had boiled and the pot had been swung over the soft flame of the seal-oil lamp to keep it warm. The boiled fish was delicious; I ate three big sections, two pounds of fish, topped by a mug of strong black tea. I ate with my fingers, picking the fish out of the pot. In this way there were no dishes to wash, a necessary consideration when all the water must be obtained from ice melted down over the seal-oil lamps. Breakfast over, Idlouk and I donned our outer caribou skin clothes. The bulkiness of the thick fur transformed me into a huge bear-like figure, but the appearance of weight was deceptive; the clothes were as light as down.

In the clear night air outside we felt little of the cold; only nose and chin reacted to the touch of frost, all else was buried deep under snug warm skins. At my call the dogs jumped to their feet, anxious to be off. A last-minute check to see that all harnesses were straight and Idlouk gave a soft command. The dogs flung themselves forward, jerking the sled free from the grip of the frosty snow. We jumped aboard as it shot by, bumping and crashing through the rough tidal zone ice. We were on our way. It was a little past eight in the evening as we pulled out of camp, but time of day meant little when it was dark the clock around. In the long night of winter, as during the long day of summer, we disregarded the clock, eating when hungry, gong to bed when we needed rest. For two months we had paid little attention to the correct time of day.

Travelling through the rough broken ice Idlouk and I had no time for anything but work. The sled jumped this way and that, often it overturned spilling the load over the ice. Dogs became tangled in the traces or jammed under pieces of ice; toggles clacked, traces snapped; on more than one occasion the main trace broke when hooked under a hummock, releasing the dogs who promptly disappeared into the darkness. With great difficulty we rounded them up. Often I walked ahead of the team carrying the small kerosene lantern trying to pick out the best path through particularly bad ice. At such times, progress was slow and our patience sorely tried, particularly as we knew that not far away there was probably a good route through; but how to find the clear paths in the pitch darkness was a problem we did not solve. A few times we accidentally stumbled on a good route, but usually we manhandled the bucking sled, shouting encouragement to the straining dogs, thankful when we broke clear of the rough going onto smooth ice once more.

Sitting on the sled as it moved swiftly over the flat expanse, Idlouk and I relaxed and talked about many things. Idlouk had never seen anything but pictures of southern Canada, although two of his daughters had been there and one to England as well, and he knew very little about the lands so far to the south. He listened amazed as I told him about our cities and towns, about the people in such places, how they lived and how they worked. I told him of the ways in which the great quantities of food necessary to feed so many people were sown and harvested, moved across country to the people in the cities who grew no food of their own; about the long freight trains that rode over the prairie hour after hour, carrying wheat from which the flour he used in his bannock was made; of the great herds of cattle that roamed the western plains, supplying meat for much of the land's population.

He was interested in the huge bridges that spanned our rivers and streams; the Lion's Gate at Vancouver, the Quebec at Levis. He asked about the tall buildings that rose up into the sky and he was unable to understand fully how water flowed from taps at such a height above ground. My stories of automobiles carrying my wife and me on trips of four and five hundred miles in one day, of planes that travelled beyond the speed of sound, made him shake his head in bewilderment; and small wonder when we moved so slowly over the snow.

Although Idlouk was fascinated by the technology of my world, he was more deeply interested in the people and the ways in which they lived. When I spoke of the cities with their innumerable houses set row on row, with their apart-

11

ments and tenements and housing projects, he shook his head slowly; he could not understand how people lived under such conditions. One evening he asked me to explain what the lists of population tables in my pocket dictionary were and I tried to give a concept of what the figures meant, to this man who in his youth had had no use for any quantity above fifty and rarely beyond twenty-five. I noted on a small piece of paper the number of people at Aulatseevik and beneath this the population listed for a number of places in Canada and the U.S.A.,* a series of notations that ran like this:

Aulatseevik	31
Ottawa	154,951
Toronto	667,457
Montreal	903,007
New York	7,454,995
Canada	14,000,000
U.S.A.	131,669,275

As the length of the figures grew so did Idlouk's amazement. The number for Aulatseevik seemed to shrink and shrink in the face of the massive figures listed for the cities and countries to the south. I told him that of the 7,454,995 people of New York city, 1,888,924 lived on one island not much bigger than the island of Aulatseevik on which his camp was situated. He shook his head, closed the book and put the list of figures inside. His mind could not accept the fact that so many people could live and work in such a confined space. As we travelled along on the sled under the broad sweep of the star-filled sky, he said, "Since you told me of all those people living on one small island I have not slept well at night. I awaken thinking about the men and women and children all crammed into such a small space, pushing and shoving, fighting for air to breathe. I see people stacked up one atop the other and I become one of them striving to climb upward to reach open air. I awake in a sweat, light a cigarette, and for a long time I cannot sleep.

* 1951.

I lie there thinking of what life must be like for all those poor people in New York."

"When I am in my house," he continued, "I am happy for a while for it is warm and there is always food. But after a few days I grow tired of the house; I grow tired of many people* so close to me. I want to get away, off on the hunt, out into the open spaces of the ice-covered sea where I can look out and see no other soul. Then I breathe deeply; I am happy; I feel like a man again. A few days on the trail and I am ready to return to my camp. I am glad to be back with my family, in the warmth and comfort of my house. For a few days I like my home, but I get restless again and I must go off on the hunt or a visit to the traps. How people in your land can live day after day, month after month, year after year in the same house and not go off to hunt I do not know. I could not do it. I would like to see our land, but I could never live there. For I like the sky over my head and the feel of the snow-covered ice beneath my feet. I like to look about and feel myself free."

Idlouk could understand the life of the people who lived on the farms and in the small villages, or the fisherfolk on the coasts of the sea. He sensed that the same elements he knew were present in their life; the sky, the sea, the broad sweep of land uncluttered by man, the slower tempo of life, the close association with sources of food. Huge numbers of fish in a seine or freezers full of beef amazed but did not bother him for he understood such things. Man must have food and the more men, the more food. But to tales of life in the cities he could not listen long without becoming restless. His mind found it difficult to envisage a life in which there was so little contact with the vital problem of gathering or reaping food. As an Eskimo this was his sole reason for existence on earth. He lived to eat and all his energies were poured into this one channel.

Our conversation was abruptly interrupted; the dogs

* Aulatseevik, population thirty-one!

suddenly started to sprint over the ice. They had caught the smell of an aglo up ahead. Idlouk peered at the snow as we dashed along while I pulled the harpoon free of the lashings and reached for the harpoon line kept in readiness in the box at the rear. As quickly as they had started the dogs stopped and milled about on the snow. Idlouk dashed forward and chased them on. Bending low over the ice, he pricked a tiny hole in the hard surface of the snow. In a few seconds he straightened and said, "Here is a fine aglo, Kingmik. Wait by it; I will take the dogs on."

I dropped from the sled and took up position on the snow. Hurriedly I scraped the crunchy crystals of loose snow from beneath my feet and stood motionless bent over from the waist, harpoon resting lightly across my knees. At my feet only the tiny cut on the snow marked the aglo. The dogs had smelled it, otherwise we would never have known it was there.

Alone in the night I crouched; waiting over invisible seal holes seemed to have become an integral part of my life. Somewhere out in the darkness the dogs were resting and Idlouk was running in a wide circle over the ice. Five minutes passed into ten; ten into fifteen, and still I waited, motionless. Nothing moved, no sound broke the quiet of the night, not even the familiar low rustle of wind blowing snow over snow.

Swooooooooooooosh! My heart jumped into my mouth and I jerked upright so badly startled by the sudden sound that I nearly let out a cry. A seal had risen in the hole. Totally unconscious that I waited above, it had come up boldly and let out air in a long bubbling gasp. I could hear the seal plainly as it bobbed up and down in the hole at my feet, the water slip-slapping on the icy sides of the hole, the sound of each breath like the escape of a jet of steam.

Slowly my arm rose in the air, poised for a moment and then flashed straight down. Through the handle I felt the harpoon head bite deep, then all hell broke loose below. The handle was jerked roughly from my grasp, a tremendous splash sent water surging up through the snow. The sealskin line slackened and then suddenly pulled taut as the seal took off for the depths. I was jerked from my feet and almost lost my hold on the end of the line. Lying across the top of the hole, now clearly visible in the broken snow, I hung on for dear life as the seal dashed madly about.

The line went limp and I scrambled to my feet. Hand over hand I hauled in, trying to take slack as fast as the seal rose up from below. In a moment the big head broke surface and two beady brown eyes stared up into mine. I grabbed for the harpoon handle that had remained tied to the line and worked it free just before the seal submerged with a splash and was gone again. Jamming the harpoon into the snow I braced the line around it to take up the shock as the seal reached the limit of the line. The handle bent under the strain and I had to throw all my weight on the line, but the seal could not jerk free. The harpoon head was firmly set.

Once again the line went slack. This time I let it go limp, jumped to my feet and jerked the harpoon handle from the snow. Handle raised above my head I waited. The slush on the water stirred and the round head of the seal broke through. As it did my arm came down and the pointed steel shaft plunged into the brain. The seal went limp, bobbing gently up and down.

Twice more we hunted at aglos as we moved over the ice; twice more we got seals, though not so large as the first. Steering a course by the stars overhead we headed north by north-west until the dark shadow of high rock hills loomed in sharp silhouette against the star-studded sky. Low down on the black mass of the land, three tiny lights twinkled and danced as we approached, gradually resolving into the lights of three small houses set on the darkened shore. The dogs caught the scent of the camp and spurted ahead until the sled flew over the snow. Howls broke from their throats, answered by howls from up ahead. Through the rough shore ice we dashed and pulled to a stop on a windswept beach. Dark figures came from the houses, calling to see who had arrived, and in a moment we were shaking hands with the hunters of the camp known as Kownuk, good neighbours some forty miles from Aulatse-evik who would be our hosts for the night.

Five families made up the Kownukmiut camp. Their houses were unlike those at Aulatseevik being made of sealskins sewn together and stretched taut over wooden frames. The interior walls were papered with pages from magazines after the universal fashion of the land. In the largest of the houses lived an elderly couple; with them their daughter and her husband who had two small children of their own. The old lady was a likeable person, nimble tongued, quick to share in all humour of the camp life. Often I stayed in her house while on hunting trips in the winter, sleeping on the platform that was so short that a box had to be placed on the floor so that my long frame could stretch out while I was asleep. All winter she and I carried on a friendly feud, for early in my stay I had said that I thought highly of Noahkudluk, Idlouk's youngest son, but did not think much of Pauloosee, the next in line. Unknown to me, Pauloosee was the old lady's favourite for she had helped nurse him during an illness when he was a small boy.

Every time I visited the camp of the Kownukmiut, I went up to the door of her house and shouted that Kingmik had come to stay that night. Always the reply came back, "Take your sleeping bag elsewhere, Kingmik, for if you are such a poor judge of men that you prefer Noahkudluk to Pauloosee, I do not care to have you in my house even for one night."

I took my bag to the house next door. But when time came to retire, my sleeping bag would be unrolled on the platform of the old lady's house, the box on the floor for my head. "Come in, come in," she grumbled, "if you are going to stay in the camp for tonight, you had better sleep here where I can keep an eye on you. You may have fooled Idlouk into thinking you are a fine man, but you haven't fooled me."

As is still the practice with the old people of the

Tununermiut of north Baffin Island, the first child of the daughter had been given to the grandparents to raise as their own. The little four-year old boy, although living in the same house as his mother, was cared for by his grandmother. He slept beside her, she cut up his meat, made bannock for him. She wiped his nose and comforted him when he was troubled. Being a small boy he could not go far afield in the dark winter months, and spent long periods in the house in close contact with his grandmother. In so doing he unwittingly spent long periods in close contact with death.

For the old lady was gravely ill. Her face was seamed, her once robust frame so shrunk that she was little more than skin and bones. Only rarely did she stir from her position crouching behind the seal-oil lamp. Her body was racked by fits of coughing; in front of where she sat was an open tobacco tin into which she spat fluid brought from clogged lungs to her throat. Her tired body was slowly disintegrating under the ravages of tuberculosis.

How often I awakened in that little house on the shore of Eclipse Sound to hear the muffled, choking cough so near. With unseeing eyes I stared up into the darkness, wondering how the tired body retained the spark of life under such an attack. After each tremulous intake of air the coughing intensified, each breath became a labouring gasp as air was sucked in through the partially clogged throat until her whole body was doubled up in the effort to draw a single agonizing breath. Seconds passed as she gagged and gagged, struggling for air, drowning in the fluid that rose from her lungs. Often I have thought, "This is it, she is about to die." But the hoarse rattle of inflowing air broke the spell and the coughing shook her body again.

Slowly the choking cough subsided. Hunching forward, the old lady reached shakily for the tobacco tin near her head and expectorated from deep within her mouth. She sagged back onto the sleeping platform, strength gone, and drifted off into a troubled sleep. Beside her the little grandson slept on, unaware that he slept side by side with death.

I lay awake. Long ago I had lost my fear of contracting this disease. While I lived with the Eskimos I must live with it; I must eat bannock mixed by hands that wipe tubercular phlegm from mouth to chin; I must sleep face to face with mouths that cough the germs into the stifling air of the small crowded houses. I take what precautions I can and for the rest I say, "Iyonamut, it is something that cannot be helped." But what of the little boy, and his grandmother who carries death in her throat? Soon the old lady will die and be buried beneath the rocks on the hillside back of the camp. This will be good, for while she still lives she is a source of infection for all who come near. She is my friend, who has given me food and shelter on countless nights, has repaired boots and mitts torn on the hunt; but I wish she would die, for until she does no one with her is safe.

CHAPTER
2

WHY DO I go North? What is it that draws me to the vast, inhospitable land beyond the northerly limit of tree growth? Is it true that the Arctic has a fascination for certain people and that "there is no cure but to put them on ice"?

Until January of 1946, I had not seen the Arctic nor an Eskimo. My knowledge of both was extremely vague; I knew they existed, but little more. My first trip to the Arctic was not taken through any basic urge to go North; I went because of my interest in film.

Shortly after my discharge from the Canadian Army in the spring of 1945, I went to work for the National Film Board of Canada. Because of my Army experience I was asked to supervise the motion picture and still coverage of the joint Army-Air Force Exercise Musk Ox that saw ten snowmobiles and forty-seven men travel three thousand miles across the barren lands of Canada's Arctic. New Year's Eve of 1946 found me at Churchill, Manitoba, on the edge of the Arctic tundra. This was my first look at the Arctic, and I was impressed. I found it very stormy, very bleak, and very barren. I missed the comforting shelter of the trees. Although enjoying the experience of working in the Arctic for the first time I had no thoughts of repeating the venture.

However, in January of 1947, I returned to Churchill, this time to direct the footage for another film on the Arctic, GOING NORTH. On this trip I flew two hundred miles north of Churchill to the settlement of Eskimo Point on the west coast of Hudson Bay, in order to shoot scenes on the Eskimo for inclusion in the film. At Eskimo Point I met my first Eskimo.

After my plane landed on the sea ice in front of the settlement, I went directly to the Roman Catholic Mission at the invitation of the late Father Paul Dionne, who a year later disappeared without a trace while on a canoe trip on stormy Hudson Bay. As I was standing by the stove warming myself after the long cold plane ride, the outer door of the Mission opened and an Eskimo, clad from head to foot in clothing made of caribou skins, came quietly into the room. I could not see his face at first as the parka hood hid it from view. He walked to a bench set against the far wall and sat down. With a quick toss of his head he threw back the parka hood and smiled at me across the room.

I was too dumbfounded to smile in return. For he did not at all resemble my preconceived ideas of what an Eskimo should look like. Rather he resembled a tall tanned Scot; thin aesthetic features, blue eyes, strong mouth, small black moustache. He might have been the trader or the policeman but for his dress, his deep colour, and his jet black hair, cut bowl fashion. Son of a white father and an Eskimo mother, he was one of the best hunters and trappers in the district. With the other members of his group, he lived on the products of the hunt, eating the flesh and fat of the animals he killed, utilizing their skins for clothing.

Before I could recover from my surprise, he pulled a paper-wrapped parcel from under his parka and set it on the floor at his feet. He unwrapped the parcel to disclose a good-sized rump of raw caribou meat and, taking a small knife from an over-the-shoulder pouch, he settled down to eat. I watched, fascinated. There was a moment's pause for the selection of a cut, a few quick movements of the knife, and a large piece of meat was popped into his mouth. He rolled it around, then gave a blink and a tremendous swallow, and the meat slid reluctantly down his throat. This continued for perhaps five minutes during which time he must have consumed three pounds of meat. Then he returned the knife to the pouch, wrapped the remainder of the meat, and leaned back against the wall. He gave one tremendous belch and grinned at me once more.

How could this man and his brethren live in a land where the white man has so much difficulty in existing? Why did he choose to remain in the Arctic, living in much the same manner as his forefathers of five thousand years before? What was he thinking as he sat across the room from me, eyes slowly closing from the combined effects of food and heat? Ever since that day I have been searching for answers to these questions.

Until 1951 my interest was related directly to film. I was, and still am, to a certain extent, a film maker, and until 1951 the Eskimo presented a problem in film. Outside of Flaherty's famous NANOOK OF THE NORTH, no film on the Eskimos had attempted to be anything but a very superficial coverage of an interesting and remote primitive people.

Out of my preliminary research on the Eskimo came the two films, ANGOTEE—STORY OF AN ESKIMO BOY and LAND OF THE LONG DAY. My wife and I, with a young camera-man, Jean Roy, spent fifteen months in the Eastern Arctic gathering the footage from which these films were made. In that fifteen-month period I came to know individual Eskimos as friends and neighbours. For the first time I stopped thinking in terms of "Eskimos", and thought of my friends, Singeetuk, Aliuk, Idlouk and Kadluk.

In the fall of 1952, after returning from the North, I wrote a report outlining my observations on the Eskimos. I felt we were not helping the Eskimo to help himself, but rather letting him drift with the times; I felt, too, that our lack of initiative stemmed from the fact that we had all too little knowledge of the Eskimo himself, and his daily life on the land as it is lived today.

Before we could do much to help the Eskimo, we should have to know how much of his old culture still remained and what had happened to his personality as an Eskimo. The only way to do so was to go into the country and live in close contact with the Eskimos. My wife and I decided to go into the Arctic to set up a contributing family unit at an Eskimo camp. For at least a year we hoped to live at the camp with only the resources available to us that were available to the Eskimos. We wanted to become Eskimos, at least as much as it was possible for us to do so.

When I could not get support for this project from the responsible government department, I resigned from the staff of the National Film Board and sought financial assistance from private groups that would enable me to carry out such a plan. In the fall of 1952, the Arctic Institute of North America agreed to supply funds, the project to be carried out during the period February, 1953 to October, 1954. But it was not until April 5th of 1953 that I finally left for the Arctic, and I had to go alone. On March 23rd, my wife gave birth to a daughter under such circumstances as to rule out any possibility of her joining me in the country with the baby in the summer.

Although this change did affect some aspects of the project, the over-all idea remained the same. I would go North for the period of one year to live as an Eskimo with an Eskimo group. I would take only my rifle and ammunition, personal clothing, sleeping bag, and my small still camera and film. I had a reputation as a picture taker to play down so I planned to use the camera only rarely for the first few months, and thereafter only when necessary to record important aspects of the trip. I wanted the people with whom I would be living to have no doubts as to why I was in their country. I wanted to be accepted as an Eskimo.

Many people have asked why I chose the Pond Inlet area of north Baffin Island for my experiment. They felt that Pond Inlet was a "good" area in the Arctic, that few problems existed there in relation to the Eskimo, and that I would be far better off to go to one of the "problem areas" such as the Ungava region or along the south coast of Hudson Strait. To me this was entirely wrong. The Eskimo problem is universal; it is present wherever there are

22

Eskimos. I had been in the "problem area" of Chesterfield on the west coast of Hudson Bay while shooting the film ANGOTEE. It was here that I first made up my mind to go back to the Arctic. At Chesterfield I saw much of the demoralizing effect of close contact with the white man on the local Eskimo population. But it was not until I got to Pond Inlet that I began to discover something of how an Eskimo could live in his land.

At Pond Inlet lived Idlouk, the one Eskimo I have met who has come reasonably close to establishing a balance between the old way of life in his land and that thrust on him by the contact with the white. Here, in the success of this one man in adapting himself to the changing conditions, perhaps lay the key to the successful development of the Canadian Eskimo as an Arctic citizen. I wanted to find that key. Living in the Pond Inlet area with Idlouk as my teacher, I would be able to extract the maximum benefit from my Arctic schooling.

3

THE SETTLEMENT of Pond Inlet on north Baffin Island is a long way from Montreal. It is almost 2,000 miles due north of that city, the equivalent air distance between Montreal and Calgary, or Vancouver and Sault Ste. Marie. Although a great many airfields are scattered throughout the Arctic, the Pond Inlet area remains difficult of access to anything but charter air flights. The closest airstrips are at Resolute Bay on Cornwallis Island to the east and at Frobisher Bay on southern Baffin Island. Beyond either of these centres travel is by ski-equipped Norsemen or Dakota in the air, or by dog sled on the ground. As my grant from the Institute did not run to the charter of a plane for such a flight, I planned to go as far as I could by schedule and non-schedule planes, and the rest of the way by sled.

Logically it would seem that Resolute Bay, being only three hundred miles to the west of my destination, was the better jump-off point for the dog team trip. On the morning I left Montreal heading east for Goose Bay, a second aircraft was taking off heading west for Winnipeg and was then going north to Resolute Bay, reaching there in just two days. I was expecting to take six to reach Frobisher, counting stopovers on the way.

However, the three-hundred-mile distance between Resolute and Pond Inlet is not a good travel route. Few Eskimos know this region well, and the ice in Lancaster Sound, which would have to be crossed, is an unknown factor, changing in outline from year to year. Dog feed for such a trip would be a problem. For these reasons I elected to go by plane to Frobisher Bay on southern Baffin Island and from there up the east coast to Pond Inlet by sled. This coast is well known to the Eskimos, and arrangements had been made through the Hudson's Bay Company posts for Eskimo guides with dog teams for the three stages of the thousand mile trip. I expected to reach Frobisher Bay in six days, and Pond Inlet in six weeks, as long as no delays developed *en route*. Delays did develop, however, to an exasperating degree.

From Montreal to Goose Bay, Labrador, is normally a five-hour run for the schedule flight, but it took us three days to make the trip.* We had covered about two-thirds of the distance when an adverse weather report from Goose Bay forced the pilot to turn south and proceed to Moncton, New Brunswick, there to await clearing conditions to the north. The end of the first day found me, along with the other passengers, in a hotel in Moncton. The next day we remained there, for the weather showed no sign of improving. On the morning of the third day, the weather at Goose was reported to be favourable, but the airport at Moncton was buried deep in fog. It was not until noon that it cleared sufficiently for us to take off. Three hours later we arrived at Goose Bay, coming in through intermittent overcast, and landing in a light drizzle of warm rain.

At Goose Bay I ran into further delay. The flight north to Frobisher, scheduled to leave the following day, had been postponed for an indefinite period due to engine trouble in the ski-equipped Dakota that was to make the trip. By this time I was becoming settled into the routine of "get forward while you can, relax when you can't". In the Transient Officers' quarters at the air station, I settled down to polish off back correspondence, and relax. I had ample opportunity for both; it was not until five days later that the plane was able to make the flight.

* Today I would be able to purchase a ticket on a commercial airline for a direct three-times-a-week flight, Montreal to Frobisher Bay.

Despite the delay I was in excellent spirits, for the aircraft, when it did leave, was re-scheduled to make only a brief stop at Frobisher Bay, and then fly on farther north to the settlement of Clyde River on north Baffin Island. This would take me to within three hundred sled miles of my destination. As the delays encountered *en route*, plus the delay in getting started on my trip, had made it doubtful if I would be able to follow through with my plan of going north from Frobisher by sled before the spring thaw set in, this was a wonderful break.

However, my joy was short lived, and the trip very nearly came to an abrupt end on the airstrip at Frobisher Bay. We left Goose Bay early in the morning of April 14th. The weather report from Frobisher Bay was excellent: visibility twenty miles, ceiling 10,000 feet. But soon after passing the halfway point on the trip, we began to run into scattered storm clouds, and the weather reports, coming in from Frobisher to the plane in flight, told of similar conditions there. By the time we arrived over the airfield, coming in on the directional beam, it was ceiling zero, visibility zero. Passing over the station at about three hundred feet, we could barely make out the buildings through the driving snow and fog.

The pilot, Flying Officer Turtle, handled the situation with superb skill. Banking the plane steeply he made a tight turn to line up with the runway and keep it in sight. It kept appearing and disappearing through holes in the curtain of snow and fog. On the landing run we lost sight of it altogether for a minute and, when we broke clear, the plane was still some 200 feet up and directly over the approach end of the runway, when it should have been almost touching down. To continue on and come round again would have meant losing sight of the strip altogether and perhaps being unable to find it again. Flying Officer Turtle made a quick decision and dropped the plane straight down. It fell almost free for two hundred feet, then, with a stomach-sinking lurch, flattened out and touched down. We hit heavily, bounced into the air again, hit, bounced, hit and bounced again. Then the plane hit and held, and we rolled to a stop with only about fifty feet of runway to go. I sat quite still and offered up a silent prayer to God and to the skill of Flying Officer Turtle, in about equal proportion.

Snow fell at Frobisher for three straight days. In that short space of time, all my carefully laid plans disintegrated. So much snow fell that any chance I had of getting North by sled was ruled out. The going was so slow, and the spring season so far advanced that I would have been lucky to reach Pangnirtung, only 200 miles up the coast. The aircraft, after waiting two days for clear weather to the north, finally gave up and, taking advantage of a momentary break in the overcast, took off on the return flight to Goose Bay. The only bright spot in an otherwise dim picture was that the flight to Clyde would take place as soon as weather conditions improved.

I spent a month at Frobisher Bay. I did not enjoy the month at all, for I had to spend most of the time keeping one eye on the airstrip, and the other on the weather. Most flights in the Arctic are unscheduled, and in many cases take-off times and destinations are laid on very short notice, usually known only to the crew involved. Almost every day planes flew north, many of them passing directly over Clyde River, but as they were not ski-equipped, they could not land on the sea ice to the north. To see the planes heading north, knowing they were passing the very place I wanted to go and yet not be able to go with them, was discouraging. On one occasion an RCAF Lancaster from the Photographic Squadron at Rockcliffe arrived at Frobisher on a direct flight from Ottawa, spent the night there, flew a mission as far as Clyde, and on the following day returned to Ottawa, covering, in the short space of three days, ground it was to take me thirty-six days to cover.

All through April and early May, the weather at Frobisher was very mild. Snow fell often, always soft and wet. By the end of the third week in May, the runway was clear and the roadways at the base were deep in puddles of water. On the land the rocks were beginning to show through the snow cover, soaking up the heat from the high-climbing sun. On the sea the snow on the ice became soft and deep, and in many places huge puddles formed under the snow. Weather reports from other stations on Baffin all told the same story, even on north Baffin, where spring is usually a good month behind the areas farther south. The missionary from Pond Inlet, on his spring patrol to Clyde River, had had to cut his visit short and make a dash up the coast for home, reaching Pond with some difficulty because of deep soft snow and open cracks in the sea ice.

In the wake of this continuing warm weather came more discouraging news. Idlouk, the Eskimo with whom I was planning to live for the next year, had started out from his camp to come down the coast to Clyde River by sled so as to be there when I arrived and take me back to his camp. He sent word by wireless that he had been forced to turn back on his trip because of open water at Cape Bowen, one of the exposed points of land, just three days' journey out of Pond. It began to look as though even if I did manage to get as far as Clyde River, I still would not be able to get to my final destination until the boat came in the summer.

On May 6th, the aircraft returned to Frobisher, and I thought my long wait was at an end. But a scant three hours before the plane landed, a message came from the nurse at Cape Dorset. An Eskimo woman was extremely ill. She would have to be evacuated to hospital immediately.

The plane went off to Cape Dorset where it picked up the sick woman and, stopping at Frobisher only long enough to refuel, took her back to Goose Bay. With that I gave up all hope of getting to Clyde River, and began making plans to stay with an Eskimo family at Frobisher Bay until the boat came in August, and I could complete my trip. But on May 12th, the day dawned clear and cool, with not a cloud in the sky. A message came through that the plane was on its way once again. I was on the runway half an hour before it was due to arrive, sitting on my gear, anxiously scanning the sky to the south. About 11:30 a.m.

a small dot appeared in the sky quickly resolving into the form of the Dakota. A closer examination revealed that the plane still had the skis mounted. This meant it was going on to the North. Slowly the aircraft made a wide sweep over the field to line up with the runway. As the plane settled into the long glide for the strip the motors were suddenly gunned and it pulled clear, beginning to circle the airfield again. My heart sank. Something had obviously gone wrong.

After five minutes of circling, the plane lined up with the runway once more. This time it came on in, making a perfect landing in front of the hangar, the metal skis with wheels protruding through slots kissing the asphalt with a light hiss of scraping metal. Slowly the plane pulled up to the hangar, wheeled about and stopped, rocking gently. I waited, wondering what had happened to make them circle as they did. What was wrong? The gyro compass had gone out as the plane settled into the landing run. Would they go on North? No one knew. I would have to wait and see.

While the crew lunched at the base and tried to repair the compass, I sat at the plane and waited. In an hour they returned. The verdict: they were going North. The weather was perfect right up the coast and they would not need the gyro compass. We would take off for Clyde immediately. My long wait at Frobisher was over.

THE FLIGHT north was anticlimatic, a scenic cruise of interior Baffin Island by air. The country around Frobisher is rugged, low rocky hills deeply indented by parallel valleys running inland to the north-west. The tops of the ridges had soaked up the sunlight and were quite bare, but the valleys were still deep in snow. As we came in sight of the indentation of the east coast at Cumberland Sound, I could see large patches of dark blue, stretches of open water near the bottom end of the long Sound. Over towards Pangnirtung on the north coast of the Sound, a tremendous ice cap and mountain range stood out clearly against the horizon.

Beyond the Sound we flew over the mountain ranges that

run up the east coast of Baffin Island and almost entirely cover the northern portion of the island. It was a wonderful sight; vast icefields of gleaming, sparkling white stretching off into the interior as far as the eye could see; ice hundreds of feet in depth, remnants of the mighty glaciers that once covered most of Canada and northern United States. Through the ice cover, and around its edges, rose the mountains themselves, reaching up four, five, six thousand feet into the sky, many of them with sheer faces of bright coloured rock, red and brown usually, dropping to the ice-covered sea. Here was a world of ice and rock, of scoured-out glacial valleys, and deep rocky fjords. Everywhere the sun on this rugged land bounced back to the eye in a myriad of sparkling, silvery snow crystals, and in the lee of the high cliffs and rounded hills, the shadows glowed a dusky blue.

As we neared Clyde River we flew directly up the coast. A few miles out to sea the land-fast ice ended in a ragged edge of solid floe. Beyond this were open water patches, some a few feet in width, others a mile or two across. Beyond the open water lay the drifting pack ice of Baffin Bay, mile upon mile of brilliant but desolate white, stretching off to the horizon.

To anyone viewing the land for the first time, it must seem impossible for people to live there and like it. From the air there seems to be no piece of land big enough to set foot on, let alone build a home. From the air one looks out over miles of rock and snow and ice, with never a sign of game. We, from the south, look upon this land with an eye that has been conditioned by hundreds of years of slow development to an existence that has its root deep in the soil. We live by the land; we till its soil. On it we build our homes; across it run our networks of highways. We look at the rocky wilderness of north Baffin and say, "This land is of no use; minerals perhaps, but not much more."

The Eskimo hunter has no such background of attachment to the soil. He lives by the sea. From it he obtains his food, the seals, the walrus, the polar bears. From the sea mammals he obtains materials for much of his clothing, fuel to heat his house and cook his food. The ice cover of the sea is his winter highway and his hunting ground. He often builds his house of snow on the ice cover. He spends the greater portion of his life on or close by the sea. When we draw a map we outline the peninsulas of the land; when the Eskimo draws a map he outlines the bays and inlets of the sea. Perhaps his closest counterpart in our way of life is the fisherman who builds his home on some rocky ledge of land facing out to the sea on which he spends so much of his life.

As our aircraft flew up the coast of Baffin Island, we passed over mile after mile of ice-covered bays and inlets. Through the binoculars I could see the seals asleep on the ice beside the breathing holes, only occasionally disturbed by the sound of the plane. Off Clyde River itself, the shore ice extended out five miles with only one large open water patch a few miles to the north of the entrance to the harbour. As we came in over the settlement, I could see the twin lines of gas drums marking the runway on the smooth ice of the bay. In a few moments we touched down, the metal skis thumping and clunking on the hard packed snow. I had reached north Baffin at last.

CHAPTER

4

CLYDE RIVER settlement consisted of a Hudson's Bay Company post, a Department of Transport radio and weather station and a radio beacon station. It was a small settlement, even for the Arctic, and in the spring of 1953 appeared to be a good deal deal smaller than it actually should have been. In February of that year, fire had destroyed the main building of the radio station, completely gutting the living quarters of the six-man crew. Fortunately they managed to save the radio equipment by throwing it out of the windows into the snow, and in twenty-four hours had the radio set up in another building and the station back on the air.

The officer in charge of the radio station offered me bed and board for as long as I wished until I could get North. Both the American and Canadian personnel of the station made me very welcome, putting me up in their already crowded quarters. That night I spoke to Pond Inlet by radio and discussed with Idlouk the possibility of getting North by sled. The discussion was carried on in a roundabout manner. At that time my knowledge of the Eskimo language was meagre, but the Hudson's Bay Company post manager at Pond, Pete Murdock, spoke Eskimo fluently. He acted as interpreter. I spoke to him through the short wave radio at Clyde, he translated into Eskimo for Idlouk at Pond, received the replies from Idlouk in Eskimo, translated into English, and then sent the replies back to Clyde in morse code by key, as his station at Pond could not transmit voice. At Clyde, one of the radio operators picked up the message as it came in, transposing and typing it for me to read. All this deepened my resolution to do two things; learn the Eskimo language, and learn to read and send morse code.

The outcome of the discussion was that I should try to reach Pond by sled. I would hire an Eskimo guide at Clyde and start out up the coast in two days' time. In the meantime, Idlouk would start out from Pond, leaving immediately, and come down the coast to meet me, the probable point of meeting to be somewhere along the stretch of coast between Capes Hunter and Adair. If either of us managed to reach this stretch of coast and found no trace of the other party, we were to turn back, as this would mean that open water had prevented our getting through. We both felt that we had a reasonable chance of making contact; everything seemed to depend on the ice around Cape Bowen. If the wind had brought it back in to shore, Idlouk would be able to come on down to meet me. If not, he would have to turn back, and I would have to wait in the Clyde River area until the summer before going to Pond.

I had no difficulty about a guide for the trip. Simonee, perhaps the best hunter and traveller in that area, agreed to take me North. His salary was to be $5.00 per day for the total time he was away from his camp, plus a ration of food for his family while he was gone. Simonee had already been to Pond on a trip for the Hudson's Bay Company earlier in the spring and he knew the route well. He quickly made arrangements for someone to look after his family while he was away, and, on the third day after my landing at Clyde, we pulled out of the settlement and started off to the north.

In May on north Baffin, the sun shines night and day, when it is not hidden by the clouds. It is much too hot for the dogs to travel by day, so we did all our travelling during the night hours, taking advantage of whatever frost might come along. The sun is much lower in the sky at night, and the temperature, which can go to forty above in the day, often drops below freezing during the night. This hardens the snow, and the sled slides more easily.

We had two sleds, instead of one as originally planned.

33

Simonee had decided that his brother Jacko should come on the trip as well. As we planned to live completely by hunting, the extra man and his dogs made no difference to the food supply. Jacko would travel ahead with an almost empty sled, breaking trail and hunting seals for food for ourselves and the dogs. This was to be my first experience of living on the land as an Eskimo. I had logged a good many sled miles prior to this trip, but always I had had sufficient food and fuel to last for any trip. Now we had only tea and a small quantity of hard-tack biscuits; the rest of our food we would hunt on the way.

Simonee's brother, Jacko, is a rather unusual Eskimo. He is a hunchback, his spine so deformed that he stands a bare four feet high. Despite his deformity he is an excellent traveller and hunter, is married, and has a family of four. His deformity is actually an asset when riding on the sled. On an empty sled the driver always sits up forward on the cross slats very close to the ground, or to the snow. Jacko is beautifully built for such travel. He can slip on and off the moving sled with a minimum of motion and effort. When he is moving among his team of dogs, it is hard to pick him out for he is not much taller than his biggest dog.

It took us four days to reach Cape Adair, the first point at which we could possibly expect to make contact with Idlouk. Travelling during the night hours, usually between seven or eight in the evening and nine or ten the next morning, we slowly wound our way up the coast. We travelled on the sea ice, keeping close to the shore, as the ice to seaward looked as if it might go out at any time.

At first the coast was low, composed of gravel and clay deposits rising to the high hills of the distant rocky mountains. But about fifty miles above Clyde a series of fjords cut deep into the coast. Here the rocky hills came right down to the shore, steep cliffs rising up for as much as one thousand feet out of the ice-covered sea. Scott Island, in particular, was a wonderful sight. Situated at the entrance of Scott Inlet, it is one massive chunk of dark rock, roughly seven miles long by three wide. On all sides it rises sheer out of the sea. The eastern end of the island comes to a point, and looks much like the bow of a huge warship with overhanging prow thrust out to sea. The Eskimos call it *oomeeakjuak*, the big ship.

Although the prow of Scott Island was in sight for a long time, it was not until the third day of travel that our sleds rounded the tip of land to the south, and the island lay in full view. Ahead was the smooth ice of Scott Inlet, and on the ice, looking like scattered bags of coal, lay dozens of seals sleeping by their breathing holes in the heat of the spring sun. The dogs saw the seals as soon as we did, and in a moment both sleds shot forward at breakneck speed. When he wants to go, the Eskimo husky dog really moves, and nothing short of the sled overturning will stop him.

It was very exhilarating, bowling over the ice with the wind on our faces; the excitement of the dogs caught up with us as well. We shouted at the dogs, urging them to greater speed. Seal after seal looked up, stared for a moment at the hurtling sled, and then scrambled madly for the breathing hole and the safety of the sea. But there was always another one, and another, and the dogs kept right on going, never for a moment slowing down.

We had travelled for about a mile like this, when Simonee thought he would try for a seal. While the sled was moving along, he worked his rifle free of the lashings, and slipped a round into the breech. As the dogs bore down on one seal, he suddenly stood up, and with a running jump leaped clear of the sled. Quickly he sat down on the snow, took aim and fired. No luck! The seal dived down into the hole. The shot frightened the seals for some distance around and in a twinkling all had dived through the holes into the sea. One minute there were black dots by the dozens, the next there was nothing to see.

The dogs ran on for about half a mile before I was able to bring them under control. As they slackened speed, I jumped from the sled, and with the whip brought them to a halt. When they were quieted, I turned to see how Simonee was making out. Although he was about half a mile away.

35

I could see him quite clearly. Instead of coming towards me as I imagined he would be doing, he was heading off at right angles to the sled, stopping at every step to reach out with his rifle and plunge it into the snow. At first I couldn't imagine what he was doing, but as I looked about my glance fell on the sled, some thirty feet away, and my heart stood still. Where the sled stood the ice was slowly sinking, and a big pool of water was forming, creeping out over the snow.

Instantly I knew what was wrong. We had run onto a patch of very thin ice; no wonder there had been so many seals out on view. Cautiously I stamped one foot lightly. I felt the ice give under my feet. I could not go back to the sled for fear my weight would send it through. With infinite care, I moved slowly away from the sled, taking long gliding steps, quietly calling to the dogs. Languidly, still hot and puffed from their run, they got up, stretched, and milled about. I kept calling and making the pursing whistle that is used to call the dogs to feed, trying to get them to move the sled before it went through the ice, or, at best, bogged down in the slowly deepening pool of water. One or two started in my direction, but the others stretched and walked about, or rolled on their backs in the snow.

Nothing I could do would make the dogs move, make them aware of their plight. Probably never before had the high cliffs of Scott Island echoed to such epithets as that day resounded over the emptiness of north Baffin. The dogs still refused to move. Then, to my intense relief, I heard Simonee calling. All the dogs jumped quickly to their feet, and, as one, dashed off in the direction of his familiar voice, dragging the sled free of the water. I quickly moved over to meet the sled, and as it went past, I jumped aboard. Swinging around in a wide circle I headed back toward Simonee, who continued his slow walk over the snow. As the sled moved along, I took out the harpoon handle and jabbed it into the ice. It went through so easily I was startled into nearly letting it go. The ice on which we had been walking was only about four inches thick and rotten from the heat of the sun. To this day, I do not know how we escaped going through.

When the sled reached Simonee he jumped quickly aboard and whipped up the dogs, heading straight to sea. Half an hour later, and some two miles off shore, we halted on thick ice for a cup of tea. Simonee then told me that sometimes the ice in Scott Inlet acts in this way. Apparently the current sweeps around the island with considerable force and if the winter is mild with a lot of snow, the ice cover on the inlet is thin. As he talked, he chuckled to himself, saying what a pair of fools we must have looked, shouting and yelling on the fast moving sled, completely unaware that at any moment we might go through the ice to a watery grave. It was not long before I started to laugh with him.

We had no trouble procuring food either for ourselves or for the dogs. Everywhere there were *ootook* as the Eskimos call a seal asleep on the ice. Usually we waited until just before stopping, to make our kill for the day, and then pitched camp right beside the dead seal. Our diet was seal meat and tea, with an occasional hard-tack biscuit thrown in for a treat. At the sleeping stops we usually boiled the meat, but during the short stops on the trail it was eaten raw. I had eaten raw meat before, but to eat it as a staple food was a new experience, and at first not a pleasant one. Raw meat is soft and slippery, hard to handle until one gets to its devious ways. I soon became accustomed to the sweetish taste and in a few days knew just what cuts were the best: the flippers, the heart and liver, the small ribs and adjoining meat.

Seal meat is not fishy in taste as so many people seem to believe. In appearance it is somewhat like beef, except that it is much darker in colour. In taste it is stronger, with a flavour all of its own.

The hardest thing to get used to was the simplicity of the meal. For the first few days I found I could eat only so much meat, then I wanted something else, anything else, before I went back at the meat again. When the meat was boiled I solved this by sipping at a cup of broth, the water

37

in which the meat had been boiled. This helped considerably, although it was not quite the right type of drink, being very fatty in itself. Something sour, like a big glass of grapefruit juice, would have been just the thing.

On May 20th we rounded Cape Adair and travelled up the coast to Cape Hunter, pitching camp on a tiny piece of snow-free ground on the south side of the Cape, our first camp on land since leaving Clyde River. All along the coast we had been watching for signs of Idlouk coming down from the north. But there was nothing, no tracks of any sort, no black dots ahead that would signify an approaching sled.

At Cape Hunter, Simonee and I climbed the big hill back of the camp. With binoculars and telescope we surveyed the sea ice to the north. Although the day was overcast, we had a good view, right up to the high land beyond Buchan Gulf. What we saw did not encourage optimism in the possibility of making contact with Idlouk. At Cape Hunter, immediately below where we sat, the open water at the floe edge was only a half mile off shore, one hundred yards of ice-free water beyond which drifted the moving pack ice of Baffin Bay. At Cape Lord Rutherford some ten miles to the north, the floe edge cut into the land and open water lapped at the foot of the Cape, completely cutting off travel in the direction from which Idlouk would have to come, or we would have to go. Farther up the coast at the next point, Cape Cargenholm, the floe again cut in to the shore. Both capes were cut off; to all appearances we could go no farther.

My map, the latest edition of the eight miles to the inch Topographic Series, showed only high cliffs along all the shore of the fjords in this area. I questioned Simonee about the possibility of an inland route that would take us around the exposed capes. He said that he was not sure there was one. As it turned out, this was a masterpiece of understatement. There *was* an overland route some twenty miles from where we sat. By going inside Dexterity Island and Bergensen Island, we could have reached a point on the south coast of the next jutting peninsula where there was only a narrow strip of low land separating Paterson Inlet from the lower end of Maud Harbour. I discovered later that this crossing is marked on the old maps.

For a long time afterward I was puzzled by the attitude of Simonee, and why he withheld information on this crossing. I believe now that it stemmed from two main causes. First of all, as I discovered later, Simonee and Idlouk were not the best of friends in the spring of 1953. When Simonee had gone to Pond Inlet that spring, he had engaged in trading with Idlouk and had come out of the deal with one of Idlouk's best dogs. Idlouk had not been happy about the manner in which the trading had been carried out, and Simonee was not anxious to renew acquaintance after such a short time had passed.

But more important than this was something that had occurred on our trip up the coast. About forty miles above Clyde we had stopped briefly at an Eskimo camp to have a cup of tea. Only the women were left at the camp, all the men having gone hunting almost a month before. The women were very worried about their men, as they had planned to be gone only about ten days. They thought the men might have been blown out to sea on a loose piece of ice. Everywhere along the coast the ice was breaking off and moving about with wind and tide. Along this coast hardly a year goes by without a hunter or two being blown out to sea on moving ice. Sometimes the hunter is fortunate and the wind blows the ice back in again. At other times he is not, and nothing is ever heard of him again.

We had been watching for traces of the men all along the way. We found the spot where they had left some gear and gone out to the floe edge to hunt. Just before reaching Cape Hunter we had spotted a loose dog off in the distance, but could not get near it. But not a sign of the men themselves did we see. At the time we were searching the ice to the north for some sign of Idlouk, we thought these hunters had been blown out to sea and lost.

Knowing this, and with the ice rapidly breaking up, Simonee was not anxious to go farther north. If Idlouk had not been able to get down to a point where we could see him from Cape Hunter, it probably meant that he had been forced to turn back at Cape Bowen. It would have been risky for us to have gone farther up the coast, fail to make contact with Idlouk, and then find that we could not get back to Clyde again. We would then have had to camp on the coast and live there, hunting for our food, until someone came to get us with a boat in the summer. Simonee could not take this risk, for if he did become stranded, there would be no one to look after his family. Not being able to tell me all this in English, and knowing I would not understand it well enough if he spoke in Eskimo, he simply said he was not sure of a land crossing to the north. He was not lying, for we could not have been sure of the crossing until we got to it. He was just skating along the thin edge of the truth.

I decided to wait at Cape Hunter for three days, in case Idlouk had been able to get through, but was being held up by slow travel conditions. I knew him to be a very tenacious person, and if he could get through at all, he would do it. Idlouk knew this coast far better than most of the Eskimos of north Baffin, having travelled it many times with the missionaries on their annual trip to Clyde. We would wait until midnight of May 24th, then, if there was still no sign of him at that time, retrace our path to Clyde. Our wait at Cape Hunter proved to be a very exciting affair.

On the afternoon of the 22nd, we awoke to a miserable day; overcast, snowing, and a cool wind out of the north-east. Although there was not much hope of seeing anything in the overcast, Simonee and I walked across the headland to the far side, and began to search the sea ice to the north for some sign of Idlouk. It was the kind of day in the Arctic when you are not sure that the black dot you see is a pebble at five feet or a very large boulder half a mile away. I could see a few seals asleep on the ice, but not much more.

As I was studying the outlines of a large iceberg about a mile to the north, a slight movement caught my eye. I watched if for a long time, trying to make out what it could possibly be. It was far too erratic in movement for a sled. I called to Simonee, who had been looking over a different sector of the ice, and he swung his telescope in the direction I pointed. After a long study, he lowered the glass and said excitedly, "Nanook." It was a polar bear.

Here was a chance to get enough meat for ourselves and the dogs to last us on the trip back to Clyde; it would be a welcome change from the seal. At Clyde, Simonee could get twenty dollars for the skin if it was a good one, ten or fifteen if not.

Back at the tent we quickly harnessed up the dogs, put the box with the primus stove and tea on the sled, and closed the tent up tight. We might be gone for some time. Leaving the two pups behind, we set off on the hunt with both sleds. First we backtracked across the point of land to have another look at the bear. He was still on the ice and a little closer, shuffling along at an ambling trot, stopping every so often to sniff the wind for scent of a seal.

Down the steep slope on the other side of the point of land, the sleds shot like bobsleighs on an icy runway, overtaking and passing dogs, but fortunately not hitting any, so that there was little noise. We moved out through the rough shore ice, all commands to the dogs given in whispers now. They were roundly cursed, also in fierce whispers, when they started to growl or howl. Simonee had not bothered to bring his rifle; he concentrated on driving the dogs. I had still camera and binoculars; Jacko would be the hunter for that day.

For about half a mile we moved steadily towards the bear. He gave no sign of having seen the oncoming sleds and the dogs had neither seen nor winded him. Then suddenly he stopped his aimless ambling and swung about. He had seen us. His head weaved back and forth as he sniffed the air, but he could not get our scent. Turning slowly he set out over the ice at a loose shuffling trot. Every few hundred yards he stopped, wheeled about to look at us, then started off again. He showed no sign of being at all concerned. He just wanted to keep out of our way.

At last our lead dog caught sight of the bear. Immediately he started to howl and lunge ahead through the snow. The other dogs took up the cry and soon the sleds were tearing along, both teams in full cry. Our pent-up excitement let loose, we shouted encouragement to the straining teams. But for all their efforts the dogs were being left behind. At the first cry, the bear had taken off in full flight, heading for the open water at the floe edge. Despite the slow shuffling appearance of his run, he was rapidly drawing away from the sleds. Leaning forward, Simonee began to cut the traces of the dogs, while Jacko, following close behind, did the same. One-two-three-four-five, quick as I could count, the traces were slashed and the loosened dogs began to pull away from the sled. In a minute there were fifteen dogs strung out over the snow, hot on the trail of the fleeing bear. But as the dogs were released, the sled began to slow down and we dropped behind.

Up ahead the loose dogs had come upon the tracks of the bear, and the scent, added to the sight, brought renewed howls over the snow. But even with the dogs loose the bear seemed still to be pulling away. I said so to Simonee, who laughed and said not to worry. The bear would get hot with all the running and would tire within a mile or so. The dogs could keep the pace all day if necessary. It began to look like a long, drawn-out affair.

At the barrier of rough ice along the edge of a narrow crack, the sled slowed down and Simonee tried to loose three more dogs. But the main trace got away from him, and all our dogs ran off leaving us stranded with the sled. Fortunately we were still the lead sled, and as Jacko came up, we threw the primus box aboard his sled and continued on our way.

The five remaining dogs could not pull all of us, so we took turns running ahead of the sled, following the well beaten track of bear and dogs. Here and there his mighty foot prints showed through, but mostly they had been obliterated by the tracks of the pursuing dogs.

The bear, the dogs, and ourselves ran for some three

miles before the bear began to show signs of tiring. By this time he was about a mile ahead of the nearest dog with the rest strung out in a long line behind. As the bear slowed down, I could see the lead dog quickly close the gap. It caught up with the bear, which immediately turned to fight. In a few minutes all the dogs had come up, and were drawn up around the bear in full battle array.

Fifteen minutes later, we arrived on the scene. What a scramble was going on! One big white bear surrounded by some thirty yapping, howling dogs! They had him cornered, but could not do much more than keep him that way, and worry his flanks and heels. The bear was no mean adversary. Already there was blood on the snow where some hapless dog had caught a clip from a massive paw, or a nip from the big teeth. The bear swung about in circles, trying to keep the dogs from flanks and heels. Every so often he charged into them, moving like lightning, and the howls of the dogs testified to the effectiveness of the charge. Several dogs were limping away from the field of battle, or lying in the snow licking their wounds.

I moved about taking colour shots with the still camera, wishing for a little sun. I had no pictures of a bear hunt and this was too good to miss. Moving into position for a close shot of the bear, I was suddenly yanked backward off my feet by Simonee. Without realizing it, I had worked around until I was upwind of the bear. One smell of man odour and, in such an enraged state, he would have been on me in a flash. With the speed of his movements I doubt that I could have got out of the way.

Jacko was also moving about, trying to get into position for a shot. It was difficult job to hit the weaving bear without shooting one of the bounding, leaping dogs. He had to wait until the bear was in the clear. The moment came. The bear dashed into a group of dogs, sending them flying in all directions. He slid to his knees as he wheeled about, then rose facing directly to where we stood. For a brief moment he was in the open, stationary, with no dogs near. Jacko fired. The bear lurched, and stumbled to his knees, but he was up again in a flash. Jacko fired again, and the bear went down once more. He rolled over and over, struggling to rise to his feet. But the wounds were mortal, and the bear collapsed into the snow. The mighty head flayed back and forth for a moment and then was still. Blood made a deep crimson stain on the fresh white snow. As the bear went down, the dogs were on him, swarming over the body, biting and tearing at the fur. We dashed up, drove them off, and turned to have a good look at the kill.

Even in death the bear was a magnificent animal. Although small for a polar bear, he was some six feet from nose to tail. The long white fur was stained yellow in spots, smeared with the fat of the seals he had killed and eaten. The mighty jaws with twin rows of interlocking teeth could crush through bone as if it were paper. The paws were nine inches across the pad, five toes each tipped with an inch-long claw. Those teeth and claws had played havoc with our dogs, a number of whom now sat licking wounds, their blood mingling with that of their late foe. None had been killed, fortunately, although in a bear hunt this is not an uncommon thing.

The bear was cut up on the spot, the meat, fat and skin loaded on the sled, and the guts given to the dogs to eat. The liver was left behind untouched, as it is poisonous, being overly rich in Vitamin A. We had a quick cup of tea, harnessed up the dogs again, and started back for the tent. On the way, we picked up the abandoned sled and towed it back to camp. That night we had boiled bear meat for supper, the first of many such meals to come.

I did not enjoy that meal of bear. At that time, my memory was still too strong of the tales of people becoming seriously ill with trichinosis from eating infected bear meat. With every mouthful I could see huge quantities of trichinosis germs invading my system, then laying me low. But a few bears later, with memory dulled and hunger sharpened, I ate cooked bear meat with gusto, although I still cannot eat bear meat raw without murmuring a short, silent prayer.

CHAPTER
5

ON SUNDAY, the 24th of May, a vicious storm swept out of the north-west. For eighteen hours the wind blew with gale force and wet snow plastered the land. Lying in our sleeping bags in the wildly tossing tent we alternately ate, dozed, and talked, and hoped the tent would not come down around our ears. We had to eat all the meat raw as we dared not light the primus for fear the tent would come down and catch fire. Without the primus we could have no water and so chewed mouthfuls of snow to quench our thirst.

For eighteen hours we did not stir from the sleeping bags, lying three in a row across the rear of the tent, heads to the forward end. In the short space beyond our heads was the primus stove and box, and the stack of meat and fat from the bear, as well as the meat from a seal. This pile of raw meat did not improve the atmosphere in the tent, although one soon gets used to such things. On awakening we would reach out, pick up the knife, cut off a piece of meat and start eating. I ate seal but the others dug into the bear. Enough snow blew in through holes in the tent for us to have ample for drink.

I lay in the sleeping bag listening to the sound of the storm. Out towards the sea I could hear the rumbling and grumbling of the ice in movement, huge pans shifting ponderously under the pressure of the wind, cracking and breaking, overriding and smashing the smaller pieces that stood in their way. It seemed strange that this should be the 24th of May. In the world "outside" all the land would be bursting into life, the tremendous world of nature stirring,

sending up its colour everywhere. On north Baffin I seemed
to be on another planet, all wind and cold and snow, a vast,
turbulent emptiness, a gigantic deep freeze.

Late Sunday night the storm blew itself out. What a
change it had made in the land and on the sea! Everywhere
the land was blanketed with heavy wet snow, while out to
sea, the long dark lanes of open water had spread a vast
lacy network across the ice. In every direction the ice had
been split and torn apart, and was now interlaced with
cracks in which seals swam and played. As I looked out over
the ice, I hoped that Idlouk had been forced to return to
Pond, for if he had been on the ice travelling when the storm
hit, there would have been little chance for him to reach the
shore. Off Cape Hunter the open water of the floe edge was
only a scant two hundred yards away, and the crack at the
edge was now half a mile across. Fortunately, the land-fast
ice to the south remained firm; the highway to the south remained open.

The storm destroyed any last hope I may have held that
Idlouk would get through. At midnight Simonee, Jacko and
I packed our gear. I walked over the point of land for a last
look to the north. There was little but open water and ice.
Sadly I walked back to the sled and as soon as the snow
hardened with the night frost, we started on the return trip to
Clyde.

Then occurred one of the strangest weather freaks I have
ever seen in the Arctic, a country not noted for the stability
of the weather pattern. In the wake of the storm came clear
skies and high winds. The temperature dropped sharply,
falling quickly to well below zero. Everywhere the snow
hardened, the open leads of water in the sea ice froze over,
and we could travel with ease either night or day. Instead of
our duffel cloth clothing, we wore parkas of caribou skins
during the coldest hours of the night. The long mild spell of
spring had come suddenly to an abrupt end. Although it was
the end of May, it felt more like the beginning of March.

This was the weather I had hoped for over the past two
months, but now it seemed to have come too late. Our sleds

slid easily over the hard snow so that we were able to make forty and fifty miles a day, but we were going in the wrong direction. There were no more detours around cracks or patches of soft, deep snow; straight down the coast we went, stopping only to eat or drink, or snatch a few hours' rest. We did not bother putting up the tent, but slept in the bags on the sled, or in a cleft in the rocks when near the shore. We did not have to rush; it was a pleasure to move so easily after all the pulling through soft, wet snow.

We reached Clyde in three days' travel. That night I spoke to Pond by radio and learned that Idlouk had not returned. They had recieved no word of him since he had left to come south. This meant that he had either been able to get through and was being held up by extremely slow going, or that he had become stranded on the coast or on the ice. I decided to wait at Clyde for two days, and if in that time he had neither turned up at Clyde nor returned to Pond, Simonee and I would start back up the coast to look for him. But this proved to be unnecessary, for on the night of the second day after our return, without any fanfare or fuss, Idlouk showed up at Clyde.

How can I express my feelings on seeing him? For two years I had been looking forward to the day when I would meet him again and become his "son". For two months I had been striving to make contact with him, against great odds. For two days I had been intensely worried, not knowing where he might be, or what had happened to him on the trip down the coast. We did not say much; we shook hands, and looked long into one another's eyes.

Idlouk had not changed in the two years since I had seen him last. He was still the same cocky, smiling individual. Thirty-eight years old, father of eight living children, Idlouk is still a young, vigorous personality, always giving the impression of being ready for anything. He is short, as are most of the Eskimos of north Baffin, standing about five foot one. With his black hair cut after the fashion of the white man, he looks much less the Oriental than many of his neighbours in the Arctic, although the slightly slanted eyes and high cheek bones betray his Asiatic origin. In May his dusky skin was burnt brown by the spring sun and wind. Against this tan, his strong white teeth stood out sharply, whenever his mouth broke into a wide smile.

Idlouk is the best hunter, trapper and traveller on north Baffin. In a land where the majority of the Eskimos just get by (and this applies to the majority of the Eskimos on north Baffin), he lives a full life. His camp is never without food. If there are foxes to be had, he will get them. And he has used his money wisely, not all of it, for that would be asking too much, but most of it. He owns a forty-foot gas-powered boat that provides him with safe, convenient transportation in the summer, and is a source of revenue when it is hired by whites coming into the area. He has an eighteen-foot canoe and outboard in which he can hunt the small whales that abound in these northern waters. He keeps his equipment in tip-top shape. On north Baffin Island his success is unmatched by any other Eskimo, and throughout the Canadian Eastern Arctic by very few.*

With Idlouk was his son, Paneeluk, the eldest son living with his father. From the two I put together the story of their trip down the coast.

They had left Pond Inlet the same night I spoke to Idlouk on the radio, a little over two weeks before, in such a hurry that they had forgotten to bring the tent, having to pick one up at the first Eskimo camp encountered on the way. At first the going had been slow but steady through soft wet snow, although it was not as soft nor as deep as when they had tried to come down three weeks before. At Cape Bowen they found the ice had come back in, and had no difficulty getting around the exposed Cape.

Once beyond Cape Bowen, they had run into very deep soft snow, and the pace had been slowed to a crawl. For three days they made only ten miles a day, and the average for the last part of the trip was only twenty. They had no

---

* In 1955 Idlouk moved to Resolute on Cornwallis Island, where he lives now.

further trouble with open cracks in the ice as Idlouk knew well the land crossing from Maud Harbour, and kept inside all the islands in this area. He was amazed when I told him that Simonee had said he was not sure of this land crossing. When the storm of the 24th of May hit, they had been safely camped on land.

The night they crossed over from Maud Harbour to Paterson Inlet was the same on which I had taken my last look to the north and then turned back for Clyde. We had been only twenty miles apart. Idlouk reached our old campsite about noon on the following day. He had been very disappointed at finding me gone, but by then the cold weather had improved travel conditions to the extent that he decided to come right on down to Clyde. He said that he could see the tracks in the snow where I had walked up to the point day after day, watching for him, and he had known how anxious I must have been to get a sight of him coming down from the north. He and Paneeluk camped on our tentsite and, after a few hours' rest, started down the coast.

On their trip they had met the hunters from Clyde, whom we had supposed to be lost on the ice. These men had gone to Pond Inlet to work in the coal mine for the month of April, neglecting to tell their families of their intentions. This is unusual for Eskimos, although they can act on the spur of the moment in many things.

With these men they had a bear hunt on the ice, Paneeluk shooting his first bear just to the south of the spot at which we had shot ours. Their hunt was even more exciting than ours, as they had three sleds all racing along after the bear. The people were not all from the same camp, and there had been a great deal of competition as to who should get the bear. At the critical moment, with the three sleds racing neck and neck over the ice, the bear turning to hotfoot it over the snow, and the men about to start cutting the traces, the dogs smelled the dead seal the bear had been eating when discovered. The teams of the other hunters turned to dash for the dead seal, but Idlouk's lead dog had his eye glued to the bear and refused to be led astray. He kept the sled straight on after the bear, Idlouk and Paneeluk laughing and shouting taunts at the other men, who were unable either to stop the dogs or get them turned in the right direction. Idlouk and Paneeluk caught up with the bear, the dogs cornered him, Paneeluk shot him, all in much the same pattern as we had followed with our bear. They had taken only as much meat as they required for the rest of the trip down to Clyde, and cached the remainder under the rocks on the nearby shore. The skin was brought to Clyde and sold to one of the Department of Transport personnel.

Normally all trade on north Baffin is carried on with the Hudson's Bay Company. However, at Clyde, with the Department of Transport and United States Air Force stations, a good deal of trading is done by the various men of the stations. While I was there, the big item in trade was bear skin, and there seemed to be a few smouldering between the members of the stations, on the one hand and the Hudson's Bay Company post manager, on the other. All wanted bear skins, but only the men of the stations were getting them, as they were giving much the better bargain in trade. Among the personnel of the stations another small feud was smouldering between the Americans and Canadians, nothing that amounted to much, but enough to make itself felt at all times.

In trading directly with the Eskimos, some difficulties had arisen. Although the Americans had no cash (no paymaster had visited Clyde for some time) they had cheap American cigarettes. Against these, offered in trade, the Canadians could not compete. Consequently the Canadians had given up trading, and the Americans had cornered the market in bear skins. Although the Eskimos invariably received a good bargain in trade, usually in items such as clothing, cigarettes, lighters, etc., and in all probability got more dollar for dollar than they would have received from the Hudson's Bay Company, they could not get many of the items they needed. Certain staples are essential to the

Eskimo of today: ammunition, tea, kerosene, primus stove, flour, to mention a few. All these things he can get from the Company, but only if he has the money, or the skins to trade for them. But in selling his skins to the Americans, he could get no money; he had to take goods from them, and not always the goods he really needed.

An example of this occurred while I was in Clyde. Jacko sold the bear skin he had shot on our trip to one of the Americans. Having no money, the American offered other items, starting with a cigarette lighter and cigarettes, which Jacko declined, and ending up with the offer of a winter p... plus two cartons of cigarettes, which Jacko accepted. r... he value of these items was roughly fifty dollars. On the surface, this was a good bargain,* and Jacko could not refuse it, for it was probably nearly three times the cash value he wou. have received from the Hudson's Bay Company post manager for the skin. But he did not really need the park... whereas he was short of kerosene and flour, items he could only purchase at the Bay store with money or skins to ...de. By trading with the American he and his family did without some of the necessities of life in his land.

Now that the contact with Idlouk had been made, I felt my problems were at an end, and anticipated no trouble in getting to Pond Inlet. In this I was quite right. We rested Idlouk's dogs for two days and, on the night of May 31st, pulled out of Clyde. Once again I was headed to the north.

As on the previous trip we had two sleds, but this time with different Eskimos. I rode with Idlouk, while Paneeluk came with Simeeonee, an Eskimo from Clyde whom I hired to help us with our load for the first half of the trip. The weather had remained cold, but there was nothing to guarantee that it would stay that way for long. We felt we could make much better time with the load on two sleds, taking full advantage of the good travel conditions for as long as they lasted. Simeeonee was to accompany us only

---

* But not today when bear skins can bring $100.00 to $125.00.

51

as far as the land crossing, and then return. In this way there would be no danger of his becoming stranded to the north in the event of the ice going out.

As it had been on all stages of my trip from Montreal, the final portion of the journey was anticlimatic. The trip turned out to be an easy one, ten days from Clyde to Pond, slow time for such a trip, but not bad considering our load and the time of the year.

Once again we lived off the land, or rather off the sea ice, hunting our food as we went along. Seals on the ice were still plentiful and at Idlouk's cache on the coast, we picked up the remainder of the bear meat. As before, we travelled by night, taking full advantage of the frost. It was cold, well below zero most of the time, which was strange for the month of June, even on north Baffin. We wore our caribou parkas for a few hours every night, something one does not ordinarily do after the month of April. Every night we were able to ice the runners of the sled so that it slid more easily over the snow. I had never seen that done in June before, and often not even in May.

All the wide cracks of two weeks before were still frozen over, and there had been almost no new movement of the sea ice at the floe. We reached the land crossing and bade goodbye to Simeeonee, who then returned to Clyde. The land crossing was done easily, a low pass between high cliffs, about one hundred feet in elevation at the highest point, and not more than a mile across. On either side the hills towered up in jagged cliffs to a height of one thousand feet or more.

Simeeonee had barely left us when Paneeluk spotted two sleds approaching from the north. We wondered who they could be. Idlouk had asked Pete Murdock, the Hudson's Bay Company post manager at Pond, to have one of the Eskimos from his camp come down to meet us, but all the men had been out hunting, and we did not expect to meet anyone until reaching the Eskimo camps some miles up the coast at Coutts Inlet. The approaching sleds came on very quickly, and in a few minutes we met them head-

on, in a tangle of fighting, biting dogs. When we got the dogs sorted out, we discovered we would have company for the rest of the trip. One of the sleds was that of Merkoshak, the Eskimo who works for the Hudson's Bay Company at Pond Inlet. I knew Merkoshak from my trip in 1951, and we talked of old times. With him was the clerk of the Company post, Jim Rex. I had not met Jim before, but in a few minutes we were sitting on the sled, chatting easily, as though we had been pals since birth.

Jim told me that Murdock, on being unable to notify any of the men from Idlouk's camp to come down to meet us, had begun to worry about us making the trip so late in the season. He asked Merkoshak and Jim to come down the coast to make contact with us and lend a hand in getting to Pond. On the way down, they had picked up Merkoshak's brother and his sled, as he was not doing anything in particular and seemed to be anxious to make the trip. We were very glad to see them; on parting from Simeeonee just half an hour before, we had taken all the gear on our sled, and it was a heavy load for the dogs to pull. Now we distributed the gear among the three sleds and, thus lightened, set out for Pond.

During the "heat" of the day we did not travel, but slept in the tent, usually pitched out on the sea ice. In putting up a tent on the ice in the spring, the practice is to bury the pegs in the soft snow cover, as the snow is usually not hard enough to hold them if they are just driven in. But on our trip, we had got into the habit of tying the guy ropes along one side of the tent to the sled. This saved us a good deal of time and effort at the stops. With the dogs running loose, as they usually are at the stops, it provided no hazard, but when they were tied to the sled, as they were whenever we pitched camp in front of an Eskimo encampment, we were asking for trouble.

One night, or rather one day, we were camped on the sea ice directly in front of an Eskimo camp on the coast. As usual we had tied the guy ropes to the sled, and on this occasion had not even bothered to upturn it. As there were almost sixty other dogs from the camp roaming about, itching for a fight, our dogs were all tied to the sled. I remember dreaming I heard a dog team approaching our tent, gathering speed as it came until it seemed to be flying along. Closer and closer it came until, with a tremendous rush, the dogs swarmed over the tent and beyond. At that moment I awoke to find myself in a flurry of flying snow and howling dogs. One minute Idlouk, Paneeluk and I were sleeping peacefully in the cozy tent, next our tent was whisked from over our heads, dragged helter-skelter over the snow behind our team of dogs which was in turn dashing after another team in the direction of the Eskimo camp.

We lay in the sleeping bags and howled. The Eskimos at the camp dashed out of their tents to see what the commotion was all about, and they howled too. Laughing, the boys set about cornering our dogs and rescuing the wandering tent which was rapidly being torn to pieces under the feet of a swarm of fighting dogs. We could not give them much assistance as we were all sleeping "raw". We watched and chuckled at our predicament, lying in the open on the ice, waiting until the tent was put up around us to get up and share in the joke. The Eskimos at that camp will not soon forget the time when Kingmik* and Idlouk were left sleeping out on the ice.

The remainder of the trip to Pond was uneventful. On the morning of June 12th, our sleds rounded the small jutting point of land, and there just a quarter of a mile ahead lay the settlement of Pond Inlet. Seventy easy sled miles across the ice of Eclipse Sound lay Idlouk's camp, my home for the year to come.

---

* I am known to Eskimos on north Baffin as Kingmik, which means "Dog", a name given to me in 1951 because of the close association of sound in "Dog" and "Doug". On the west coast of Hudson Bay I am known as Adjeleeuktik—The One Who Takes Pictures.

CHAPTER
6

IN 1953 Pond Inlet settlement consisted of a Royal Canadian Mounted Police detachment, a Hudson's Bay Company trading post and store, an Anglican and a Roman Catholic Mission.

The census of 1951 established the total Eskimo population of north Baffin Island at 582—128 in the area of Clyde River on the east coast, 209 in the area of Arctic Bay to the west of Pond Inlet, and 245 in the Pond Inlet area itself. They belong to the Tununermiut group of Eskimos, a classification noted by Rasmussen in his monumental studies of the Eskimos some thirty years ago. Outside of the small number of Eskimos recently moved to the far north islands, the Tununermiut are the most northerly Eskimos on the North American continent. Today they are rarely referred to as the Tununermiut group, but are known by the name of the post or settlement into which they trade: Pond Inlet, Clyde River, and Arctic Bay. Almost the entire population of the area is Anglican. The story told is that the Anglican and the Roman Catholic Missions both reached the area in the same year, 1926, but the Anglican missionary had his Bishop with him, and he promptly baptized all the Eskimos who came in to see the ship. Most of them have remained Anglican to this day.

As they live largely by the hunt, the population in each area is scattered widely over the land, or, more accurately, along the miles of sea coast, for they are a sea culture people; only rarely do they hunt or travel on the land. Small groups, usually three to five families, will set up a camp at a certain location and from this main campsite hunt and trap over the surrounding area. In the Pond Inlet district there are eight such camps on the shores of Eclipse Sound and two more on the east coast of Baffin Island above Coutts Inlet.

The main campsite of each group remains fairly static, but the population of the group fluctuates considerably from year to year. Idlouk's main campsite is called Aulatseevik. It is situated on the southernmost tip of Curry Island which is in the lower reaches of Eclipse Sound. The camp has been located there for the past eleven years, but in that time only he and his family have remained as original members of the group. Other Eskimos and their families have come and gone, sometimes moving through wanderlust, sometimes because they have been unable to get along with Idlouk whose driving personality makes him different from most of the Eskimos in the area.

Each spring Idlouk and the other members of his camp move from Aulatseevik to a tent-site about ten miles to the west. Here, on a narrow shelving gravel beach that has been blown clear of snow over the winter, the families move into tents. All during the spring thaw and run-off, the gravel beach is free of wet and damp, which makes it a desirable site for this time of year. At the time of my arrival in the Pond Inlet area in June of 1953, Idlouk's group of people were living at this location. The population of his camp was twenty-nine, plus seventy-four dogs and pups. I do not jest when I include the dogs and pups in the tabulation of the numbers at the camp. Dogs eat more food than humans do. In the Canadian Eastern Arctic today the dog is rapidly eating the Eskimo out of house and home.

The twenty-nine people were divided into five family units living in four separate tents. One unit was made up of Idlouk's aged parents, his mother, Agnowyah, age approximately 67, his father Akomalik, age approximately 73. With them lived their two grandsons Elijah and Danielee. The parents of the two boys had both died some years before, and they had been raised by the grandparents and watched over by Idlouk, their father having been his elder brother. Much later in my stay, Idlouk told me the story of his brother's death. His brother had gone away on a trip with the missionary and on his return found his wife had died in his absence. He had been very fond of her and grieved over his loss. He would have no other woman to take her place, and within a year he himself became ill and died. Idlouk is convinced he simply did not want to live without his wife.

For a few years he missed his elder brother terribly, for Idlouk had regularly turned to him for advice. About that time, Idlouk's father and mother had gone to work for the Anglican missionary at Pond Inlet and Idlouk had been left alone with his family. He said that he was very worried for a while, as it is hard for one man to hunt food for his family and his dogs and also operate a successful trap line. I have often wondered if this period in his life helped form his present vigorous, restless personality.

A second family unit at the camp was headed by Kadluk, an Eskimo slightly younger than Idlouk, who had been at this camp for eight years. In facial features he looked like a white man, his father being the late Gaston Herodier, who spent some time on north Baffin Island thirty odd years ago. Kadluk had never seen his white father, nor even a picture of him, but when Herodier died in 1929, he left his estate to be divided evenly among his three sons in the north. Kadluk's inheritance is administered by the Canadian government. Each year Kadluk receives a payment of $400.00, mainly in interest, from the invested funds. He is one of the few Eskimos in the Canadian Eastern Arctic, born of Eskimo mothers and white fathers, who have received anything from their fathers other than their appearance.

When his Eskimo father died in 1944, Kadluk came to live at Idlouk's camp. Idlouk is a shrewd individual, and the acquisition of Kadluk with his $400.00 annual inheritance was a worthwhile addition to the camp. The two men and their families have got along together extremely well over the years, Kadluk's carefree, happy-go-lucky temperament providing the foil for Idlouk's more ambitious drive.

Kadluk and his wife, Lydia, have five children, all of them as white in appearance as their father. This seems to be the pattern with the offspring of mixed unions in the Arctic. For the first generations, the white blood shows through very clearly in the facial appearance of the children, but it does not seem to remain. Eventually as the children marry within their own group, the Eskimo features return to predominance. Today it is extremely difficult to tell if an Eskimo is of pure blood or not. I have known two or three cases in which I have assumed Eskimos to be "all Eskimo" only to discover that one of their great-grand-parents had been a white man. To the Eskimo this matter of mixed blood is of no importance. The heritage of the Eskimo is the life he lives in the far north land, and not the blood of his father or his grandfather.

The third family unit at the camp was headed by Kitchooalik. He also is not Eskimo in appearance and, in addition, is quite tall, the tallest Eskimo I have met on north Baffin Island, where the people are short in stature. He is not an original member of the Pond Inlet group, but comes from Cape Dorset on southern Baffin Island. He was one of the group of Eskimos moved to Devon Island in 1926 by the Hudson's Bay Company when it opened a new trading post in the far north islands. The post is no longer open, and all the Eskimos have either returned to Dorset or drifted off to other locations. Kitchooalik is the only one of this group left on north Baffin Island.

Kitchooalik is a very energetic, restless, boyish personality, a good hunter, but only a mediocre trapper. His family always has food, but rarely do they have much money. This is a little surprising as most of the Eskimos moved to Devon from Dorset were good hunters and trappers.

Kitchooalik is the husband of Rebecca, Idlouk's eldest daughter. Many people in Canada and England know Rebecca well. When she was a very young baby, her parents gave her to Idlouk's parents to raise as their child, this being the custom at that time. Shortly after this, Idlouk's parents went to work for the Anglican missionary at Pond, the late Canon John Turner. Canon Turner took a fancy to Rebecca and brought her up almost as his own child. When Canon Turner married and moved to open the new mission at Moffet Inlet with his wife and family, Rebecca went along, helping Mrs. Turner to look after her children. At Moffat Inlet, Canon Turner met with the tragic accident in which he lost his life. He was accidentally shot by a .22 rifle. The ensuing air rescue by the Royal Canadian Air Force made news headlines for weeks. Canon Turner was evacuated from Moffet Inlet and flown to Winnipeg, where he died in hospital a few weeks later.

Rebecca, who had been flown out with Mrs. Turner and the children, went with Mrs. Turner to her home in England where she lived for about one year. But she could not adapt herself to life in a country whose climate and customs were so different from her own. In 1949 she returned to north Baffin Island to take up her life as an Eskimo at the camp of her father. For a few months she was terribly unhappy. Having spent the biggest part of life living with the Turners in their house, followed by a year in England, she was not really an Eskimo at all. The transition was a drastic one for her. Fortunately she had a good friend and adviser in Mrs. W. Heslop, the wife of the Hudson's Bay Company post manager then at Pond Inlet. Mrs. Heslop, sensing something of the struggle the girl was having in trying to adjust herself to the new way of life as an Eskimo on the land, did all she could to ease the shock of transition.

While my wife and I were living at Idlouk's camp in 1951 during the filming of LAND OF THE LONG DAY, Rebecca and Kitchooalik were married at the Anglican mission at Pond. Kitchooalik was a widower at the time, his wife having died in the spring of that year. Although Rebecca and Kitchooalik had met only briefly, Idlouk arranged a marriage between the two. This is the custom of the land; no father considers his job of raising a child completed until he has arranged for a good partner for the married life. I remember that the missionary's wife was scandalized by the speed with which the match was arranged and the marriage completed, but Idlouk is a very practical person. Good husbands are not easy to find in the Arctic today, and Kitchooalik was a fine catch. Besides, Kitchooalik had a three-year-old daughter to look after, and she needed a mother very badly.

Kitchooalik and Rebecca soon became inseparable, and today are a happy married couple. Besides the step-daughter, Rebecca soon had a daughter of her own, but unfortunately this child died when she was only a year old. Why she died no one knows; she simply became ill and died. This is often the case in a land devoid of any but the most rudimentary medical facilities. When I arrived at the camp in June, Rebecca's second child was well on the way.

A fourth family unit was headed by Oodleteetuk, Idlouk's eldest son. He was married in 1952 to Ishoogituk, Kadluk's youngest sister. The couple had no children; the first was expected to be born not long after the arrival of Rebecca's baby. Both families were hoping for a son. A son will be the most important member of the group when he grows up, the hunter and provider. Oodleteetuk and his wife shared the same tent with Kitchooalik and Rebecca in the summer, and the same house in the winter. With their small families, there was ample room for all.

Idlouk's was the fifth family unit at the camp, and the largest of all. Idlouk and his wife, Kidlak, both thirty-eight years of age, had had a total of nine children, one of whom had died. I have already mentioned Rebecca and Oodleteetuk. Next came Peneeluk, the boy of sixteen who had accompanied his father on the trip to Clyde River and return. A year and a half younger than Paneeluk is Leah. Many people in southern Ontario will remember Leah as the little Eskimo girl who spent four months living with my wife and me near Ottawa while she recuperated from an attack of tuberculosis. She returned to her father's camp on the ship in the summer of 1952. After Leah came three

boys, Mosesee, age nine; Pauloosee, age seven; Noahkudluk, age five. Last there was Ruthee, the only member of
the family I had not met before; she had been born after
my wife and I left north Baffin in 1951.

On June 15, 1953, the population at Aulatseevik increased by one. That day I became *ilningwah* to Idlouk
and his wife, meaning "in the likeness of my son". The
arrangements for this induction into the family were simple.
A son in the Eskimo family has no say in how he conducts
his daily life, often even after he has married and is raising
a family. He takes orders from his father as to where he
goes, what he does, how he conducts his daily life. Working
within such a relationship I would not be able to interfere
with the pattern of the family or camp life throughout the
year, and yet I would be able to participate in and observe
every activity. The only deviation from this pattern occurred when two activities happened to conflict by taking
place at the same time, but in different areas. Then I had
a choice as to which one I should undertake. Other than
this, I took orders as I would have done had I really been
Idlouk's son.

Although I had been living as an Eskimo ever since leaving
Clyde River on my first try to reach Pond Inlet in May, I
now took up my role as Idlouk's son, a working member
of an Eskimo camp.

LATE JUNE on North Baffin Island is the time when the
snow leaves the land and the sea ice is covered with water.
In a normal year, spring comes late to north Baffin, but
usually by June warmer weather has come to stay. Since
early in April there has been no darkness on the land; from
the middle of May the sun has not set below the horizon,
but, when not hidden by the clouds, circles endlessly in the
sky. The sun does not rise as high as in southern Canada,
but the land, being under the rays for twenty-four hours
a day, soaks up the heat.

The high rocky outcroppings are the first portions of the
land to become snow-free, the dark surfaces quickly ab-

sorbing heat from the sun. The snow cover slides away from the steep rocky slopes, small balls of snow rolling down the hills, gaining size and momentum until shattered on the sloping beach or the rough shore ice. The hard packed snow becomes wet and soft, here and there turning to water which trickles away over the rocks under the snow. Each day the water trickles increase in volume until the soft tinkle of the first June freshet becomes the thundering roar of the full July run-off.

With the first touch of warm weather in May, the birds come up from the south; gulls, kittiwakes, murres, ducks, birds deriving their existence from the sea are the first to appear. The little snow bunting, of course, has long before arrived; his is a late winter arrival rather than early spring. He generally reaches north Baffin early in April, joining the ptarmigan, raven, snowy owl and gyrfalcon, all of whom winter in this far north land.

Close upon the heels of the sea birds come the land species, the plovers, the longspurs, the jaegers, heading for their summer breeding grounds on the rolling plains that intersect the rocky land. In late May the first formations of snow geese appear, long wavering V's of pure white winging high overhead, clearly etched into the bright blue sky. By the middle of June the birds are settled on the breeding grounds, laying their eggs in shallow nests on the ground. In the Arctic, all birds nest on the ground or on the ledges of the rocky cliff faces that rise up out of the sea.

Bylot Island, in particular, is a haven for almost every species of bird that makes its summer home north of the Arctic Circle. Although the island is largely ice cap, tremendous fields of glistening white ice rising in the interior to a height of three thousand feet and more, the snow-free rocky ledges of the east and west coast and the low rolling plateau that covers the southern third of the island attract hundreds of birds. Using the illustrations from Peterson's *A Field Guide to the Birds*, Eskimos have identified thirty-three different species they have seen in this area.

As long as the Eskimos can remember, they have looked forward to the return of the birds to their land, to the taste of fresh eggs eaten raw or boiled. Snow geese eggs are the favourite, with murre coming a close second. Under white man's law, the gathering of these eggs is forbidden, but few Eskimos in this area pay much attention to this. The Eskimos know it is against the law to take the eggs, but, having no clear concept of what a law is, or means, they do not pay much attention to it.

"Perhaps the policeman would catch you (meaning arrest) for taking the eggs," said one old Eskimo in answer to my query, "but then you are a white man. He would not catch me for this is my land, not the white man's. He (the policeman) does not understand geese. I do, just as my father did before me. The policeman tells me I must not take eggs. And why should I not take eggs? Must I who am hungry for the taste of fresh eggs stand by and watch the foxes and the weasels eating eggs? No, I like eggs."

I can understand and sympathize with his feelings. For I too have come through the winter on north Baffin, living almost entirely on the meat and fat of seals and narwhals and rabbits. I too have looked forward to the day when high overhead I would see the first flight of geese winging their way north to the breeding grounds on Bylot Island, and my mouth has watered at the thought of a meal of fresh eggs. The law forbidding the gathering of eggs is a sound one when viewed from our side of the tree line, but it will always be impossible to enforce unless something else takes the place of the egg in the Eskimo diet.

Despite the reawakening of the Arctic in springtime, many of us, brought up on the adage "April showers bring May flowers", might find spring on north Baffin a rather desultory affair. Ice still covers the sea and will do so until the end of July or early August. Deep drifts of winter snow cling stubbornly to the land. Temperatures barely rise above freezing even when the sun rides high in the sky. Often it rains, a cold wet drizzle that soaks clothes and tents and sleeping gear.

To the Eskimo, however, spring is the best season of the year. The month of June brings an almost holiday-like air to every camp. The meat caches are empty, but it does not matter, food problems are over for a while as seals are plentiful, sleeping on the ice. The rivers are running and there is water for tea without laboriously melting ice. On the trail he sleeps in the open; there is no need to build a snow house at the end of each travel day. Trapping is over, winter with its dark and its cold is a long way off. Until the fall, the Eskimo is master of time.

I love spring in the Arctic, the sights and sounds it brings to north Baffin Island. For the first time in nine months the ear delights to the muffled tumbling of water over the rocks under the snow; to the rushing roar of snow-fed streams and rivers racing down to the sea; to the dull echoing rumble of far-away landslides as huge masses of frost-cracked shale and rock thunder down the steep slopes. The eye is dazzled by the unbelievable brilliance of the sun on the white snow, by the intense blue of the spring sky, by the sight of the first flowers bursting into bloom through the melting snow cover, or in the puddles of water in the rocks. The nose, so long atuned to the strong odours of blood and fat and decaying meat, gratefully picks up the delicate scent of the land, the smell of wet earth and moss. There is even new flavour to the water; you can taste the land in it.

I love the feeling of existing without regard to time, the endlessness of the day. There is no darkness to regulate the daily life; you sleep when you are tired, eat when you are hungry. I like to hear the shrill cries of the children as they play on the rocky shores or out on the sea ice, running about with reckless abandon chasing birds and dogs; or to see them stretched out full length by the cracks in the sea ice for hours at a time jigging for fish.

But late spring of 1953 was a time of cold and snow on north Baffin; the weather was more suited to March than to June. All the cracks in the sea ice in which the sea birds usually feed were frozen over. Gulls roamed the rocky coasts like ravens, seeking out the opened winter cache sites hoping for a morsel of food pecked from between the rocks. On the land, snow covered the feeding and nesting grounds of the snow geese, and almost every day in our travels over the ice we saw geese resting well away from the land. Some were nesting and the female sat on the eggs up to the neck in wind-blown snow. Drifts formed down-wind from every nesting bird just as they form in the lee of the ice hummocks on the sea.

The cold weather did not bother the seals; everywhere they lay by their breathing holes basking in the hot sun, sometimes playing like children rolling over and over in the snow, diving into the hole and then quickly clambering out again onto the ice. Usually the young seals cavorted about; the older ones alternately slept and kept one eye on the surrounding ice, always on the watch for hunters and for bears.

On north Baffin, the seal is the mainstay of life for the Eskimos. In fact this is true for the majority of the Eskimos in the Canadian Eastern Arctic. They eat its meat; they use the fat as fuel for the seal-oil lamps which cook the food and heat the houses. The skins are sold at the Hudson's Bay Company store, or they are made into boots and mitts and trousers. Remove the seals from the area and, unless fed by the outside world, the Eskimos would cease to be.

All winter the seals live under the thick ice cover on the sea. Being a mammal, the seal must have air to breathe. Starting when the ice cover first forms on the sea in the early fall, the seals keep open a series of breathing holes in the ever thickening ice. At the surface the holes are only big enough to allow the seal to stick its nose out of the water to breathe, and, after the first heavy snowfall in late November or early December, are invisible but for a slight concave depression in the snow. The holes open out vertically into cigar shaped openings to the sea in which the seal rests while it breathes. Beneath the ice the seals feed on small fishes and plankton that abound in these northern waters. Larger seals will eat large fishes as well.

In the spring when the hot sun melts the snow cover on the sea ice, the seals enlarge the holes at the surface by scraping the ice with their teeth and with the sharp claws of their front flippers. They then come out on the ice to bask in the hot sun. Usually they appear in April, although at certain locations it is possible to see seals on the ice during any month of the year. By May, wherever there are seals, they are out on the ice, first beside the breathing holes and later beside the cracks that form in the ice. They will lie singly or up to three and four at a single hole. Along the cracks, which can extend for miles, they often lie in groups of twenty to thirty, hundreds of them for as far as the eye and the telescope can see.

Day after day throughout April, May, June and July, the Eskimos hunt the seals. Travelling by sled they move over the ice from frozen-in iceberg to iceberg, using the bergs as vantage points from which to search the surrounding ice for seals in the best position for a kill. Today the kill is made with a rifle, usually a 30.30 calibre or a .300. At times the small bore .22 is used, chiefly by the younger boys. The hunter gets into position for a shot by stalking the seal behind a white screen. The screen, made of a square yard of white cloth stretched taut over two wooden cross slats, is used as a portable blind. To the seal it looks like a piece of ice.

A seal on the ice sleeps in short naps, ten seconds to a minute or so in duration, rarely any longer. Then it lifts its head and looks all about. If it sees, hears or smells anything strange, it will immediately slide into the hole, beside which it has been lying, down into the sea. The hunter must move forward while the seal sleeps and crouch motionless behind the screen when it looks around. Many seals adopt a definite time pattern for sleeping and looking around, and the hunter can move forward using this time pattern, always going down a few seconds before the seal is due to look up. Others follow no pattern and then it is necessary for the hunter to watch them continuously as he moves forward, ready to sink down behind the screen at the first sign of movement on the part of the seal. While crouched behind the screen, the hunter observes the movements of the seal through a small slit cut in the cloth for that purpose.

In an area which has not been extensively hunted, the stalking of seals is not a difficult job. Seals are curious by nature and often their curiosity overweighs their caution. They will often stay to watch when they should have looked and dived. In the Pond Inlet area seals are wary, and seem to be growing increasingly so as each year goes by. There are lots of seals, but they are getting more difficult to hunt. Idlouk's totals of seals get lower each year, and he and the other hunters from his camp must roam farther afield to get the seals they need for food and clothing. In 1951, although a newcomer to stalking seals on the ice, I was able to do quite well at it. In 1953, I had a good deal of difficulty in holding up my end as a hunter at the camp.

A seal is stalked up to the wind, for seal can smell danger from a long way off. The hunter must move to the sun if the sun is shining so that his shadow will not fall on the screen. Both of these factors often mean long walks, circling around a seal for a mile or more before the stalk itself begins. Deep soft snow makes stalking tedious; overcast days make it almost impossible to judge distance when peering at the seal over the top of the screen or through the tiny slit. Having to stalk through pools of water on the ice is noisy enough to cause a seal to go down; new ice on these surface pools will crinkle badly at every step. On one occasion I missed getting seals for an entire morning when gulls from a nearby rookery frightened the seals with their cries as they came circling overhead.

The ideal situation for a stalk occurs when the day is sunny but slightly hazy, and shadows are not so sharply defined; when the hunter can stalk both to the wind and the sun and keep a partially snow covered land horizon behind him; when there is smooth ice or light snow underfoot; and when the prey is a young seal whose curiosity has not been blunted by previous contact with danger. Twice I have hunted seals under such ideal conditions, and each time have been able to get within eight yards of the seal and observe its movements for twenty minutes through the slit in the screen before making the kill. In each case the seals saw the screen, but it did not alarm them.

Before the coming of the white man and his rifle, the Eskimos stalked seals without a screen, armed only with a harpoon or a knife. This art has been lost by most of the Eskimos with whom I have come in contact in much the same way as most of us have lost the art of driving a horse; something better has come along. Idlouk is one of the few Eskimos I have seen hunt the seal in this way. He does it remarkably well and every so often, when the conditions for such a stalk are right, he will go after a seal without the screen, armed only with his harpoon. Under his guidance I have tried it, but so far have not managed to get any closer than fifty yards before the seal has become alarmed and gone down into the hole. When this happens Idlouk always tells me that my feet are too big to be taken for seal flippers, or that all seals can spot a white man from a long way off.

I watched Idlouk make a kill this way on a day when it was too windy to use the screen to good advantage. Carrying only the harpoon, with his white parka cover covered by the dark blue one I wore, he walked to within three hundred yards of the seal, taking advantage of every piece of rough ice as cover. He then lay down full length on the ice behind a piece of ice and when the seal was asleep, rolled quickly out into the open. In about thirty seconds the seal looked up from its nap, searched the ice and immediately spotted Idlouk. Through the binoculars I could see the seal rise up on its front flippers for a better look. Idlouk immediately imitated the movements of the seal. His arms held close to his sides, he raised his head clear of the snow. With knees pressed tightly together, he waved his lower legs and feet in imitation of the movement of the hind flippers. Then he slumped down, to all intents a seal asleep on the ice.

The seal was completely fooled. Every time the seal slept, Idlouk crept forward; every time the seal looked up, Idlouk became a seal, looking around, waving his feet, sleeping on the ice. He was careful always to keep a three-quarter outline of his body towards the seal to disguise the telltale hump of his shoulders.

It took him two hours to get within fifty yards of the seal; another half an hour, he was twenty-five yards away. The seal was still not in the least suspicious. At about ten yards, Idlouk carefully readied the harpoon, working by feel alone, his eyes glued to the seal. At the slightest sign of movement, Idlouk became a seal, even making the rasping cough the seal uses when out of the water. Harpoon in position he waited. The seal raised its head and looked over at Idlouk. I held my breath; one false move and the seal would be gone, a three-hour hunt wasted. But all was well; the seal's head went down to start another nap. It was his last. The moment the seal's head touched the ice, Idlouk jumped to his feet and dashed forward. The seal looked up at the noise, saw Idlouk coming, and scrambled madly for the hole. For a moment I thought it was gone, but Idlouk's arm flashed into the air and down again. The harpoon, thrown on the dead run, buried itself in the seal's arching back. A quick tug on the line and the harpoon head came free of the handle, pulling flat under the skin and the fat. The seal was hooked. Hardly pausing in his stride, Idlouk swung his fist as the seal raised its head. In one swift blow he crushed the skull, killing the seal instantly. The long hunt was over.

It was immediately after this hunt that Idlouk first talked to me of how he felt about the coming of the white man to his land. I have often heard the opinion expressed that the Eskimos would have been better off if the white man had never gone into the Arctic, and that the solution to the problems of the Eskimo was to remove all white men from the area and get the Eskimo back to his old way of life. I do not hold with this view, and I have yet to meet the Eskimo who does. Most Eskimos are terribly confused by

69

the impact of our culture on their own, but no one I know would want to return to the old way of life. Sitting together on the dead seal, enjoying a meal of raw liver and seal heart with a mug of tea, Idlouk talked to me of the old days in his land. "I am glad I do not have to live as my father and my grandfather did," he said, "for stalking seals on the ice without a harpoon or a screen can be a hard job. When the sea ice is covered with water, the hunter's clothes get soaking wet as he crawls through the puddles after the seals. With wet clothes he soon becomes cold and miserable. If the snow is deep and soft, it is backbreaking work to crawl the long distance to the seal. And if the hunter runs into a streak of bad luck in his hunting, he often starves to death with his family.

"Not far from here there is the grave of an Eskimo who died from starvation when the hunting in his area failed in 1922. I was only a boy at the time, but I remember. Today we might go hungry, but we know that we can always get food from the white man to help us over the bad times, where before we would have starved to death. I hear many white people speak out against the store. Sometimes I do not understand the money I get for my furs, and the money I must pay for my goods, but I never forget that if it wasn't for the store of the white man I wouldn't have my rifle, my ammunition, my seal screen, my steel knife, my tobacco and my tea. And I would not want to be without any of them."

CHAPTER

7

FOR A WEEK after my arrival at the camp I led a leisurely
life. After being on the trail for over a month my sleeping
bag and caribou sleeping skins were damp. Sealskin boots
and mitts were badly in need of repair. Each sunny day
Kidlak hung the sleeping bag and skins out on the rocks
back of the camp. She made new boot bottoms for one
pair of sealskins, and a complete new pair with double soles
for wear on the rocky land around the campsite. She made
a new pair of sealskin mitts as mine were worn into holes
at the fingers, and she promised that, as soon as I brought
in three fine young seal skins from the hunt, she would
make a pair of sealskin trousers for me. Due to circumstances beyond my control, the trousers were not made until
the spring of 1954.

Idlouk was anxious to get back to his regular life—the
hunt. June and July are important months for the Eskimos
on north Baffin; the skins of the young seals are at their
best and bring two dollars and fifty cents at the store. As
the trapping season had been over for two months, this was
the first chance Idlouk had had of making money since
that time. He could sell the skins of the larger seals for one
dollar at any time, but this was hardly enough money for the
amount of work involved in preparing a skin for sale. The
skin must be thoroughly scraped to remove the fat, washed,
and dried staked out on the hillside, or over a wooden
frame. During the best drying months in the spring and
early summer, the Eskimos are busy with the skins of the
young seals. During May and June the skins of the older

seals are unfit for anything but dog food; the hair is moulting. The skin can then be peeled off in long strips.

To make up for time lost while on the trip to Clyde River, Idlouk decided to do two jobs at once; go after young seals, and at the same time put in caches of seal meat along the route of his winter trap line. This meant a two hundred mile journey to the bottom of Paquet Bay, east and south of our camp.

I accompanied Idlouk on this trip. On the night of June 22nd we left the camp and headed north and east over the ice of Eclipse Sound. We travelled light, taking only the small sled and ten dogs. Our load consisted of a small canvas tent, very old and full of holes, two sleeping bags with caribou sleeping skins, a single large polar bear skin as a ground sheet and a sled cover, rifles and ammunition, harpoons and harpoon lines, grub box with primus stove, extra fuel, about ten sea biscuits, and a quarter of a pound of tea. We each took rubber boots as an extra item of clothing, but otherwise had only the clothing we wore: sealskin boots over socks of heavy duffel cloth, heavy trousers and shirt with over-trousers and parka of duffel cloth with windproof covers. This is normal clothing for spring travel on north Baffin Island. Few Eskimos of today bother with trousers or parkas of sealskin; these items having been superseded by duffel cloth bought at the store, which is vastly superior to sealskin for such use.

When well sewn, sealskin boots will keep water out, but the boot itself soaks up water and gets very damp. This gradually dampens the duffel sock next to the boot, and soon the feet are clammy and cold, particularly on the bottom where the foot comes in contact with the snow ice. In a rubber boot the foot becomes damp but not wet, and the felt insole keeps a dry insulation between the foot and the ice. This does not apply in the fall of the year when the ice surface conditions are somewhat the same, but when the air temperature is well below freezing. Then the rubber boots are not warm enough, and the sealskins are much the better footwear.

In addition to being a more comfortable type of footwear in late spring and early summer, rubber boots save the Eskimo housewife a good deal of work. Sealskin boots, that have been wet, harden on drying and must be chewed or scraped soft, and stretched into shape before they can be worn again. They wear out very quickly. An Eskimo mother with husband and three children to look after can usually keep her family well supplied with sealskin boots. Once the number of children in a family gets beyond three, she does not have enough hours in her day to keep up with the demand for dry boots. I have often seen smaller children kept in the tent for two or three days, unable to go out to play until new boots were made by the overworked mother.

Although I refer to our "grub box", this word does not really apply, for an Eskimo rarely has any grub in the box. A white man travelling in the Arctic usually has a well stocked grub box, food of all kinds, two primus stoves plus a good quantity of fuel for the trip. But with the Eskimo, the only grub in the box is a bit of tea and sometimes a few hard biscuits or bannock. A quart of kerosene is considered ample for a seven day journey. On this trip we expected to be gone for at least seven days, probably ten, and for that time we would hunt food for ourselves and the dogs on the way.

The first day out was overcast but bright. For eighteen hours we hunted over the ice on lower Eclipse Sound, working our way toward the narrow channel that separates Frechette Island from the mainland. The seals on Eclipse Sound were wary and it was not until noon that we made our first kill, twelve hours after leaving the camp. In the next six hours we shot only two more, one of them a young one with a fine skin. They were all shot at a range of two hundred yards or more, which is a long shot for this type of hunting. A seal's head is no bigger than a small saucer and is rarely over six inches above the surface of the ice. The seal must be killed outright, for if wounded it will slide into the hole and be lost. For a kill, it must be shot in the head.

About eight in the evening we made camp on a tiny snow-free gravel beach at the southern tip of Frechette Island. The campsite was a pretty spot facing almost due south and backed by the high rock walls of the island. A few yards from the tent a small stream ran down over the rocks in a series of tiny waterfalls; the water danced and sang, the first sign of spring we had seen since the warmer weather of a month before. We fed the meat of the young seal to the dogs, keeping only enough for supper and breakfast for ourselves. The other seal, along with the fat of the young one, was cached under rocks on a small point of land near the campsite. A cache is simply a shallow depression among the rocks in which the seal is placed and then covered over with rocks which lie about in abundance. This keeps foxes and bears from the meat. Our supper was boiled seal ribs followed by a hard biscuit and a mug of strong black tea.

After five hours' sleep, we were awakened by the patter of rain on the canvas walls of the tent. In half an hour the old canvas was sopping wet, leaking badly in half a dozen places. In order to keep the sleeping bags and skins dry, we immediately broke camp and loaded the sled, covering everything with the big bear skin to keep off the rain. Breakfast was raw seal meat and tea eaten in the open. By the time we moved off, our outer clothes were soaked.

As we travelled across Tay Sound to the mouth of Paquet Bay, the rain came down steadily. In an hour we were both soaked to the skin. An oilskin slicker would have kept us dry, but such clothing is almost unknown to the Eskimo, although the store rarely runs short of light cotton shirts and silk bandanas. Not a seal was to be seen in any direction; we seemed to have the entire area to ourselves. Heading along the east side of Paquet Bay, we ran into a strong head wind that drove the rain down in sheets. With the temperature barely above freezing, we were nearly frozen, as uncomfortable as it was possible to be.

In Paquet Bay we began to see an occasional seal on the ice. Here and there a lone seal braved the wind and the rain to lie beside the breathing hole. But they did little sleeping. Stalk after stalk ended in failure, the seal going down before we could get close enough for a shot. In the high wind, the screen snapped and cracked like a pistol, and once it was blown right out of my hands as I was settling into position for the shot. In twelve hours of travel and hunting, we shot only one seal. Twice we stopped to have a biscuit with a mug of tea, and on the second occasion had raw seal meat from the kill. It was impossible to be comfortable under conditions such as we met; when stalking seals I was far too warm, when travelling on the sled I was much too cold. There seemed to be no in-between. Underfoot, the rain was softening the snow; here and there puddles of water appeared on the ice. We both changed from sealskins to rubber boots which are much warmer and drier under such conditions.

Near another small stream running down a narrow valley cut into the high rock walls of the bay, we pitched camp. The rain still poured down and the tent leaked in a dozen places, but we needed the rest and what warmth our sleeping bags would give before they too became soaking wet. For supper we had boiled seal meat and another mug of tea. There were no more biscuits; they had been used up during the day. With only the one seal, we did not feed the dogs; they could easily go for a day or so without food. As on the night before, the seal was cached under rocks on the shore.

After the long wet day Idlouk and I were both very tired. In spite of the steady drip of rain from the holes in the tent, I quickly fell asleep. It was eight hours later that I came out of a deep sleep to hear Idlouk muttering hoarsely to himself. He was propped up on one elbow, groping around in his sleeping bag.

"I feel as though I am swimming," he said.

He very nearly was. A puddle of water an inch deep had formed in his sleeping bag while he slept. One of the guy ropes of the tent had pulled loose in the wind, allowing the tent wall to sag. The rain ran down the groove into the hole where the rope had been, and from there down onto the top of the sleeping skin, which held the water in a small lake. It had not reached me, but my bag was almost as wet from other leaks in the tent. Now everything we had was soaked.

Breakfast was a cup of tea and the last of our seal meat eaten raw. Then we broke camp. The rain still pelted down and the wind howled between the high rock walls. The dogs were hungry and reluctant to travel, but travel they must. Regardless of the weather, we had to hunt to eat.

For eighteen hours we worked our way slowly down the bay, stopping to hunt every seal we saw on the ice. They were few and far between, seals being better off in the sea in weather like this. Even at places where normally a lot of young seals frolic on the ice we saw nothing, or just one or two, and neither of us could get close enough for a shot. Half way down the bay we found a solitary gull nesting on a rocky cliff. The two eggs in the nest were anything but fresh; in one the young gull had begun to form. Idlouk ate his egg with relish. I ate mine.

That night we pitched camp without having made a kill. Six cache sites had been passed and we had been unable to put in a single seal. We were both very hungry, the hunger that comes from strenuous physical exertion and no food. Without food I was having a hard time keeping warm, the twice daily cup of tea only momentarily providing a spark of inner warmth.

For the first time I began to sense something of what it means to hunt in order to eat. Prior to this, stalking of seals had been a sport, an exciting game. I had always gone off to hunt in high spirits as one goes into a football game or a boxing bout. Now I hunted with grim resolve. I was hungry, damned hungry. I was cold and wet. Hunting was no longer a game, it was a business. Hunger drowned compassion, I was primitive man hunting for his meat.

And yet I was not really primitive man, for I had not

yet learned patience, the patience that comes only after generations of such a life. Idlouk was hungry, but calm. I was hungry and short tempered. I cursed the seals, the rain, the dogs, the Arctic. None of this helped; I still got no seals.

That night we went to bed without food, in wet clothes and wet sleeping bags. As long as I lay in one spot I slept well, as heat from my body gradually warmed the wet clothes where they came into contact with me. But every time I changed position new contacts would be made, and I had to warm them slowly before getting back to sleep again.

The following day brought no improvement in the weather. Rain still came down steadily and the wind still blew. Once more we harnessed up the dogs and started off down the bay. Far ahead the high rock walls gradually petered out and we could see the dim outline of the low rolling plains that run inland from the lower ends of all the deep sounds in this area. If we did not get a seal today, perhaps we might be fortunate enough to see caribou on the plains and close enough to the edge of the sea ice to hunt without a long walk inland. Hunting of caribou on north Baffin Island is permitted only from mid-August to mid-September, except in the case of starvation. We considered ourselves hungry enough to be starving.

For another twelve hours we travelled down the bay. By now the surface of the sea ice was covered with pools of water. Seals on the ice were more plentiful, but in the wind and the rain they were not doing much sleeping. Try as we might, neither of us could get close enough for an effective shot. We were getting very tired from the long unsuccessful stalks after seals. At the end of a stalk I did not have the strength left to hold the rifle steady enough for the long shots we were forced to try. For the second day in a row we were forced to pitch camp without having made a kill. The dogs were very hungry now; all day they had had to be driven to move at all. Both of us were beginning to feel the effects of the long period without food. We had lost much of our feeling of hunger, but we could not get warm, even after the mug of hot tea. There was no thought of turning back. I was an Eskimo son, I had no say in what we did. And Idlouk was an Eskimo. He said, "This sort of luck cannot go on indefinitely. Does it not say in the Bible that one must not be downhearted by adversity for tomorrow will bring a better day?"

This time our camp was on a small point of land on the west side of Paquet Bay about ten miles from the lower end. Back of the tent the land sloped gently upward in sharp contrast to the steep rocky cliffs of our previous campsites. After putting up the tent, Idlouk spied two ducks in one of the small pools of sea water near the shore. Hunter overcame fatigue. I went after the ducks while Idlouk climbed the small hill back of the camp to search the surrounding hills with his telescope for a possible sign of caribou. I thought he was wasting his time for it was a number of years since caribou had been seen close to the sea on north Baffin Island.

For about fifteen minutes I worked my way slowly and carefully along the shore trying to get into position for a shot at the ducks. I managed to reach a sheltered spot immediately above the little pool in which they swam. Slowly I raised the rifle and took careful aim. Ordinarily I would have scorned to eat sea duck but now in anticipation I could taste the flesh in my mouth.

Before I could press the trigger, a shout rang out. Away went the ducks in a flurry of flapping wings and splashing water. For a moment I was tempted to try a shot on the wing, but fortunately did not. Looking inland I could see Idlouk standing on a small hilltop, silhouetted against the grey sky, waving his arms excitedly. This could mean only one thing. He had spotted caribou. A thousand to one chance had paid off.

The caribou, a single big bull, was grazing peacefully along a hilltop about three miles away. From Idlouk's vantage point I looked at him through the telescope. He stood out clearly against the horizon, alternately grazing and raising his head with its tremendous spread of antlers, to search the land around for danger. We watched him for about ten minutes, making sure of the direction in which he was feeding and then quickly ran down to the camp. It was the work of but a few minutes to change from rubber boots to sealskins which would be lighter for walking in case the hunt turned into a long drawn-out affair. Closing up the tent with rocks, we took rifles and ammunition and were on our way. The dogs were left behind; their work would come later, providing we managed to get the caribou. Fortunately the wind was such that they would not get the scent of the caribou and go after him before we could make the kill.

We walked south for about a mile, keeping on the sea ice along the shore. This was roughly the same direction in which the caribou was moving as he fed, always drifting into the wind. Then we took to the hills, leaving the sea ice and climbing steadily up the long gentle slope from the shore. We had not seen the caribou since leaving the vantage point of the hilltop, but if our calculations were correct, we should intersect his line of movement a mile or so inland from the edge of the sea.

It was a tough job walking over the soft snow and broken ground, often through pools of water that had formed under the snow. After the first half mile I was very tired, and Idlouk was not in much better shape. We moved along together, often stumbling to our knees on the broken ground and on the small rocks hidden under the snow. Coming up over a rise, about forty minutes after leaving the sea ice, we spotted the caribou. He was about half a mile from us, moving along at right angles to our line of approach. He would graze for a minute or so, pawing the snow away from the moss and lichen, and then raise his head to look about. At times he would stand motionless, watching some object that had caught his eye. Then, satisfied that it did not presage danger, his head would come down and he would resume feeding, always moving upwind.

Idlouk motioned to me to be very quiet and to take his arm. Linked together, we moved up over the top of the rise and out into full view of the grazing caribou. Between us was a wide shallow valley, with no cover of any kind, across which we would have to go before we could get into position for a shot. Thus began one of the strangest hunts I have ever taken part in on land, with hunter and hunted always in full view. It was much like stalking a seal on the ice without benefit of the screen.

Slowly we moved along in the same direction the caribou was feeding, always angling in to intersect his line of march. When the caribou raised his head to look about, we froze on the spot. Close together, motionless, we must have looked like a dark rock to him. When he began to feed we moved again, keeping in a low crouch, taking long gliding steps, carefully easing our feet down into the snow.

A quarter of a mile of this and I was dead beat. With muscles already fatigued from three days of ceaseless stalking of seals and no food, I found it torture to freeze in awkward positions, absolutely motionless, in full view of the caribou. But Idlouk was as firm as a rock. Eyes glued to every movement of the grazing animal, he glided along, taking me with him, sensing rather than seeing the hummocks of uneven ground. Even before the caribou's head had swung up to look about, he would anticipate the movement and freeze. In spite of my fatigue I was fascinated by the intensity of his bearing. Something of his feeling communicated itself to me. Everything else was forgotten, all that existed was the caribou and I. I had no pity for the animal about to die. Without his flesh and fat *I* might die, and the sense of self-preservation runs strong in every human breast.

We had reached a position about three hundred yards from the caribou when I stumbled slightly on a hidden rock. The head swung up with a jerk, antlers etched into the grey of the sky. I thought, "I've done it, we've lost him."

Jumping high in the air, the caribou ran off to the right. But he was still curious about what had caused him to run. Swinging around in a wide circle he cut in toward us as we still crouched motionless on the snow. About two hundred yards away, he slowed down and swung around to face in our direction. There he stood, motionless, front legs splayed out wide ready for instant flight. Slowly I sank down into a sitting position on the snow and raised the rifle to my shoulder. Idlouk began to grunt, the pig-like noise of the caribou. The big head swung about trying to get our scent, eyes straining to see what we could be. With the caribou head-on, I aimed for the heart. A short prayer, a long breath, and I squeezed the trigger. At the sharp crack the caribou went down, but he was up again almost instantly. I had not allowed for wind drift, and the shot had struck the left shoulder, breaking the leg and badly dazing him. On three legs he set off in the direction of the beach while we jumped up and ran after him, stumbling and falling over the uneven ground. All fatigue was for-gotten.

The caribou ran about half a mile, and then swung about to face us again. Idlouk quickly dropped down and fired, but the shot missed. Away went the caribou. Then suddenly he collapsed in the snow. Slowly he struggled to his feet and faced in our direction. Idlouk took careful aim and fired again. This time he went down to stay. As we ran up to him, Idlouk drew his pocket knife. Reaching the animal he grabbed the wildly threshing horns and, with a quick slash of the knife, cut the animal's throat. The caribou jerked and then was still. Our supper lay at our feet.

Suddenly I was terribly hungry. Idlouk showed me how to slit the tips of the antlers, peel back the velvet and eat the gristly substance from within. While chewing on this, we worked together cutting up the animal. First the hide was removed. Next the four legs were taken off, the car-cass gutted, and the head cut free. As we worked we ate— small pieces of back fat, strips of meat from the lower legs, tidbits of liver and heart, a mouthful or two of the stomach contents. Nothing had very much taste, it was just food. Famine to feast. Two hours before we had had no prospect of food; now we had enough to last us for the rest of the trip.

Once the main work of cutting up was completed, I

took the rifles and walked back to our camp to get the dogs and sled. Getting the sled up over the partially snow-free land was a back-breaking job, but much easier than trying to get the meat down onto the ice. I knew; I had made some carries such as that on a few occasions before. Besides, with the dogs up at the point of the kill, we could feed the entrails to them. No Eskimo on north Baffin would ever think of feeding any other portion of the caribou to the dogs unless it was a matter of life or death. Caribou meat is too highly prized for that.

In my absence Idlouk completed the cutting up. The caribou was now in six main pieces, the four hams, the body cavity and the head. Inside the body cavity he placed an assortment of small parts, the liver, the heart, a portion of the large intestine. He saved the lining of the smallest of the three stomachs and stuffed it with the contents of all the stomachs, a greenish mush of predigested lichens on which the caribou had been feeding. Later on I got to like this dish very much; at the time I cared little for its acidy taste.

All the meat, except the forelegs, was loaded into the large chest cavity and the loose stomach skin folded over the opening and hooked to the backbone, thus making a closed container that could easily be loaded onto the sled. The remains of the entrails were fed to the dogs, which had been standing by, kept back only by the repeated cracks of the long whip. They fell on the food like wolves, for they were ravenously hungry.

Back at the tent we boiled a tremendous pot of caribou meat. The meat was tough, but I cannot remember enjoying another meal so much. After two mugs of strong tea, still clad in wet clothes, we crawled into the wet sleeping bags and soon were deep in the first sound sleep in well over two days. Cold, damp and hunger were forgotten.

The killing of the caribou marked the turning point in our luck. We awoke twelve hours later to find the sun shining down out of a clear blue sky. The wind moderated somewhat and changed direction, blowing out of the west.

Idlouk and I stripped down to the skin and spread clothing and sleeping gear out on the rocks to dry. For two or three hours we alternately ate and played tag over the rocky hills, trying to keep warm while our clothes dried. With the temperature barely above freezing, conditions were not quite right for bathing in the sun.

MANY YEARS ago, before the establishment of settlements on north Baffin Island, the barren ground caribou played an important part in the life of the Eskimos of this area. Although basically a sea culture people, the Eskimos of north Baffin consider caribou meat one of the greatest delicacies of their land. The skins are unmatched for winter clothing, both in lightness and in warmth. Caribou fur has an extremely high insulating value, largely because of the unique construction of the hair which consists of thin hollow tubes. For travel in winter, boots, socks, mitts, pants and parkas of caribou skin provide the best protection known against the intense cold.

"When I was a boy," said Idlouk's father, Akomalik, as we talked together not long after my trip down Tay Sound and Paquet Bay, "we used to hunt caribou nearly every fall. Our camp was in Tay Sound, not far from the place you have just been. We went there late in the spring, before the ice moved out. There were many caribou in those days. I have even seen them killed on our little island of Aulatseevik. But that was long ago.

"My father and I, along with the other hunters from the camp, would go inland from our camp by the edge of the sea. Not far inland, though; we were never out of sight of the sea. From the tops of the high hills we watched for caribou. Sometimes we would see none, but usually there were lots of them. When we saw a herd the hunters went off in different directions to surround it, but keeping out of sight. When everyone was in position, we would show ourselves, all at once in a large circle around the herd. The animals did not know where to run. They dashed off one way only to be stopped by a hunter. They tried another path, but

83

once again a hunter blocked the way. Where there was open ground and no hunters to cover it, we put up piles of rocks in the likeness of man, and these fooled the caribou. They became confused and ran around in circles.

"In a while they became used to having the hunters all around them, as we did not try to kill them. No, not yet we didn't. But as soon as the caribou quieted down and began to feed, we shouted, and waved our arms and ran about. The caribou became alarmed again and ran off only to be turned from escape by the hunters and by the piles of stones that looked like hunters. They ran around in circles not knowing where to go. This went on for a long time, often for two days. Never did we give the caribou a moment to lie down and rest, nor did we get any rest ourselves. But we could go longer than the caribou without sleep. The caribou must get some sleep every day, or he gets very tired from running.

"When we had the herd very tired, all the hunters moved forward, walking slowly toward the caribou as they lay on the ground. If we were careful we could sometimes walk up close enough to kick them. They were so tired. Then we shot them. Some of us had rifles while others used the bow and arrow. We used to get rifles from the whalers who came to our land, but sometimes the ships would not come and we would run out of ammunition. We would have to use the bow and arrow again. But it didn't matter, for the caribou were weary. I have seen hunters slit a caribou's throat before it could scramble to its feet and be off.

"Throughout the fall and early winter, we lived on the meat from the caribou, while our women made warm clothes from the skins. When the meat caches were empty we left the area and journeyed over the ice to Mitch-imatellik (Pond Inlet). From there we hunted seals at their breathing holes during the dark winter months. Early in the spring we would journey to Sengeeriak (Button Point) at the floe edge. Here all the Eskimos would come in the spring, hoping the ships of the whalers would come."

The generation of young people growing to adulthood

on north Baffin Island today sees little of the caribou. Many of the young men know nothing of the land back of the coasts as they do not go there to hunt caribou any longer. The large herds no longer came down the valleys from the interior of the island to the coast regions. There are a number of contributory causes for this, the greater numbers of rifles used and the increased availability of ammunition for high-powered, large-bore rifles being a major one. The introduction of the high-powered rifles undoubtedly resulted in a much higher yearly kill, and decimation of certain herds of caribou. But one other factor pertaining to the rifles is often overlooked. This is the amount of noise made by high-powered large bore rifles. I believe the noise and confusion of the hunts when everyone had a rifle and lots of ammunition did much to cause the herds to change their migration routes.

According to the older Eskimos, a fairly large herd of caribou used to move in a sweeping circular path of migration around the north and east portion of Baffin Island. This movement centred on Eclipse Sound. Old Eskimos still remember the days when they hunted caribou in the sea from their kayaks, spearing the animals as they crossed from the mainland to Bylot Island at Low Point, swimming across Navy Board Inlet. They still talk of the year when a large herd of caribou, crossing in the fall from Bylot Island to the mainland near where the settlement of Pond Inlet now stands, crashed through the thin ice and were drowned in the frigid waters.

This movement no longer takes places. In 1947, the last of the caribou on Bylot Island were killed. Now they are found on north Baffin only in the interior valleys, well inland, to the south of the sounds running out of Eclipse Sound. I do not think this herd was wiped out, for outside of the big kill on Bylot Island, the Eskimos speak of no other large killing. I think the herd changed the path of movement so as to avoid the north coastal region with its noise and confusion and death.

Another factor that affected the course of such a movement was the increase in the number of dogs in Eskimo camps. Idlouk told me that few things frighten caribou like the smell of dogs. He said that in the old days the Eskimos had only a few dogs and when they camped near the lower ends of the sounds in the fall to hunt caribou, they always camped by a swift-flowing river. The dogs were kept close to the river and were restrained from wandering in the hills back of the camp. All excreta was thrown in the river so that the dog odour was kept to a minimum. With the increase in the numbers of dogs and the extension of travel routes along winter trap lines, it was no longer possible to maintain such conditions. Dogs became frequent travellers into areas where caribou had previously grazed unmolested throughout the winter months and the noise and smell would soon tend to make caribou avoid such places.

CHAPTER
8

EARLY in July, much of the ice on the sea remained hard, but snow on the surface had long since melted, covering the ice with pools and lakes of water. Some of the lakes were four and five miles long, great puddles of fresh and near fresh water on the surface of the salt sea ice. Close inshore, the rise and fall of the tide broke the ice to pieces so that leads of open water separated the main body of the ice from the shore at high tide. Off every rocky point cracks formed in the ice, long leads of open water from five to fifty feet wide and more, cutting for miles through the thick ice cover on the sea.

Along such cracks the seals came out to bask in the hot sun. Sitting high on the hilltop back of the camp, looking out over the ice through the telescope, I saw hundreds and hundreds of seals sleeping or playing on the ice. Beside the holes they lay singly or in pairs; along the cracks they were thick as flies, clustered in groups of fifty to one hundred. There were so many that it was next to impossible to stalk them, there were always too many looking about. Most of these were second year seals that had spent the winter at the floe edge in Baffin Bay, off the entrance to Pond Inlet, before migrating down into Eclipse Sound in the summer. They are very thin, long and slim in body, and there is so little fat on them that it is not worthwhile stripping it off for use in the seal-oil lamps. The skins are not as valuable as those of the first year seals. If we were short of food we ate their meat, but if not, the dead seals were put in the caches to use as dog food next winter. We did not bother even to remove the skin.

We used the floe edge technique of shooting them in the water while standing on the ice at the edge of the cracks. If the cracks were narrow, they were easily retrieved, but at the wider cracks it was necessary to have a second hunter waiting in his kayak on the water, ready to dash out and harpoon the seal after it was shot, and before it could sink. The kayaks were taken out to the cracks on the sleds.

When travelling on the sea ice by sled, we often saw second year seals bobbing up and down in the breathing holes. Singly they rarely came out on the ice. We hunted them in the holes by selecting a spot near a series of such breathing holes, then sitting on the ice with rifle and harpoon ready. If a seal bobbed up in a nearby hole, it would spot the hunter sitting motionless on the ice, become very curious as to what he could be, and bob higher and higher in the hole trying to get a better look, often pausing at the peak of a bob with half the length of its body out of the water, hind flippers gyrating madly to keep it balanced there. At such times the seal made an easy target.

On being shot, the seal slid slowly back into the hole and down into the sea. The moment the hunter fired, he dropped the rifle, picked up the harpoon and dashed for the hole, harpoon raised ready to throw. The hunter had to sink the harpoon into the body before it got too far down, and to do this the harpoon was often thrown on the dead run.

It is possible to lose seals that have been shot while sleeping on the ice beside the breathing hole or crack. The ice around the hole is usually slippery and wet, and the seal lies with its head beside the hole, often almost hanging into it. When shot it will start to slide slowly along the ice into the hole where the momentum of the plunge will take it under the ice, impossible to retrieve. The blood from the wound will help the seal along the slide.

Most seals on the ice in large numbers seem to get along

together reasonably well. They lie side by side along the cracks and each one pays almost no attention to its neighbour. There is no seal community, or group. With seals it is every man for himself. They have no form of warning or danger signals that can be used by one seal to warn others. Sudden movement on the part of one seal will, of course, frighten others around so that all will go down into the sea, but this is not because of any universally recognized warning system. Eskimos realize this, and govern stalking practices accordingly. It is an advantage in that if a seal among a lot of seals is frightened by the hunter and dives into the hole, only those in the immediate vicinity will dive after it. However, it is a disadvantage when stalking a number of seals along a crack or beside a series of holes, for the hunter must keep an eye on all of them; there is no such thing as one or perhaps two seals acting as a lookout for the rest.

Although much of the sea ice was covered with water, there still remained many small islands of ice. These islands were low, rounded hummocks, as little as two feet in diameter or as much as five hundred feet, and of every possible shape. As the sun beat down on the ice, the surface of the islands melted and the water ran off into the puddles and lakes nearby. Being salt ice, it melted into jagged splinters or crystals that cut the bottoms of our sealskin boots. It was necessary to have extra soles put on our boots, and to make tiny boots of sealskin for the dogs to keep their feet from being cut to ribbons as we travelled over the sea ice. When we were stalking seals, the ice surface on the islands crunched and crackled with every step, particularly during the cool "night" hours when the sun was low on the northern horizon. To stalk silently on such a surface was impossible. It was necessary to stay in the lakes and rivers on the ice surface, avoiding the islands of ice wherever possible. This usualy lengthened a stalk considerably as it was impossible to travel in a straight line. Often I spent two to three hours winding my way along the tortuous paths of water, slowly pushing each foot forward through the water step by slow step, not daring to lift my foot clear for fear of the noise it would make. My feet became paralyzed with the cold, muscles became aching knots, for it was not possible to crouch low enough behind the screen to rest without sitting down in the water.

The worst moments of such a stalk came when I had approached near enough for a shot. Then I had to get out of the water onto the ice and sit down for the shot. Three steps might be all that were required, but they were three steps on ice that crackled at the slightest touch. Too much noise and the seal would be gone and a three-hour hunt wasted. This happened to me all too often.

If a cold snap set in, and one can set in at any time of the year on north Baffin, where no month is entirely free of snow and ice, then new ice formed on top of the pools and rivers on the sea ice, and it too crackled with each step as badly as the ice on the islands. It was then impossible to stalk quietly.

One method of hunting under such a condition is to drive the dogs straight for the seal on the ice, whipping them into a fast run. The seal looks up, sees the onrushing sled and does one of two things: stays on the ice to watch, or dives into the hole. If the seal does not dive, the hunters immediately start to shout, a long steady drawn out Ooooooooooooooh, as loud as they can. The combination of the sight of the onrushing sled and the steady sound of the voice seems to fascinate the seal. It looks up, straining to see what is making such a noise. It rolls over and over, makes as if to slide in the hole, then rises to look again, baffled but still curious. It strains its body upright, resting on outstretched front flippers.

When about a hundred and fifty yards off, one of the hunters picks up his rifle and with a running jump leaps clear of the sled. Doubled over he runs quickly off to one side, drops to his knee and fires a quick shot at the seal. If the seal is very curious he will not fire quickly, but will sit down and take careful aim. With practice this method can account for a good many seals.

A slight variation is used for young seals. The hunter, after spotting a young seal, prepares the screen and then starts to walk steadily in a straight line toward it, holding the screen in front so that only his head is visible above. As soon as the hunter is spotted by the seal he commences to hum, a low steady sound that covers the crunching footsteps. This seems to fascinate the young seals as much as the louder shouting from the onrushing sled fascinates older ones. Using this method, I have often walked to within fifty yards of a young seal, carefully sat down, and then shot it easily.

Throughout the fall, winter and spring, the seals float when killed in the water. But early in July they start to sink. Throughout July, August and early September hunters always carry the harpoon as well as the rifle. Many reasons have been advanced for this sinking. The Eskimos believe it to be caused primarily by the lack of fat on the seal in the summer. In summer the layer of fat which completely encompasses the seal's body shrinks in thickness. From being as much as three inches, it will rapidly dwindle to a half inch or so. Without this fat the seal sinks very quickly when killed.

The decreased salinity of the sea water due to the large amounts of fresh water dumped into it by the spring run-off has been cited as another factor affecting the buoyancy of the seal. Water in the wide cracks in the sea ice in the late spring and early summer can be fresh enough for the dogs to drink. I have seen seals shot in such cracks sink slowly down to a depth of six or seven feet and there remain suspended in the water as the current carried them slowly away. The fat on the body has not been sufficient to keep them afloat in the upper layer of water with its reduced salinity, but sufficient for them to float in the sea water below the surface layer. This summer sinking applies only to the mature seals. The first year seals which retain their body fat through the summer of the first year of their existence do not sink and can be shot in the open water without fear of being lost.

Every day in July the hunters of Aulatseevik, myself among them, roamed far and wide over the ice in the never-ending hunt for food. Usually we went off in pairs, each pair with sled and dogs moving off in a different direction, to be gone sometimes for only a day, sometimes for three or four before coming back to the camp for a rest. On such hunts we lived completely off the land, or rather off the products of the sea, eating most of the meat raw, caching what we and the dogs could not eat in some convenient place so that it would serve as dog food during the long winter night to come.

On a few occasions all the adults and most of the children at the camp went out together on an organized hunt, five or six sleds moving over the ice together. On such organized hunts we would be gone for as little as a day, or as much as three days, and rarely did anyone think of sleep in that time. It was hunt and eat, from the time we left, until the time we returned to camp, everyone completely stuffed, thoroughly exhausted, and soaking wet from splashing through the deep puddles on the ice.

The main purpose of these hunts is to get the skins of the young seals. The skin is the property of the man making the kill while all meat and fat is communal property.

The weapon generally used on such hunts is the seal harpoon. It consists of a long steel shaft about shoulder high that is rounded off at one end and has a sealskin line wound about the other to form a rough handle. Onto the rounded end is fitted the harpoon head which is readily detachable. The head is made of steel fashioned to form a broad flat point that tails off into flanged flukes curving back from the main axis. Attached to this head is a long sealskin line. The steel head has a ball socket which fits over the rounded end of the harpoon handle. With the head held in place, the sealskin line is run along the handle to a spot about two thirds of the way to the top where a small metal loop is fastened. At this point on the sealskin line a tiny thong of sealskin has been sewn. This thong is threaded into the metal loop, the main line pulled taut and the thong wedged under the loop. The harpoon head is now firmly attached to the handle, yet a quick tug on the line is all that is needed to free the small thong and allow the head to drop free of the handle.

When harpooning a seal the harpoon handle is gripped in one hand and the coiled line in the other. Standing over the seal hole waiting for the seal to rise, the hunter, if he is right-handed, holds the harpoon head to the left across his knees. Both feet are kept flat on the ice, and together. There must be no movement of the feet as a sound could easily carry down through the ice and frighten the seal. The hunter stands back about two feet from the hole, invisible to a seal rising up from below. He rests by bending over from the waist, and putting his elbows on his knees; otherwise he stands upright, eyes glued to the hole ready to spot the tell-tale rise of water in the hole that signifies the approach of a seal. When this happens, he slowly raises the harpoon high, arm straight above the head. The moment the seal's head breaks the surface, down goes the arm and, if he is a good hunter, the harpoon head enters the seal's body at the thick neck.

Such accuracy comes only after long practice. Eskimo men and boys play games to ensure that they get practice without having to wait for seals. In one such game a broomstick is used for a harpoon. The player stands on a patch of clear snow or earth, both feet together, knees straight. About two feet to the front and slightly to one side the broom handle is thrust into the snow, making a neat round hole. Then without moving his feet he raises the broom handle high and tries to plunge it down into the same hole, putting all the force he can into the drive.

When the harpoon head enters the seal's body, thrust in deep through the layers of fat, the hunter gives a sharp tug on the line held in his other hand. The line comes free of the handle which is quickly withdrawn leaving the harpoon head buried deep under the fat and flesh. By this time the seal has taken off for the depths. The hunter drops the harpoon handle, grabs the line with both hands, and hangs on. When the seal reaches the limit of the line, it is pulled up short. The harpoon head is pulled backward and the curved flukes pull it flat under the skin. The seal is safely hooked.

My first organized hunt was one of the most unusual events of my life as an Eskimo. We had five sleds, each with four or five hunters, ranging in age from old Akomalik and his wife to little Noahkudluk, Idlouk's youngest son. As we moved off from the camp there was a lot of confusion and laughter; dog teams became tangled and people ran from sled to sled, pushing one another off onto the ice and sometimes into the water. About three miles out on the frozen surface of Eclipse Sound, all sleds stopped by a large frozen-in iceberg, while the male hunters climbed the berg and with their telescopes searched the ice around looking for the best spot to go after the young seals. To the north and west lay much rough ice, ideal places for the seals to have their *aglos* as the Eskimos call the openings under the snow in which the young are raised. Here and there black dots that were sleeping seals were visible on the ice, a few of them being identified as young seals.

Once the area was decided upon, everyone readied his harpoon, then jumped aboard a sled. In a moment five sleds were racing over the ice toward a nearby area of rough broken ice about a mile away. Here three young seals had been spotted asleep on the ice. Speed was essential now for the first sled on the spot might get in a quick shot at a seal before it went down, and then would have first chance at covering the best holes in the area to await the seal coming up.

Faster and faster the sleds flew over the ice, dogs urged on by voice and whip. The sleds slammed down into puddles of water throwing up sheets of ice-cold water over the occupants at the front. They did not mind; being up front they would be first off the sled in the race for the holes. I was with Idlouk on his big sled along with Oodleteetuk and a visiting Eskimo, Kyaklooapik. Our sled slowly drew ahead of the others as we approached the nearest seal.

The seals had seen us coming from some distance off. Being young, their curiosity got the better of their caution and they squirmed around on the ice, necks craning into the air as they attempted to make out what we could be. The sight of the onrushing sleds was too much for two of the seals; they quickly dived into the holes, but the third one was curious. It stayed out on the ice as if hypnotized by the fast approaching sled.

When we came within three hundred yards, it was still there, straining for a better look. Now we all started to shout at the top of our lungs. The seal rolled over and over, almost standing on hind flippers. Two hundred yards and it was still there. Then the dogs caught sight of it and the sled leaped forward with a jerk. When a hundred yards off, I dropped my harpoon and snatched up the rifle from the sled. With a running jump, I leaped clear and ran quickly to one side so as to get a clear line of fire. Dropping to one knee I took quick aim and fired. No luck, the shot went wild. I had not time for another, for at that moment the dogs reached the seal.

They were on him in a flash. The careening sled, with nothing to hold it back, slammed into the fighting, snarling dogs. Idlouk and Kyaklooapik leaped into the fray. Both had dropped their harpoons and were trying to catch the madly squirming seal with their bare hands and keep it clear of the dogs. What a mêlée! Idlouk, Kyaklooapik, joined by Oodle-teetuk and myself, ten dogs and the seal all fighting like fiends in a raceway of rushing water about one foot deep beside the seal hole.

Idlouk got the seal by a front flipper, but the seal and a dog bit his hand and he had to let go. Then Kyaklooapik dropped on it and tried to pin it down beneath his weight, while we kicked and slashed at the dogs to get them away. But the seal was strong and slippery. It squirmed out from under Kyaklooapik, rolled under two or three dogs and reached the edge of the hole. Idlouk grabbed a hind flipper as it started to slide into the hole, while Oodleteetuk and I fell on him to keep him from being dragged into the hole.

95

But Idlouk couldn't keep his grip. With a mighty flip and a splash the seal was gone, leaving us lying in a heap in the foot-deep water.

By this time the other sleds had come up. Quickly everyone ran off over the ice, searching out the other breathing holes in the vicinity. In five minutes twenty hunters were scattered over the ice in an area of about a square mile, each motionless over a seal hole waiting for the seal to come up. Idlouk, Oodleteetuk, Kyaklooapik and I retrieved our harpoons from the overturned sled, and covered off holes but the best ones were taken by people from the other sleds. Now all we could do was wait. It was only a matter of time until the seal came up in one of the holes.

Five minutes went by and there was no sign of the seal. Not a sound could be heard as everyone stood motionless. Then, a shout rang out from my left. Kitchooalik had spotted the seal's head in a hole no one had noticed. Quickly one of the small boys nearby moved over to cover that hole. All was quiet again.

I stood motionless, eyes glued to the tiny whirlpool in the hole at my feet. Small chips of ice bobbed and chuckled in the swiftly racing water, sucked under from time to time only to bob up again in a different spot. I was soaked to the skin, water dripped from my clothes hitting the ice in a steady rhythm of musical pings. With such noises I was sure no seal would come my way, but, already a little more like an Eskimo, I stood patiently, no thought for anything but the seal.

As I waited I became conscious of another sound. Far off to the south where the sheer rock cliffs of our island lay deep in the shadow of the afternoon sun, a dull muted roar grew in volume until it filled the air all about. It was an awe-inspiring sound. Heavy and pulsating it came, as if giant machines were grinding rocks and stone, rending the earth to dust. The air about me quivered and trembled, tremors ran through the ice under my feet. I looked about with apprehension, half expecting to see the far-off land sink into oblivion or suddenly disappear in a flash of flame. Near me stood Agnowyah, Idlouk's old mother. As the sound built up, she dropped her harpoon to the ice and looked wildly about. She shrank down to the ice, eyes gazing terror-stricken at the distant land. All the hunters' heads turned to watch.

We could see nothing, but we knew it was a landslide. Tremendous at it was, we were too far out from shore to do anything but note the direction from whence the sound came. Later I visited the place of the slide on the north shore of our island, and I found an entirely new valley. The slide had started in a small snow field near the top of the island. At first it had been all snow, but as it gained momentum and weight the slide tore off rocks and soil, ripping a tortuous path that gradually widened from three yards to over three hundred, rushing between rocky cliffs at express-train speed until finally it poured off the land onto the sea ice which cracked and buckled beneath the massive weight.

Slowly the sound died. Fitfully it flared up once or twice, then was heard no more. Agnowyah rose to her feet and picked up the harpoon, her normally brown face pale. She looked over in my direction, but appeared not to see me. I could see her lips moving as if in prayer, and I wondered if she prayed to the God the white men had brought to her land, or if she prayed to Seela, a god she knew well in her youth, the shadowy being who lives somewhere between earth and sky, and threatens mankind with all the mighty powers of nature.

Another five minutes went by and still we waited by the holes. Then out of the corner of my eye I saw movement. Fifty yards away stood Kadluk, slowly raising his harpoon. For thirty seconds he stood motionless, harpoon held high above his head, while I watched, my breath caught in my throat. Suddenly, in a movement too fast to follow, his arm flashed down, and his shout ripped through the quiet air. I saw the released shaft of his harpoon drop to the ice as he grasped the taut line with both hands and braced himself for the pull.

As I ran over, he started to haul in the line. Hand over

hand the line came slowly reeling in. The seal was not a big one, and pulling it was not a difficult job. With a splash the seal's head broke clear of the water; Kadluk dragged it, fighting, out onto the ice. He pulled it clear of the hole and stepped up close to its side. Stooping over slightly he waved his left hand inches away from its nose. The seal's head lifted and the jaws opened as if to bite. Quickly Kadluk swung a roundhouse right, hitting the seal flush on the top of its upraised head. The seal collapsed on the ice, killed instantly by the single, crushing blow.

For the next three hours we continued to hunt seals on the ice. Kadluk got another and Idlouk got three. No seals came up to the holes I watched, although they came to holes close by. It was a cold job, standing motionless by the hole watching and waiting for the seals to come. The wind dried my outer clothing, but I was still wet to the skin. Kitchooalik stepped onto a snow-covered hole and went in the water up to his hips. That made five of us with clothes wet through.

After Idlouk's second kill everyone agreed that it was time for lunch. Three primus stoves were lit, and Kadluk prepared to cut up one of the tender young seals. He and Kitchooalik first removed the skin, working very carefully so as not to damage it with knife cuts. The skinned carcass was then slit from throat to hind flippers, and the ribs pulled back and pressed flat. Then everyone gathered around the kill and started in to feed on raw meat cut right out of the carcass within half an hour of the kill. As I was new to this type of feast, Idlouk showed me how to sample all the better portions, parts considered by the Eskimos to be the tastiest of them all. First there was a small slice of heart, followed by a snack of the steaming liver. With each piece of meat taken, a small square of fat was eaten too, and this gave piquancy to the taste. Next I tried the meat from the shoulder, or the flipper as it is often called. This was delicious, but a little difficult to separate from the bone. I refused an eyeball, taking instead a section of the lower ribs with bits of meat and fat attached.

We stood around the seal in a circle, eating and talking, moving around constantly, always searching out a tastier piece of meat or fat. The younger boys dashed back and forth between the carcass and the primus stoves, getting them lit, filling the kettles with fresh water from the surface pools on the sea ice, putting in the tea, and letting it boil. Good natured banter flew back and forth, no small part of it directed at me.

"Perhaps Kingmik finds Eskimo food too much for his stomach. I noticed he refused an eyeball."

"Ah, but he's still a white man. We have to make allowances. Give him a little time."

When all had eaten their fill, mugs were filled with strong black tea. Tobacco pouches came out and everyone relaxed sitting on the sleds, sipping tea and smoking, belching slightly as they talked. Beside the sled lay the remains of the devoured seal, now a heap of fat with some small bits of meat and bone. These the dogs would clear up before we pulled away. Sitting on the sled beside me, Idlouk asked if I would like to try one of the old-style dishes, one that not many Eskimos bothered with today, as it takes too long to prepare. I said yes, I would like to try.

Putting down his cup of tea, he retrieved the head from the remains of the seal. Smashing the skull, he extracted the brains and laid them on the ice. Next he took the remaining eyeball, and put it beside the brains. From the thick layer of fat that once enclosed the seal's entire body, he cut a slab some six inches square. Putting the brains and the eyeball onto the fat, he proceeded to chop it up with his big snowknife. For about fifteen minutes he worked very carefully, chopping and mixing until brains and eyeball had been reduced to a pale yellow mush thoroughly flavoured with bits of fat.

Taking a bit on the tip of his knife, he tasted it, paused for a moment, and then added a small square of fat and chopped this well into the mixture. Then he tried it again. This time he was pleased at the result. Looking at me with a sly grin he said, "Now you try it."

99

Although I had not liked the sight of the eyeball as it was being chopped in, I was intrigued by the mixture. Tentatively I took a small quantity on the tip of my knife and popped it into my mouth. I rolled it around to get the flavour and then swallowed. The mixture had a pleasant taste, quite sweet, but unlike anything I had ever eaten before.

I tried another bit, then another. Idlouk helped me and in ten minutes we cleaned up the lot. By the time I was finished, I thought the taste delicious, and I have never changed my opinion to this day.

CHAPTER
9

BY MID-JULY the land was almost free of snow; only in deep gullies and clefts in the rocks did the drifts cling to the land. High up on the mountain ranges that fringe the north and east coasts of north Baffin, the ever-present icecaps and snowfields glistened shining white under the high-riding summer sun. Here and there long tongues of glacial ice flowed down broad valleys to the sea. Glacier-fed streams ran with undiminished force, rushing pell-mell to the sea, but the smaller streams, fed only from the winter snow cover, had dried up or were reduced to a mere trickle of their former flow. In places where, only two weeks before, the air had been filled with the thunder of mighty torrents plunging down sheer rock cliffs in spectacular waterfalls of a hundred feet and more, the stillness of the Arctic air was broken only by the cry of the gull or by the creak and groan of the sea ice rising and falling on the flow of the tide.

Although most of north Baffin is mountainous, and a large part of the mountainous area glacier-covered, there are extensive areas of low rolling plateau. Here and there broad valleys run between walls of rock to the sea. The north and east coasts of the island present an almost unbroken line of high rock cliffs to the sea, but south of the mountains the land becomes less rugged, in places not unlike the rolling foothills of the Rocky Mountains in Alberta. This appearance is a superficial one only. What appears to the casual glance to be smooth grassy meadow is really a hummocky, boggy semi-swamp over which walking is difficult and damp. Uplands are of course gravel and clay, arid and windswept, dotted here and there with clumps of grass and small plants. Brown is the predominating colour of these valleys and plateaux, dull brown broken only by the rippling white of the fields of Arctic cotton grass.

Much has been written about the profusion of summer plant life in the Arctic. It is true that a great many more varieties of flora grow in the Arctic than most people realize. In some localities plants grow in profusion, but this is not true of all Arctic regions. Great stretches contain nothing but rock, snow, or ice, while the arid upland plateaux have only scattered patches of the most rudimentary plant-life, mosses and lichens. Even in the localities where plants can and do grow, the landscape is viewed quite differently by different people in the area. Eyes accustomed to the splendour of plant life in southern Ontario or on the Pacific coast will see flora in the "lush" valleys on north Baffin as very sparse indeed. To anyone seeing the Arctic for the first time in summer, and having been unaware that the country contained anything but rock, ice and snow, the variety of plant life is a pleasant surprise. To the average Arctic resident in the settlements, imprisoned for months by walls of snow and ice, the sight of grass and flowers no matter how meagre gladdens the eye and the heart. To the Eskimo of north Baffin, plants are as nothing in his life; he has eyes only for the sea.

One of the chief factors controlling plantlife in the Arctic is permafrost, the permanently frozen ground that underlies almost all Arctic regions. On north Baffin, only a thin surface layer of the soil becomes free of frost in the summer. Twelve to eighteen inches down is ground that never thaws. Above such frozen ground, soil temperatures can never be very high. Water cannot seep down and must drain off in streams or rivers, or form vast shallow bogs and marshes. When walking on the land during the short summer months, one is rarely conscious of this underlying layer of frozen ground. But dig a post hole for a building foundation, and in a few moments the metal shovel rings harshly on the concrete-hard ice.

Although I knew about permafrost long before I first visited the Arctic, it was not until the summer of 1951 that I became acutely aware of its existence. While endeavouring to capture a snow goose alive so that I could take close-up photographs, Idlouk and I had to swim across a lake high up on an inland plateau. When I waded into the ice-cold water from the shore, my feet sank down through six inches of bottom mud to rock hard ice. For twenty yards or so I waded over this icy floor, my bare feet cringing from contact with the centuries-old ice that formed the bottom of the lake.

Shortly afterwards, at Idlouk's camp, I noticed a dog digging for mice. The dog found the mouse hole in the ground by sense of smell and then started to dig straight down. In a few minutes his rapidly scraping paws hit the permafrost level about fourteen inches from the surface. Here he sniffed for a moment and then started to dig horizontally along the ground immediately above the frozen earth. This is precisely what the mouse had been forced to do when digging the hole. Five minutes later, and about ten feet from the starting point, the dog reached the end of the tunnel. A short scramble, a terrified squeak, and a snap of iron jaws signified the end of the hunt.

Mosses, lichens and grasses form the principle flora of north Baffin, and all are usually found in similar localities, growing in profusion in the broad watered valleys, less evident on the arid and windswept upland plateaux. Grasses cover the bottom lands, growing to a height of six inches or more near the banks of the rivers and in the more sheltered gullies. Farther up the valley sides, where the rocky out-croppings show through, grasses mingle with mosses and lichens. On the plateaux all three grow in scattered patches in the gravelly soil. Exceptionally luxuriant grasses grow up about the burrows of foxes, and wherever there has been an Eskimo campsite established for any length of time.

The plants are not confined to any one type of terrain, but are found almost everywhere except on or near the glacial ice. As a rule they do not grow haphazardly among each other, but keep to areas suitable to their growth re-

quirements. On the gravelly, windswept plateaux the yellow
Arctic poppy dances wildly in the strong north wind. Among
the rocks of the wide river valleys are the patches of saxi-
frage, each bed a solid mass of mauve-coloured flowers, a
splash of brilliant colour that always startles the eye attuned
to the dull brown tone of the general landscape.

Arctic cotton grass borders the shallow lakes on the
plateaux and carpets the floor of many a grass-covered
valley, lending a touch of lightness to the drab monotone of
a boggy hillside. Cotton grass is important to the Eskimos.
In September the young girls and the women gather the
cotton-like tufts and store them in small containers made
from the stomach of the caribou or from the throat mem-
brane of the seal. The tufts are used to form the wicks of the
seal-oil lamps. Laid along the straight leading edge of the
lamp, the tufts soak up the oil from the shallow bowl of
the lamp and burn with a soft candle-like flame. Not all
cotton grass provides suitable tufts for use as wick material.
The discriminating housewife will gather only the large
single tuft heads, the slim three-pronged tufts being used
only in case of emergencies.

In sheltered places among the rocks dwarf willows grow,
the closest thing to a tree the Arctic lands have produced
since the last retreat of the glacial age. On north Baffin the
willows are vigorous and healthy, but small. The longest I
have seen was about three feet and the highest a mere foot
above the level of the ground. Farther to the south, particularly in the tundra country west of Hudson Bay, willows
grow to the height of a man. In that country I have seen
small sheltered valleys with willows reaching to a height of
six feet and more. On the southern plains the willows grow
long, but instead of growing vertically they grow horizontally, hugging the ground away from the almost constant
cool breath of the north-west wind. Sometimes the stem is
above the ground, sometimes it is below. I once traced a
willow back along, and under, the ground for a distance of
seven feet before coming to the root. And I have heard of

cases where willows have been traced in this way for as much as fifteen feet.

In the Arctic there are no poisonous plants and none with thorns. Most are perennial, spending many years moving from germination to the first flowering, often developing next year's flowering buds before the winter sets in. The Arctic summer is too short for annual plants to complete the life cycle in one season. In some, the flowering bud spends the winter on the plant wrapped in a fluffy cocoon of downy insulation safe from the intense cold of the long Arctic night, ready to send forth the flower at the first stimulus of heat from the returning spring sun. Such plants send flowers up through drifts of snow as though impatient to taste the light and heat so long denied them.

Some plants are eaten by the Eskimos; but only in times of extreme food shortage could they be considered a part of the diet. As summer is not usually a time of food shortage, about the only time an Eskimo on north Baffin eats any produce from the land is when he is walking in the hills hunting rabbits or geese, or when in leisurely fashion climbing the hill back of the camp to look over the sea with his telescope. Two plants in particular are eaten at such times: sorrel and the crow berry. In certain locations, known to all the Eskimos, both grow in profusion. Sorrel resembles miniature rhubarb, with a stem about six inches long. The leaves are from half an inch to an inch in diameter. Both leaves and stalk are eaten, but the leaves are the choice part. Often when rabbit hunting in the high hills back of the campsite, Paneeluk and I sat down beside clumps of sorrel and ate our way through the patch, only stopping when not a leaf or a stalk remained. I always ate with relish, for the fresh acid taste was something I missed in my regular diet of meat. At the camp I often wakened feeling hungry and, while everyone slept, quietly dressed and climbed the hills for an hour or two eating all the sorrel I could find.

Children eat almost any plant. One species, fernweed, has a tuberous root with a taste of raw young carrot. Another, the lilac-flowered vetch, has a flower that is eaten by small children. Adults rarely go out of their way to eat such plants, but everyone, if the opportunity arises, will gather quantities of sorrel which they bring back to camp in sugar sacks. Here it is put in a pan with water and then boiled. If boiled over the primus stove, about five minutes is sufficient, but over the seal-oil lamp much longer is required. Just before taking the pot off the stove, a spoonful of sugar is added to the water which is drained off. The drink is very refreshing, medium red in colour with a faint raspberry taste. The Eskimos drink it while it is still hot, but I preferred mine to cool until ice cold. When out hunting in the kayaks, Idlouk and I sometimes took a sugar bag along, and if we passed close by a place where sorrel grew, we would go ashore and gather it. But never once did we actually make a trip to gather such land produce, although it grew quite close by our campsites.

One of the reasons for this is the difference between the Eskimos and white men in food taste and food pleasure sensation. With the Eskimos, taste alone does not play the same part in eating as with ourselves. They derive pleasure, not so much from taste in the mouth, as from the full stomach. No matter how much Arctic plant life you eat, you rarely feel full. It is a pure taste pleasure sensation. Badly cooked food, spoiled food, does not bother the Eskimo very much. With them I have often eaten food that has been in contact with kerosene and gasoline. I ate it reluctantly, because it was the only food we had. The Eskimos ate it with relish.

I like to taste food first, then have a full stomach; no meal is satisfactory without both. With Eskimos food remains in the mouth for only a minimum period before it is swallowed. A filet mignon as served in our finest restaurant would not interest an Eskimo. A half dozen such and he would feel happy; with a dozen he would be content. He would eat them any way they came, raw to burned black; that would not be too important.

Eskimos will eat odd combinations of foodstuffs, at least odd from our point of view. After returning south from my period of living as an Eskimo, I found myself much like them in this regard. It did not matter very much whether my meat was fried, boiled, broiled or raw, providing I got enough of it. It did not matter whether I started my meal with soup or dessert; it was all food and served the same purpose. I had not lost my taste for fine cooking, but it was not as important as it had been two years before. I am not sure that it ever will be again.

Summer life in our camp was leisurely. We hunted daily, either on the sea for seals, or on the land for rabbits. But there was no pressure to make a kill; we always had more food than we could possibly eat. Excess food was stored in caches and would be used as dog food in the winter months. Paneeluk and Kitchooalik went off to a fish lake about a hundred miles to the south-west of our camp. Here they fished through the ice, jigging for fine Arctic char and came back to camp with nearly two hundred fish. They brought them back packed in sealskin containers, made by lacing a sealskin up into a long bag. By the time the fish reached the camp, they were not fresh. The smell was very bad, but I found the taste delicious. Some of these fish were stored under the rocks so that they would rot further and provide a dish that Eskimos consider a delicacy. I was to discover later that rotten fish is an excellent trail food in the coldest months of the winter as it does not freeze as hard as fresh fish and is easy to break up and eat in the sub-zero temperatures when fresh fish is as hard as steel.

In preparation for the open-water hunting that was soon to come, Idlouk and I painted our kayaks a pale, pale green to match the colour of the underwater ice. I made tips of whalebone for the paddle while Idlouk fashioned ivory heads for the harpoons, finely balanced barbs, a large one for whales and a smaller size for seal.

Paneeluk, Elijah and Ooingoon, Kadluk's eldest son, along with the younger boys, hunted rabbits in the hills. The Arctic hare is found in abundance throughout north Baffin. In winter it is almost pure white, but in summer the coat is a dull brown, flecked with spots of black and grey, which blends almost perfectly with the dull brown of the vegetation. Hunting rabbits in summer is not an easy task as they are hard to see, and there are no tracks to follow. At first I would tramp for hours without seeing any sign, but gradually I learned the ways of the rabbits. I watched the other hunters, the way they worked up a rocky slope, the side of the slope they hunted over in the morning, and the side they went to at "night". I soon learned that rabbits were not everywhere on the island; they had their favourite spots too.

The women at the camp were the busiest of us all. Each day hunters brought in the skins of the young seals they had killed on the ice. The skin of the seal was removed by the hunter immediately following the kill, or immediately he got back to camp. Under no circumstance must the seal be left so that the sun can beat down on the skin as this would spoil it. At the camp the skins were put inside the tent, usually in a bucket. In their spare time, between looking after the children, making boots, cooking food, the women took the skins to the rocks in front of the camp and removed the excess fat. This was done by scraping the inner side of the skin with a special woman's knife. Care was taken when scraping not to cut through the skin, as this would considerably lessen its value if it was to be sold to the store.

After all fat had been removed by scraping, the skin was then washed with soap and warm water to remove the fat from the hair. If it was to be sold at the store, used as boot tops or the backs of mitts, or for sealskin trousers, the skin was then pegged out taut on the hillside to dry. To prevent the dogs, which roam freely about the campsite, from eating the skins, the women have to take the skins high up on the hills. This is back-breaking work, for wet sealskins are heavy. Yet the Eskimo women scramble up the rocky slopes, usually with two or three sealskins plus the baby on their back, without visible sign of strain. They would never think of asking one of the men to do the job, for this is woman's work. I have often seen the boys help the mothers with such tasks, but the help is never requested. It must be given.

If the skin was to be used as boot bottoms, then all the hair was removed by boiling the skin in a bucket of water over an open fire. The fire was usually of seal-oil, poured over chunks of seal fat, which burned with an intense, but exceedingly smoky flame. After the skin had boiled for a short time, it was taken out and the hair easily scraped free. The skin was then pegged out on the hillside to dry. When dry, it was a deep yellow colour, and stiff as a board. It was then tied to the top of a pole or to the tip of the tent pole and left in the sun and wind to bleach. If left long enough, it would eventually turn white; how long this took depended, of course, on the amount of sunshine there was in any given period. All women strove for a white skin, for it made an attractive inset in the boot. But weather and necessity often forced them to use the skin long before it was white.

The children played about the campsite all day and night. There were no regular hours for eating or sleeping. Everyone went to bed when he was tired, and ate when he was hungry. Boys and girls roamed far and wide over the land in the vicinity of the camp and on the sea ice near the shore. The ice near the shore was not very safe, being full of holes and cracks, but I have yet to see a child fall in. I was always impressed by the way children played in such an area, the parents never giving a thought to their falling through the ice. Of course, the children were always together as a group and the older ones kept an eye on the younger. The very small children played under the watchful eye of the mother or an older sister or neighbour.

Small boys and girls spent a good deal of the time fishing for stickleback through the cracks in the ice. This ugly little fish can easily be jigged with a bent pin, and will even swallow bits of cloth on the end of a string. The children lay for hours on their stomachs on the ice, heads hanging out over the open water of the cracks, patiently jigging for these fish. Then they proudly carried the catch back to show their fathers who praised them for being real hunters. After that the fish were tossed aside and forgotten while the child dug into a meal of boiled seal meat.

Often the children roamed the land for twenty-four to thirty-six hours at a time without eating or sleeping. They became thin as rails from the combination of exercise, no sleep and little food. Parents worried about this but they did not do anything to stop it. "The children are happy, and after all, is this not the highest thing to be had from life?" they would say.

On the coasts of north Baffin where the Eskimos have their camps, mosquitoes are not much of a nuisance. Idlouk's summer camps were well situated in this regard, being on the windy points of small islands, and we were never bothered. I noticed the first mosquitoes at the camp on July 18th, but never saw more than one or two at a time. Inland the story was quite different, for the tundra is the home of the mosquito. In the valleys and plains to the south of the long sounds, at the bottom of Eclipse Sound, mosquitoes make life miserable from July to the end of August. Only on the crests of the hills where the high winds blow can one be free of these pests. In the valleys they rise up from the ground in clouds, getting in the hair, up the nose, in the mouth. They do not seem to bother the Eskimos very much, and in time I managed to get used to them.

Bad as the mosquitoes are on the plains of north Baffin, they are mild when compared to the inland tundra country of the central Arctic prairies. Here caribou are driven mad by the biting stinging swarms. I have seen dogs so badly bitten that their eyes were swollen shut. Some have died as a result. Around the buildings of the settlements, the mosquitoes gather on the sunny wall of the house out of the wind in such numbers that a normally white painted wall is black with their mass. They can gather so thickly on the windows as to make it impossible to see out.

Recently Canadian scientists have been conducting a research programme in the tundra country in an attempt to establish some means of effective control. Considerable data has been gathered on distribution and habits, and experimental attempts have been made at control. The scientists conducting the experiments are usually classified as Bug Men. Their researches cause the Eskimo to shake his head. As one Eskimo told me, he always had a suspicion the white man was a little crazy, and after watching two of them set traps to catch mosquitoes, he was sure of it.

On July 13th, Idlouk decided the time had come to change our campsite. Each day new holes appeared in the sea ice, cracks grew from small openings to wide rivers overnight. In another week, or at the most two, travel on the ice by sled would be impossible. Before this happened we had to get the entire camp moved across the inlet to the tip of the island about four miles away. It was from here that we would hunt the narwhal as they came down the shore of Eclipse Sound heading for their summer feeding grounds in Milne Inlet, Tremblay Sound and Koluktoo Bay.

Moving day for the Eskimo was a picnic affair of complete confusion and lots of work. No one hurried, for days were twenty-four hours long. Our day started at midnight with a big meal of boiled fish and two mugs of tea, for no one was sure when we would eat again. Then everyone set to work to take down the tents, pack up the gear, and carry it down to the edge of the sea ice where the heads of the families supervised the loading of the family sleds. The women and girls did most of the packing while the men and boys harnessed the dogs, collected all the hunting gear and loaded the sleds. The woman is the boss around the tent, and as such it is up to her to put it up and take it down, and to choose the site for the tent at the new campsite.

Moving day for the Aulatseevikmiut was much the same as moving day for all Canadians. Children ran wild about the beach as the tents came down and the household effects were carried down to the waiting sleds. Mothers worked like slaves, packing and sorting, making innumerable trips

111

between the tent and the shore looking for articles they were sure had been misplaced and finally finding them in the first place they had looked, always trying to keep an eye on the small children as they scrambled about among the piles of bedding and sleeping skins. Men were the bosses, strutting about the beach, ordering sons to bring this and to bring that, to harness up the dogs, to lend a hand here and lend a hand there, shaking their heads in amusement at the antics of the wives as they searched for some misplaced treasure among the growing mountains of gear piled beside the waiting sleds.

First to go on the sled was the twelve-foot dory, for there might be wide cracks in the ice to cross, cracks too wide to be bridged by the sled. Then we should have to unload the sled and ferry everything across in the small boat. The dory was firmly lashed to the cross slats of the sled. Into it went all the household gear, some packed in boxes, most of it loose. Eskimos are still not used to the idea of possessions, of having large amounts of wordly goods. They dash back and forth between tent and shore, making innumerable trips loaded down with small items like a kettle or a pot, or perhaps a blanket or the family clock.

Paneeluk and I carried the heavier items down to the sleds where Idlouk loaded them into the boat. Gradually the boat was filled to the gunwale, and the sleeping skins and robes were laid on top to provide a safe seat for the women and children on the short trip to the new campsite.

Every hour or two during the loading activities, some-one would suggest that we have a cup of tea, a suggestion that never went unheeded. No matter what was going on, one of the housewives immediately started up the primus stove and put the kettle on to boil. For fifteen minutes everyone but the children lay back on the rocks and relaxed, drinking tea that was as black as ink, and smoking thin, dried out cigarettes. Tobacco was in short supply now and would soon be gone altogether until we could get into the settlement for more. Of cigarette papers, there were none.

Idlouk tried lens tissue without success, newspaper with even less, and finally settled for white tissue paper that I found in the bottom of my kit bag.

Eventually everything was loaded and all the children clambered aboard. Stowed away in the bow of the boat were four little pups, too small to walk. At intervals they cried for their mother who was in harness and would run with the team. After a last look over the empty campsite, Idlouk unrolled the long whip. With a shout and a crack of the whip, the dogs were urged to get up and go. But the load was heavy and the dogs were languid from lying in the sun. They could not budge the sled. Idlouk cracked his twenty-foot whip and shouted; Paneeluk hauled in the main trace and then let it go with a jerk. The dogs leaped forward, but still the sled would not budge. It seemed to be stuck tight. Now Idlouk was aroused. He jumped in among the team laying about with the handle of the whip. Dogs leaped this way and that and howled their fright. He jumped to one side and cracked the whip again over their heads. This time they lunged forward with a will and the sled came free. Thumping and bumping, it careened through the rough shore ice. Behind, the three other sleds moved off, one by one, until a long caravan snaked its way over the water-covered ice on the sea.

IT IS AT moving time that the impact of our civilization on the Eskimo way of life is easy to see. For the Eskimo hunter of today is usually a man of property. Before the advent of the white man, he was a nomadic hunter, following the game, going through a regular cycle of movement to places where game appeared at certain seasons of the year. He moved with a minimum of effort for his possessions were meagre. In those days Eskimos had few dogs, three or four at the most, often only one or two. Families pooled dogs in order to haul sleds and gear.

Today, moving is a different story. It presents as many problems to the Eskimo as it does to ourselves. The only difference is that the Eskimo does not have to worry about finding a house; in summer his tent is carried on the sled; in winter the snowdrifts provide material for building a new home. But the amount of gear he must move is growing every year, necessitating bigger sleds, more dogs per team.

Simply by becoming Christians, many Eskimos have had to add a dog to their team. On north Baffin Island every Eskimo above the age of six has his own Prayer Book and New Testament printed in syllabic character writing. In addition, every family has one or two or often three books of the Old Testament, plus notebooks and paper for jotting down Bible quotations and references. If there are six people in a family, the total weight in prayer and other books to be carried on the sled can easily be twenty-five to thirty pounds. This weight, plus that of one small bag of flour, means an additional dog on the team.

These, however, are minor items. The list of goods introduced into the country by the white man is endless, and most of them must be carried on the sled when the family moves: flour and sugar; tea and tobacco; kerosene and gasoline; rifles and ammunition; sea biscuits; traps and sewing machines; kettles and pots; heavy dories and canoes.

The statement is often made that the Eskimos have too many dogs. This is quite true. But the Eskimo of today, dependent on the dog team for transportation, needs a good many more dogs than his ancestor of a hundred years ago. He has more goods to carry; he has larger families to transport; he must go faster than his forefather did, for he has a long trap line to tend. He is a hunter-trapper, and has to use time in much the same way as we use it in our way of life. If he is to get along in his new existence, he must make good use of his time.

In the Arctic today, the dog poses one of the basic problems of the country. The dog is rapidly eating the Eskimo out of house and home. Most sea culture groups would have little difficulty getting enough food for themselves and a few dogs, but to feed the numbers of dogs they have today is not easy. At our camp we had a total of seventy-four dogs, as opposed to twenty-nine people. Each dog ate as much per day as a human. They ate the same food, seal meat. Every day at our one camp we had over one hundred mouths to feed and the strain on the resources of the area was tremendous, not to mention the strain on the hunters who were out day after day trying to get enough food to keep ahead of the hungry mob.

As the Eskimo must have dogs to carry on his life as a hunter-trapper, the answer to this problem lies in trying to get him to develop a better breed of dog, one capable of doing the job that is expected in the country today. There is no such breed as an Eskimo husky dog. He is the world's biggest mongrel. Eskimo dogs are of every conceivable size and appearance. No attempt is made to breed good dogs; they simply mate and reproduce.

It would seem that the process of natural selection would eventually produce better and better dogs. If the Eskimo husky ran wild, this would probably be so. At the camps most dogs run loose when not working in the team, the dogs from each team tending to keep together as a unit. No attempt is made to segregate a bitch in time of heat, and to mate her with the best dog of the team. Sometimes the better dogs do father the pups, as they are usually leaders and fighters in the team. But they cannot watch the bitch all the time, and there is always a loose dog or two at every camp that is not much good for anything. All too often these dogs reach the bitch. The pups of such a union do little to add to the strength of the team or to the future of the breed.

Even when running loose, as most Eskimo dogs do in the short summer period when they are temporarily unemployed, natural selection does not always work for the best. In the summer of 1953, Idlouk's team lacked a leader and a boss. Sometimes these two positions on the team are taken over by one dog, at other times two dogs share the positions. In 1951 Idlouk had a bitch for a leader, and a huge pugnacious dog, Shugluk, as the boss. This combination worked well until Shugluk became overly vicious. He was injuring too many dogs in the fights and had to be shot.

Shortly after the move across the Inlet to the point of the island, the bitch in our team came into heat. One day we awoke to find that Idlouk's dogs had disappeared. We knew they were off in the hills selecting a new leader and boss, the winner to be the father of the pups to come. For two days Paneeluk and I roamed the hills looking for the team. I wanted to see that battle, a fight to the death for supremacy in the team. But we could not find them.

Early on the morning of the fourth day after the disappearance of the dogs, I awakened to hear Mosesee rushing down the hill back of the tent crying, "Atata, atata, Mukshuk kilikpuk."* Mukshuk was one of Idlouk's biggest dogs and, although still only a pup, should have stood a good chance of winning the fight.

Quickly Idlouk and I dressed and went outside. About a hundred yards from the camp we found Mukshuk lying in a cleft in the rocks. He was completely exhausted. His left leg had been bitten to the bone and a large flap of skin and fur hung down to his toes. One ear was nearly severed from his head. He could do little but lie on the ground and pant. We knew that he had not been the winner for he was alone and the winner would be with the bitch.

Idlouk had been worried about the dogs ever since they disappeared. Now he was more worried than ever. If Mukshuk could be taken as an indication of the fierceness of the fight, a battle royal must have taken place off in the hills. His fears were well grounded. About twelve hours later, four more dogs arrived at the camp, all limping along, bearing the scars of a terrific struggle, legs bitten, ears chewed, noses lacerated. Shortly afterwards the bitch pranced over the hilltop and down into the camp. Following her closely came the winner, Nikpee, a dog we had not conceded the remotest chance of achieving success. He did not look like a winner; he looked as though he had had a fight with a polar bear. His nose was chewed to rags, one ear sagged down over an eye, he limped badly from a bite

* Father, father, Mukshuk is coming.

on a paw. But his head and tail were high and he did not stir from the side of his mate.

We counted the dogs lying among the rocks. One was missing, Nixee, the best dog on the team, the one we had hoped would turn out to be the leader and boss. All that day the children roamed the hills back of the camp looking for Nixee, but not a sign did they find. Late in the evening, he came home, staggering over the rocky ridge back of the tents, stumbling and falling on the broken ground. In the shelter of a ridge of rock, and well away from the other dogs, he lay down, licking his wounds. He was not far from death. His head was slashed and bitten in a dozen places, one ear was gone, bitten off clean at the base. His shoulders and forelegs were covered with bites; even his tail hung limp, the tip almost severed by a savage bite.

My own reaction was to shoot him immediately, but I waited to see what Idlouk would do. He did not say much; he looked over Nixee carefully and then walked down to the edge of the sea. I followed and we sat on the rocks, looking out over the ice to where the sun at midnight still hovered over the glacier and ice cap of far-off Bylot Island. For a long time we sat, Idlouk slowly drawing on his little pipe. In a while Paneeluk came up and said, "Nixee is dead."

I do not know what Idlouk was thinking as he sat on the rocks. I did not ask, and he did not say. I suspect that he was thinking of days gone by and of the fine dogs and leaders he had driven. He was unhappy, that I could sense, for Nixee had been his favourite dog. For an hour or so he remained, grieving over his loss.

"Iyonamut," he muttered, finally, as he stood up and walked back to the tent. "It can't be helped. How about a mug of tea?"

chapter 10

I LAY FLAT on the rocks, rifle cradled loosely on my arm, looking out over the broken ice cover on the sea. Behind, the rugged stone coast rose to a height of fifty feet before levelling off sharply into a long slope to the interior hills. In front lay the broad expanse of Eclipse Sound, still ice-covered on the twentieth of July. The ice was rotten, full of holes and cracks, and rapidly disintegrating under the warm rays of the summer sun beating down out of a cloudless sky. Huge ice pans, often miles across, shifted back and forth as the combined effects of wind and tide set them in movement, creaking and groaning as they ground their way along the rocky coast. Travel by sled on the ice was still possible, but not for any distance, and only with the greatest care.

I was hunting for young seals in the open water cracks along the shore off the rocky point. I still needed one more fine skin from a young seal to complete the sealskin trousers my mother had promised me. I had been on the rocky point for almost two hours, watching and waiting. A few older seals had come up in the open water of the cracks, but they had been too far from shore. Tide on north Baffin is not very high, three to four feet in most places, but it is enough to make a difference when fishing for a dead seal. Off rocky points dead seals can often be retrieved from the sea floor as the land slopes down in gentle gradients, but off the rocky cliffs the land drops straight down into the sea. Often two feet off shore the water will be a hundred feet deep.

I had been lying quietly for about an hour before I saw the first seal. It was not a young one and too far out to be retrieved if shot, so I lay still and watched. It swam about in a leisurely manner in the open water patch, then dived cleanly only to reappear a minute or so later in another patch of water fifty yards along the shore. It swam around looking out over the ice, then dived again, this time up-ending with a splash and diving down deep to feed. I was alone again.

Another half hour passed and still I lay quietly, for who knows at what moment the seal will come. Patience is inherent in all aspects of an Eskimo's life, a patience so lingering that it staggers the modern mind; the continuous watching and waiting for game that may never come. Back and forth my gaze wandered over the broken ice, casually but intently, watching not so much for a seal, but for the sight of anything unusual in the surrounding seascape.

But at the end of three hours my patience was wearing thin. Surely if there were any young seals about they would have come along by now. I rolled over on my back to ease the cramped muscles that had been pressed close to the hard rock, and looked up into the pale blue sky. Then with a sigh I rolled over and scrambled to my feet. Picking up my rifle, I slipped the round from the breech and jumped down from the smooth rock on which I had been lying to a ledge just below. As I landed on the rock and turned to walk back to camp, a slight movement caught my eye. My head came round with a jerk. There, not thirty feet from where I stood, was the round black head of a young seal in the water, concentric rings radiating out from his bobbing head across the open water patch to the nearby shore.

I stood still as stone, cursing myself under my breath. An Eskimo would not have given up so soon. I should have known better. How many times had this same thing happened to me, waiting so long but just not long enough. What a fool I was! "Kadloonahpudlukpoongah," I muttered under my breath, "I am just like a white man still. No patience at all."

The seal bobbed up and down while it peered all about. It looked in my direction and for the space of a few seconds we stared into one another's eyes across thirty feet of open space. I held my breath, frozen to the spot. It looked away, still bobbing up and down, now and again going completely under water before coming up again a few inches away. Slowly, I sank to my knees. With infinite care I slipped a round into the breech of my rifle, working by feel alone, eyes never leaving the bobbing head. Slowly the rifle came to my shoulder while the seal bobbed along. I centred the head in my sights, and took a long steady breath. As I did, the seal's head slid slowly under water and was lost to my view. I waited for a few seconds but it did not reappear, and I knew the seal was swimming away. It would not go far, for it had not dived deep, but which way would it go?

To the left, I decided, I do not know why. Jumping from rock to rock, I ran around the point and quickly found a smooth spot on the rock. Lying full length, rifle to my shoulder, I waited, covering a patch of open water fifty yards away. Two minutes went by, three, and still no seal. I must have guessed wrongly, it had gone the other way. But no, up popped the black head again and right where I had thought. Carefully I took aim at the dancing, bobbing head and waited for it to be still. The seal rose high and held still for a quick look about. My finger squeezed tight.

The seal rolled over and floated high. Blood from the wound flowed freely, dyeing the water to a dull red hue. At last my sealskin trousers were complete.

As I rose to my feet, a new sound came to my ear. It was a long drawn out snore, as if someone lay asleep in the rocks nearby. I stood still and listened again. Once more the sound hit my ear, seeming to come from the right, across the point of land from where I had just come. I wondered what it could be, for I had thought myself alone on the point.

All was quiet for a few moments and once again I prepared to retrieve the floating seal. I jumped down from the rock on which I had lain, but as I did so the sound came again, and much closer. Instantly I knew what it was— the long drawn-out sigh of the narwhal as it came to the surface to breathe. I had known of narwhals since 1951, small whales that I had hunted from my kayak in Koluktoo Bay,* whales that had given me one of the most exciting film sequences I have ever photographed. In 1951 the ice on Eclipse Sound had gone out early in July and we had hunted the narwhals from kayak and canoe. This year with the ice still covering the Sound at the end of July, the whales were coming down to their summer feeding grounds by swimming under the ice, coming up for air in the cracks and holes that dotted the fast rotting ice cover. This year we would hunt narwhal from the ice.

Quickly I scrambled down the rocks to the edge of the sea. Near the tip of the rocky point, loose pieces of ice jammed in against the shore. Jumping from piece to piece, I managed to work my way around to the floating seal, haul it out on the ice and then half carry, half drag, it back to the shore by the way I had come. I left it on the rocks with my rifle and harpoon, quickly climbed the steep rock shore and started to run up the long hummocky slope back to the camp. The whales would be about five miles off and headed in this direction, swimming under the ice, rising up in the cracks and holes in the ice to breathe as they followed their migration route along the shore of Eclipse Sound toward Milne Inlet. They should pass right by the tip of our island. It was this very reason that we were camped where we were.

It was over a mile back to the camp, half the distance up the slope to the rocky ridge and then down the other side to the camp on the opposite shore. When I arrived on the top of the ridge overlooking the tents of the campsite, I was puffing like an old walrus. Standing silhouetted against the sky, I waved my arms, swinging them in circles

---

* Not far from the site of a proposed seaport that may be built to handle possible shipments of iron ore from a rich find on north Baffin Island.

across the front of my body and well out to the side. At an Eskimo camp, there is always someone looking about no matter what time of night or day. After a few seconds of waving I heard a cry from below, and figures ran from the tents. No need for me to shout, they would know what I had seen. My signals could mean only one thing—narwhal.

Never had I seen so much excitement at the camp. Men scurried about gathering up harpoons and lines, blowing up sealskin floats or avatuks as they are called. The boys prepared their fathers' rifles, the children ran around shouting, "Kilalogaluit, kilalogaluit, kilalogaluit," "Whales, whales, lots of whales." This was the day we had been waiting for since early in the spring. For months we had lived on a diet of seal meat. Now narwhals meant muktuk, the thick crunchy skin of the whales, delicious eaten raw or boiled, the high point of Arctic cuisine in the summer months.

Narwhals are the strangest of all the Arctic sea mammals. They are small whales from ten to fifteen feet long. When young, they are dark slate in colour, but as they grow older this changes to a mottled black and white not unlike marble flooring. The belly is almost pure white, especially in the female. Narwhals have two tusks, but it is only in the males that the tusks are seen, and then usually only one of them. It grows out of the left upper jaw, a long spirally grooved spike of ivory, growing as the animal ages, sometimes reaching a length of eight feet. It has a hollow core through which the nerve runs, for the tusk is really an overgrown incisor tooth. The Eskimos say the narwhal has toothache, like a human, and this is why so many of the tusks are broken off at the tip. The tooth hurts; the narwhal rubs it on the rocks and breaks it off. I believe this to be true, for I have seen "bad" or infected tusks. In these the tusk does not seem to be different from a healthy one, but the nerve tissue and the tissue around the skull at the base of the tusk gives off a strong, obnoxious odour. With advanced age the tusk solidifies, starting at the tip and working back towards the butt.

122

No one has yet been able to find how this tusk is used, although it must have use as it is always well polished near the tip. The Eskimos say narwhals use the tusk to spear big fish, but I have never met anyone who has actually seen this done. Some say they use the tusk to grub on the bottom of the shallow bays like the walrus in search of molluscs, but I have always found them feeding in the deeper waters off shore or at the edge of the sea ice in the spring. It is not a weapon, at least not in this age. Narwhals are inoffensive and will flee from all danger.

Some scientists are inclined to think that the legend of the unicorn is somehow tied up with the narwhal. The temptation to reason this way is very strong, for the tusk of the narwhal is identical to that commonly pictured on the unicorn, a spirally grooved spike of ivory. Some day perhaps we shall know.

Although narwhals have very poor eyesight, they are extremely difficult to hunt because of their incredibly sharp hearing, the sound of a drop of water falling on the deck of the kayak being enough to send them streaking for the depths. When hunted from kayaks in the open water, they can sometimes be cornered at the ends of deep bays. In the shallow water they cannot dive and escape, but even then they must be harpooned first for if killed they will sink and be lost. The Eskimos prize narwhal highly. The amount of meat and fat from a big one will be equivalent to that from five or six big seals. Muktuk, the thick outer skin, is an excellent food for the Eskimos or anyone else living in the Arctic lands, being rich in Vitamin C. Most of the meat is used as dog food, although strips of meat from the back are eaten dried or boiled. The long black sinews are cut off, separated into threads by the women and laid out on a rock in the sun to dry. The sinews make excellent thread, superior to caribou sinew for sewing waterproof seams on sealskin boots and clothing.

Both rifle and harpoon are used when hunting narwhals from the ice. The harpoon is quite different from that used on the seal. The handle is some five feet long and made of heavy wood. The bottom end is capped with an ivory stub in which a hollow or socket has been carved. Into this socket is fitted a thick ivory prong about nine inches long, usually carved from a walrus tusk. The prong tapers to a rounded point and is held tightly into the socket at the base of the handle by sealskin thongs, running through holes cut near the top, to holes cut into the handle. In this way the prong is securely attached to the handle, yet by simply pulling sideways on the prong, it will pull out of the socket and dangle loose still attached by the sealskin thongs.

The harpoon head is carved from ivory and is similar in design to the one used on the seal harpoon, the principle of operation being the same. The actual tip is a broad piece of sharpened metal usually cut from a shovel blade or an old saw. The harpoon head has a long sealskin line attached to it. The head is fitted onto the pointed end of the ivory prong on the handle, the sealskin line pulled taut and secured to the handle by a small ivory catch. The other end of the line is attached to a sealskin float, or avatuk, a sealskin that has been blown up like a balloon.

When the harpoon is thrown at a narwhal it is lofted through the air as it has some distance to travel. The weight of the heavy wooden handle provides the impetus that forces the head deep into the body. The moment the harpoon strikes home the narwhal rolls over and dives straight down. The float is quickly thrown into the water. As the whale dives, the line attached to the harpoon head pays out, reaches its limit, and then the float is dragged under. The drag of the float pulls on the line causing the ivory prong of the harpoon to come out of the socket. The harpoon "breaks", allowing the harpoon head and line to come free of the wooden handle, which floats to the surface. The shock pulls the harpoon head back, and the curved fins in the head pull the head flat under the fat and skin, securely anchored against any pull.

It is then merely a question of time before the heavy drag of the float pulls the whale to the surface where it can be shot. If the hunter is in open water in a kayak, he can harpoon it with a killing harpoon that has a steel tipped head. To kill a whale instantly, it must be shot in the brain, and the brain is hard to find. A narwhal has a huge lump of fat in a big hump right where its forehead should be. The actual head of the whale is about fourteen to eighteen inches back of this, the target area a small circle about five inches in diameter. As there is nothing to mark the location of the brain, only continual practice can ensure a good shot. Once the whale is killed the avatuk serves the additional purpose of keeping it afloat until retrieved.

Carrying my heavy wooden harpoon and long sealskin line, I walked with Idlouk back over the hill from whence I had come. As we walked down the hill to the shore where I had left my rifle and the seal, we could hear the sounds of the narwhals, closer now and more of them. Through the telescope we spotted them, about three miles off, long black backs arching up and down in the open water of the cracks and holes in the ice. In places the cracks were too narrow to be visible; all we could see was the smooth white ice, cut now and again by dark shadows arching up and down, the whales seeming to sheer through the apparently solid ice like knife through a cheese. While scanning one patch of what seemed to be smooth unbroken ice through the telescope, I was startled to see the long tusk of a huge narwhal rise slowly up out of the ice. Up and up it came until more than half the length of the whale was out in the open. Then it slowly slid back down into the invisible hole through which it had risen.

All the hunters were soon out on the ice. Idlouk and I carefully picked our way over the loose pans near the shore, jumping from pan to pan for a distance of about one hundred yards until we reached a belt of more solid ice. There was no movement as the tide was full and slack. We paused on the solid ice and waited to see just where the whales would come. We could hear nothing, but we knew the whales were not far off swimming under the ice, heading along the shore in our direction.

125

For a few moments all was quiet as we waited. Occasionally a shout rang out from other hunters who were working their way seaward far to our left. Once I heard a wild shout followed by laughter and I knew someone had fallen through the ice into the water. I grinned at Idlouk and he grinned in reply. "Probably Kitchooalik," he muttered, "he's just like a boy."

A slight tremor ran through the ice on which we stood. Glancing in towards shore I saw the loose pieces of ice start to move down the coast, slowly at first then gathering speed. The tide had turned and the ice was moving with it. The piece on which we stood, a piece about half a mile each way, began to move parallel to the shore. Slowly and ponderously it slid along, pushing everything before it. Looking seaward I could see that all the ice in the vicinity was now in motion, swinging under the press of the tide. Although our piece was thick and fairly intact, I was a little nervous over this turn of events. I looked across at Idlouk. He had no eyes for the ice, he was watching the open water spots for whales.

As the ice moved along the shore, our piece swung in closer to the rocks, jamming the loose pans onto the rocky coast. Ice pans began to pile up, ride over one another, the ones close in being pushed up on the sloping shore. Slowly and relentlessly the ice ground along, smashing everything that stood in its path. On shore huge boulders were driven along, or rolled up the rocks. Our piece pushed under a neighbouring floe and a wall of three-foot-thick ice slid easily over the surface, creeping towards us as though pushed by some giant hand. I looked over at Idlouk but he still had eyes and ears for nothing but whales. I tried this too, but my eyes kept coming back to the advancing wall of ice.

Closer it came; forty feet, thirty-five, thirty. I glanced over at Idlouk again and found him watching me with a grin. "You are still a white man," he said, "you have much to learn. Watch the ice carefully and see what it does."

Twenty feet, fifteen feet. Suddenly there was a sharp

crack. The ice under our feet tilted a little and then rose up about two feet. With a tremendous squelching splash the advancing piece of ice sank slowly down. Its tremendous weight had broken the piece on which we stood. We were safe enough for although the ice was considerably reduced in size, it was still thick and intact.

Over by the point, the ice was beginning to pile up on an underwater reef. Where only fifteen minutes before the surface of the ice had been flat as a field, now a massive ridge of ice blocks was forming, already about fifteen feet high and growing visibly before my eyes as more and more ice piled in driven by the press of the ice behind.

The noise of the ice was low and ominous, rumbling and grinding like giant teeth gritting and gnashing together in a rage. Sometimes the piled up pieces, often as big as a good-sized garage, tilted high in the air and fell back with a crash. The ice pans creaked and groaned like a floor in a vacant house. Our piece touched another equally big and a sharp tremor caused me to sway on my feet. A large chunk broke free and swung off to the left. New cracks appeared and then disappeared as edges over-rode one another and ice pans were forced up or shoved down below.

In half an hour we drifted over half a mile along the coast. The ice was unrecognizable as that on which we had so recently stepped. Instead of a smooth, relatively unbroken field stretching off to the horizon, now we looked over a crazy world of jumbled ice blocks of every conceivable size and shape. They were pushed helter skelter along the rocky coast and far out to sea. Off the point the ice barrier over the sunken reef was now a jagged wall of ice over fifty feet high, block after block from little ones the size of footballs to some as big as cottages, all piled together in a long ragged heap. Our piece was still intact, but it groaned and creaked under every new knock. I thought it was going to break up under our feet as each minute passed.

Quickly as it had started, the movement stopped. One minute the air was filled with the creak and groan of the shifting ice, the next all was quiet except for an occasional crash as an ice block tumbled from a lofty perch. The currents set up by the change of the tide had slackened and released the pressure on the ice. The new contours of the ice were set. It would never be the same again.

During all this time we had seen nothing of the whales. Idlouk had been watching the open water cracks carefully as we drifted down the coast, but apart from an occasional seal, we had seen nothing. The ice movements had probably sent the narwhal off in a different direction, perhaps going past the point of the island much farther out.

Idlouk decided to return to land at the point of the island and wait for the next school of whales to come through. Getting back to the land was a tough job. The ice was very rough and broken, full of holes and rotten spots where it was thin, but we managed to make shore with nothing worse than wet feet. Here we sat down to rest beside the seal I had shot earlier in the day. Kadluk came in as well and the three of us sat around the seal eating pieces of raw meat. I ate the heart and one flipper; they were delicious. We had no tea to top if off. That would have to wait. When we had finished our snack we carried the carcass up to a cleft in the rock wall of the shore and pushed it well back out of the way of ravens and gulls that haunt the coast in summer.

We all lay on the rock, face up to the pale blue sky. The sun on the rocks was very hot, although the air temperature was not much above freezing. Full stomachs and the heat of the sun made us drowsy and for some time we lay half asleep, not saying a word.

A far-off shout brought us to our feet. The whales were coming through again. Back out on the ice we went, jumping from ice pan to ice pan, splashing through the foot-deep puddles of water on top of the more solid pieces. As we ran, we fanned out, separating to cover as much of the ice as we could, Kadluk to the left, Idlouk straight ahead, and myself angling off to the right, the direction from which the whales were arriving. With the ice so badly broken, with holes and cracks everywhere, it was impossible to travel in a straight line. I had to take advantage of every solid piece of ice, running along beside a crack until it narrowed enough for me to jump across. Often I jumped from small pan to pan with ice breaking up under my feet. I had to keep going, for to stop would have meant a ducking in the sea.

About half a mile out from shore I reached a solid piece of ice and stopped to rest. Off to my left I could hear shots as other hunters fired at whales coming up in the cracks near them. But around me all was silence. Then a narwhal blew close by, and another, and another. About two hundred yards ahead of where I stood, I could see the dark backs arching through a small patch of open water as a school of about ten whales surfaced time and again to breathe, then dived before resuming their swim along the coast under the ice.

Rifle ready under my right arm, harpoon in my left hand, I walked quietly over the ice towards the whales. There was no danger of the whales seeing me, but with their incredible hearing, I had to be careful of every step. I moved to within fifty yards of them, and still they swam, diving back and forth across the pool. I had to be within twenty-five yards for the shot, for I had to shoot to kill and then get the harpoon into the whale before it could sink.

About thirty yards off I could go no farther; a wide crack stretched off to my right and left. I could easily have jumped it, but to do so would certainly alarm the whales. Putting the harpoon down on the ice, I raised the rifle to my shoulder. I had to shoot standing to be able to see the whales. Twice they dived across the pool, but I could not get in a shot. Their backs slid up so quickly and smoothly that they were gone before I could get my sights on the one small part that would mean a kill. Anything but a kill would be useless. The whale would simply dive deep and be gone.

Before I could get off a shot, the whales dived and were gone. Quickly I picked up the harpoon and jumped across the crack. I ran up to the edge of the pool and sat down on the ice and stayed very still. There would be other whales along and this was a good spot for them to come up. For five or ten minutes nothing happened, then suddenly a seal's head broke the surface about twenty feet from where I sat. It bobbed up and down a few times, then looked over in my direction. For about thirty seconds we looked into one another's eyes, then it continued to bob up and down in the pool, gradually working farther and farther away. I let it go, for I was after bigger game.

The seal was soon joined by another and another. In fifteen minutes the pool contained over thirty seals, swimming back and forth, bobbing up and down. Small wavelets from their motions splashed against the ice edge at my side. They kept an eye on me, and very few came over to my side of the pool, but otherwise they ignored my presence on the ice, although I was in full view. Every few minutes one would look around, take fright, and with a tremendous splash dive deep into the water. In a twinkling all the seals had disappeared leaving only the concentric wavelets of water to radiate out to the edge of the ice. Then a minute or two later a head cautiously broke the surface, then another and another until all were back, swimming and playing in the water.

For half an hour I waited, but the whales did not return. Still the seals swam around the water patch. I decided that as the whales were not coming back for the moment I might as well try for a seal. Slowly I raised the rifle to my shoulder and aimed at a seal quite close by the ice but on the side of the hole opposite to where I sat. Although the seal would sink on being killed, it would float for about thirty seconds or so before starting down. Being close to the edge of the ice, I would have a good chance of getting the harpoon into the body before it could sink down deep enough to be lost.

At such range I could not miss. The seal floated high, blood pouring from the open wound in the head, staining the water around to a deep red hue. Quickly I scrambled to my feet, dropped the rifle to the ice and snatched up the harpoon. Running swiftly I dashed around the edge of the ice, jumped over two cracks of open water and started up the other side of the hole towards the spot where the seal still floated high.

Just then a narwhal surfaced at the far end of the open water hole. It was followed quickly by another and another and another. In a moment four of them were swimming and diving not forty feet from where I stood.

The moment the first narwhal broke surface I stopped dead in my tracks all thought of the seal gone from my head. Once again I cursed myself for being so much the fool, for my rifle lay on the ice on the opposite side of the water hole. The whales were too far away for the harpoon, I would have to get back to the rifle, taking the chance that my foot-steps on the ice would not alarm them. Turning, I ran back the way I had come, keeping low down and moving as quietly as I could. I reached the rifle safely and sat down by the water's edge. The whales were not alarmed, they still frolicked back and forth. I chose the biggest one of the four, the only one with a tusk. Back across the pool they went, three dives bringing them to the farthest ice. Then they returned, heading directly for the spot where I sat. The long back arched up and down as I followed it in the sights. It disappeared under the water, and I moved the rifle down covering the spot where I thought it would appear again. Up it came and right in my sight. I squeezed the trigger.

With a tremendous splash the whales disappeared, all diving deep into the sea. I jumped to my feet, positive I had made a kill, but as the waves splashed up to the edge of the ice, no long dark back was visible on the surface of the sea. Quickly I ran along the edge to a point opposite where the whales had been at the time of my shot. Fifteen feet out from the ice, blood stained the water in an ever widening pool, growing and growing until the dark stain was twenty feet across. But there was no sign of the whale. I was sure I had killed it but it must have had enough kick to dive down under the ice. For half an hour I scurried over the ice around, looking in all the cracks and holes, but no trace could I find.

At the pool in which I had first shot, the blood was gradually thinning out and there was no sign of the whale. I had forgotten about the seal I had shot, but as I looked down into the gradually clearing water I saw a dark shadow drifting very slowly along the edge of the crack. I ran along to where I could see it better, and there, five feet down in the water, my seal floated serenely along, the ocean currents slowly carrying it under the ice cover. Quickly I raised the harpoon and plunged it down into the water. With a quick tug on the line, I jerked the handle free of the head and hauled the seal out on the ice. I had often heard of seals sinking after being shot in the cracks in the sea ice in the summer and then stopping a few feet below the surface, but this was the first time I had ever seen it.

For the next week we hunted whales day and night, our whole life governed by their comings and goings. Always one of the small boys was stationed on the high hill back of the camp. At the first sight or sound of whales coming through he gave the alarm and all the hunters turned out onto the ice. One moment the camp lay peaceful and quiet under the high riding sun, the next animated figures ran shouting from every tent, pulling on wet sealskin boots, picking up rifles and harpoons, anxious to be the first out on the ice. For two or three hours we dashed over the ice trying to outguess the oncoming school of whales, trying to be waiting beside the crack or open water patch in which they would come up to breathe. Often I would guess wrong. It was aggravating to wait beside a beautiful stretch of open water only to have the whales surface in another one two hundred yards away. Then a decision had to be made. Should I sneak over to where they were and hope they would stay long enough for me to get off a shot, or should I let them alone and stick with my position hoping they, or other whales, would come my way? Often I chose the wrong course.

But sometimes I would make the right move, and be waiting at the right crack in the ice when the whales came up to breathe. Standing a few feet back from the edge of the water, rifle cradled in my arm, harpoon at my feet, I would be startled by the sudden appearance of a long black shadow rising swiftly up from the depths of the sea. A moment later

132

the back of the whale broke the surface of the water, quickly followed by another and another. The air was filled with the sound of their breathing, a long-drawn-out swoosh of air as the lungs were emptied at the peak of the dive, followed quickly by a sucking intake cut off sharply as the breathing hole in the top of the head was suddenly submerged for the next shallow dive. Back and forth they swam, often passing not more than ten feet from where I stood on the ice waiting for the right moment for the shot, long bodies sliding through the dark green water with effortless ease. Most of them were females, but now and again I saw a male push its long twisted tusk up to the sky. Each time I saw a tusk thrust up from the water, a new thrill ran through my body; for the males with their long ivory tusks were the most valued of all the kills.

Carefully I swung the rifle to cover the arching back as it followed the long tusk up out of the water, rifle swinging smoothly in perfect time with the forward movement of the whale. Right and left the rifle swung, my eyes squinting carefully along the long glistening barrel, waiting for the right moment for the kill.

Crack! The whale rolled over and floated high, killed instantly by the shot through the brain. With a mighty splash the other whales dived deep, churning the water into a bloody foam as they streaked for the depths.

The moment after I fired I snatched up the readied harpoon. Pausing only a moment for a quick aim, I lofted the harpoon out towards the floating whale, already starting to sink slowly down into the water. With a soft thud the harpoon head bit deep into the body. Quickly I jerked the long sealskin line in my left hand. The harpoon "broke" and the head came free of the handle, pulling flat under the skin. I had completed the kill.

The moment the kill was made, I let out a long yell. Soon all the hunters came streaming over the ice to lend a hand in getting the carcass out onto the ice and cutting it up for transportation to the distant shore. While we worked, we ate pieces of muktuk cut from the choice spots on the

whale. The best pieces are the trailing edges of the short
flippers and along the tail; next in favour are slices from
the body near the tail. When the whale had been cut up
the meat and fat were left on the ice to be brought to shore
on sleds once the tempo of hunting died down. Then all the
hunters straggled back to camp, soaking wet from splashing
through puddles or from slipping into the water as we
dashed across the bobbing ice pans. At the camp, the women
kept big pots of muktuk and whale heart on the boil, as well
as kettles full of black, black tea. After a quick meal we lay
down on the sleeping bags or in a cleft in the rocks to snatch
a few hours' sleep before the next run of whales came
through.

On the morning of the third day I was walking back to
camp with Idlouk after an unsuccessful sortie. Suddenly
Idlouk stopped, walked back a few feet, and began to peer
intently down at the ice. I came back and looked too. I
could see nothing, until Idlouk told me to look carefully at
a small sector on the ice surface. Bending low I could see a
yellowish stain in the ice. "See that stain," Idlouk said,
"there is a piece of fat under the ice below there. Wasn't
it close to here that you shot the narwhal the first day they
came through? Yes it was. You must have killed it but it
came up under the ice right here."

With his harpoon he chopped down through the foot-thick
ice. Reaching down into the hole he fished around for a
moment, then brought up a piece of fat and muktuk about
six inches square. The edges were ragged from tearing teeth.

"Your whale has been eaten by sharks or by killer
whales," he said; "there are always some of them around
when the narwhals come through."

At the end of four days I was so tired I could hardly
see. Not one of us had more than two hours' uninterrupted
sleep in all that time. And still the whales kept coming
through. Going back to camp on the evening of the fourth
day, Idlouk and I were soaked to the skin and dead tired.
After a meal of muktuk and tea, we took off all our clothes
and Kidlak laid them out on the rocks to dry under the rays

of the midnight sun. I tumbled into my sleeping bag and was soon in a deep sleep.

Two hours later I came slowly awake to hear shouts ringing through the camp. The whales were coming through again. Idlouk was already scrambling for the door of the tent and I quickly followed. Outside we stumbled, gathering up our clothes from where they lay scattered over the rocks, dressing in a frenzy of haste. Still drugged with sleep, we ran out onto the ice, slipping and stumbling on the smooth water-washed surface. Our weariness did not matter, the whales were coming through and the winter ahead was long. Whales meant delicious muktuk through the long winter night.

In five days' hunting we managed to kill six whales. Then they stopped coming. Idlouk thought we had frightened them so badly with our continuous hunting that they had been turned into one of the deep bays to the east where they would rest and feed before continuing their journey down the coast. By that time I did not care if all the whales on north Baffin had taken off for the Antarctic. I was out on my feet, my eyes refused to focus from lack of sleep. Muktuk for the long winter meant nothing now. I would gladly starve as long as I did not have to go out after whales again. All I wanted to do was to crawl into my sleeping bag and sleep forever and ever.

But there was no chance of rest. Out on the ice lay the meat and fat from six whales, drifting with the ice as it moved back and forth under the effects of wind and tide. The meat and fat had to be brought ashore by sled and boat, and cached under the rocks. Each narwhal had to be cut up immediately after being killed, for the meat will become poisonous if this is not done. The same is true of the meat from the walrus, but not from the seal. Three of the carcasses we managed to get ashore without too much trouble for there was fairly good ice right in to the shore near where they lay. But three others gave us no end of trouble. A sled loaded with meat and fat weighs close to 1,200 pounds. Twice, loaded sleds overturned when ice gave

135

way beneath the load. In each case we barely managed to keep the load from sinking and dragging the dogs to a watery grave. Two hundred yards from shore the sleds could go no farther; a wide band of open water cut us off from land. Small boys from the camp rowed out to us in the dory and the long task of ferrying meat, fat, dogs, sleds and ourselves to shore began. It took almost a day to get the last load across, and another half day to put all the meat and fat into caches for use in the winter.

CHAPTER

11

BREAK-UP came late to north Baffin Island in the summer of 1953. Throughout the latter part of July, the ice cover on the sea shifted daily. Close to shore open water patches grew in size only to disappear quickly as the ice changed in outline under each attack by wind and tide. Often the water remained open long enough for us to use the kayaks and the canoe, but we could go no great distance by boat until the ice cover moved out of Eclipse Sound into the open sea. July 28th was the last day on which we were able to use sled and dogs for limited travel on the sea ice in the vicinity of the camp. On that date the ice finally started to move out and the sleds were pulled up on the rocks, their long travel season over until the fall.

For four days the ice moved slowly past the point of the island. From a vantage point high up on the rocky hill back of the camp, we could see the dark blue line of open water far off to the north-west across Eclipse Sound. Daily this dark line grew wider as the forward edge of the open water crept closer and closer to where we were camped. Field after field of fast rotting ice swept ponderously past the point of our island, moving east and then north heading for the open sea, carried along on the easterly current that would take it around the margin of Eclipse Sound past Pond Inlet settlement, jamming into the narrow opening of Pond Inlet itself before spilling out into the open waters of Baffin Bay. Here it would join the ice of the polar pack coming down from the waters of the far north isles, ice from Barrow Strait and Lancaster Sound, ice from Kane Basin and Smith

Sound, ice from the Arctic Ocean itself, all to drift rest-lessly south through Baffin Bay and Davis Strait, eaten away by sun and wind and water until finally disintegrating in the open reaches of the vast North Atlantic Ocean.

On the morning of August 3rd, I awoke to hear little Noahkudluk, Idlouk's youngest son, whispering to his father.

"Atata, atata, kanoeetooaluk," he said. "Father, father, what can that be?"

"That" was a new sound coming clearly through the thin canvas walls of the tent. It was the sound of the sea, the soft chuckle of tiny waves washing on an ice-free shore. The ice had gone.

Noahkudluk was enthralled by the sound. Ten months had gone by since it had been heard on north Baffin, and ten months ago Noahkudluk had been too young to under-stand what it meant. All day he ran up and down the rocky shore, throwing stones and bits of bones into the water, getting his feet wet as he paddled joyfully about in the shallows of a nearby cove. Often he stopped, listening in bewilderment to the whistle of the wind on the sea. Two days later, when a high wind brought heavy waves thunder-ing up on the rocks below the tent, he refused to go outside until his father assured him that he need not be afraid of the sea.

With the coming of open water, we took to the boats for all hunting and travel, roaming restlessly over the sea. For a few days we hunted seals off the point of the island, Idlouk, Kadluk and I in our kayaks, the others in rowboat or canoe. But the island's rocky point was not a good place for a sum-mer camp. Our tents faced due north across the widest part of Eclipse Sound and up the farther long reach of Navy Board Inlet. Under the press of the north-west wind blow-ing strongly over this long open stretch, mighty waves built up to crash thunderously on our exposed cape. On such days we were tied to the land unable to venture on the sea to hunt. We needed calmer waters than these in front of our camp, now that open water had come.

On August 8th we moved camp again, this time travelling by boat. Two days before all the men had paddled the big canoe to the campsite at Aulatseevik and there had launched Idlouk's gas-powered boat from its winter berth on shore. The boat was big, forty feet long and powered by a two-cylinder gasoline engine, but it barely held all the gear of five households, and twenty-five people as well. Loaded to the gunwale, people perched on top of the load like birds on a nest, the boat chugged slowly through the narrow channel back to the main campsite at Aulatseevik. Here the high rock walls behind the campsite provided shelter from winds out of the north, and we would have smooth waters for hunting as well as a safe harbour for the big boat. While we moved over the water, the dogs trotted over the land, herded along by Paneeluk and Elijah. They arrived at the camp hours after the boat, hot and panting from the stiff climb over the high interior hills of the island.

The campsite at Aulatseevik was peaceful after the stormy camp on the exposed cape. Some mornings the sea lay calm as water in a plate, the high hills of the land around reflected perfectly in the mirror-like surface. Hardly a minute passed that we could not see the small black heads of dozens of seals swimming leisurely about before diving down deep to feed. Twenty-four hours a day a silent hunter sat on the rocks to the west of the camp; his rifle was cradled loosely in his lap, his hands busy carving a piece of ivory or soapstone, fashioning a new harpoon head or some article for sale to the store, but his eyes rarely ceased scanning the surface of the sea. Every so often the rifle cracked and a seal floated high, blood staining the water around. At each shot the dory dashed out from the camp, manned by two or three small boys pulling desperately on the oars, trying to reach the seal before it sank. Sometimes they would be in time, and proudly haul the catch ashore. Often they would be too late and their cries of disappointment echoed back and forth across the quiet bay.

It is under conditions such as these that many of the fine Eskimo carvings are done. In some areas of the Eastern

Arctic Eskimos carve in the same way as they hunt; it is a job to be done. But on north Baffin the Eskimo carves only in his spare time and usually at odd moments snatched from some other more prosaic job. Sitting on the rocky shore or in the bobbing canoe, pipe clenched between dark stained teeth, humming an old song of the land, he whittles slowly away, stopping now and then to squint at the ivory piece that is slowly being transformed into a sleeping seal or a crouching bear. Now and again he shakes his head in disgust and changes a line here and a line there, but his eye is never long removed from scanning the surface of the sea. For he is a hunter, his responsibility to feed the women and children of his camp.

For two weeks I hunted seals in the sheltered waters of the bay. Hour after hour I glided swiftly over the smooth waters in my long slim kayak, rifle and harpoon ready for the kill. Hunting was not easy, as it was necessary to sink a harpoon attached to a float into each seal before I could make the kill. I sat quietly, kayak bobbing gently on the smooth ground swell. Minutes passed quickly as I waited and watched. Far off to the right I could see Idlouk sitting in his kayak; from the left I might hear a shot and know that Kadluk was trying for a kill. But near me nothing happened; all I could do was wait.

Without warning a seal's head broke the surface about fifty yards ahead. Slowly the seal bobbed up and down looking all about. It did not catch sight of me. Set low on the water my form merged with the dark hills behind, and the seal did not see me. It started to swim about. Slowly, I brought the long paddle forward and back. The kayak crept forward, long tapering bow knifing the water with scarcely a sound. Closer I moved to the swimming seal, moving up from behind and keeping slightly to its left. I closed the distance between us to ten yards and still it had not seen or heard my stealthy approach.

A last shove with the paddle and my right arm raised the harpoon high. The seal rolled over, lolling on its back. My arm shot forward and the harpoon arched through the air. With a soft thud it struck and bit deep. I knew the seal was hooked.

Instantly the seal came awake and with a terrific splash dived deep. I threw the sealskin float from the rear deck of the kayak and paddled clear. The seal reached the limit of the long line and the float bobbed rapidly over the surface of the sea. A narwhal could take the float under, but not a small seal. Quickly I paddled up to the float and followed close behind as it was dragged along, a boiling froth in its wake.

Suddenly it stopped. I stopped too. From under the deck of the kayak I drew my .22 and slipped a round into the breech. Twenty-five yards ahead the seal's head broke surface and it looked about. I took aim at the bobbing head. The kayak swung and tossed and I had a hard time keeping the seal in the sight. But the moment came. I squeezed the trigger. The seal rolled over and floated high.

Stowing the rifle under the deck again, I paddled up to the slowly sinking seal. First I retrieved the float and returned it to its place on the aft deck. Then I gathered in the line, pulling the seal back up to the surface and alongside the kayak. Taking a small gaff, or *nixee* as it is called, I hooked the seal by a flipper and with my free hand worked the harpoon head free of the flesh.

Kayaks are cranky craft and the job of geting a seventy-five pound seal onto the rear deck is not an easy task. First I brought the seal directly alongside the cockpit, and, as I am righthanded, on my right. I held it securely by one hind flipper and with a quick shove thrust the seal down into the water and rolled the kayak over as much as I dared to the right. Keeping the kayak tilted sharply over I pulled the seal quickly up. The water removed much of the dead weight of the body and it came up like a heavy cork. As it reached the highest point out of the water, I jerked in sharply with my arm pulling the seal's body across the rear deck of the kayak where it dropped with a thud. Quickly I straightened the kayak and the seal was safely aboard. Here it would ride out of the way of harpoon and paddle.

141

If it had been a big one, I would have left the harpoon head attached and towed it to shore.

The first time I had to get a seal aboard on a hunt, I was scared stiff. Idlouk had taught me how to do it in the shallow water near the camp. Here I had no difficulty picking up the technique as I knew that if the kayak turned over I could easily scramble to my feet. But when I had to do the same thing out in the centre of a wide bay with the nearest kayak about a mile away, I was very much afraid. The kayaks on north Baffin are not the type in which you can go completely over and come up on the other side. If you go over, all you can do is get out as best you can and either wait for help, clinging to the kayak in the frigid waters, or try to kick and paddle it to shore. Also, when Idlouk made my kayak, he did not leave quite enough room for my long legs. Instead of having my feet pressed flat against a board set in the kayak frame, I had to hook my feet under the board in order to sit flat. If the kayak went over I was not at all sure I would be able to get my big feet out from behind the board.

But pride overcame fear. To call the other Eskimos for help would not do. With a silent prayer I shoved down on the seal and tilted the kayak over to the right. Up came the seal and I jerked it across the rear deck. I straightened the kayak so quickly that I very nearly rolled it over to the left. But I had made it safely and that was the end of my fear.

Later that day I arrived back at camp to the tributes of the Eskimos who had all come back empty handed from the hunt. I glowed under their praise and proudly helped cut up the seal and distribute the meat to the tents. Meat from my rifle fed the camp that day. But I could not fool Idlouk. As we sat in front of the tent making a meal of raw seal heart and fat, he looked at me and grinned.

"Today on the water I watched you through my telescope as you retrieved your seal. I knew you would be afraid for I was afraid the first time I had to do that too. I wondered— will he be able to do it?—for I know that you are a white man, and white men are different from Eskimos in knowing the ways of our land. Then I watched while you got the seal on board and I was proud. More and more you are getting to be like an Eskimo, and like my son. There are not many white men who live with the Eskimos as you are doing, learning what it is like to live as we do in our land. I am glad that I am able to be your Eskimo father and teach you all I know. When you go back to your land, I will write a note for you. It will be to the big chief of all the white men who come to our land on the boat in the summer. It will say, 'Listen well when Kingmik talks of the life of the Eskimo in his land. For he has been an Eskimo. He knows what it is like to go hungry in the cold. He knows how to kill seals and narwhals. He knows how to drive the dogs and paddle the kayak. Sometimes he even thinks a bit like an Eskimo. Listen well when he talks, for he knows the life of my land.' "

Later on Idlouk did write that note. He wanted me to send it off to the chief in my land. I did not do so, but have kept it with me in my wallet so that it accompanies me wherever I go. Although the films I have made have won many awards and the plaques and certificates testifying to this are among my most prized possessions, not one of these honours occupies the same place in my heart as that note from Idlouk. Written in syllabic character writing, on a scrap of paper torn from a small notebook, it is my graduation diploma from the school of the Arctic.

TOWARDS the middle of August we began to make plans to go in to the settlement at Pond Inlet to meet the annual supply ship, the *C. D. Howe*. For three hundred and sixty-four days the inhabitants of this remote part of Canada have only radio contact with the rest of the world. During this time they live unto themselves, a self-sufficient existence on the top of the world. For the white residents of the settlements, the radio provides a tenuous tie with their homeland to the south, but the Eskimo has little thought for anything but *his* land. He looks upon southern Canada in much the same way that southern Canadians look upon the Arctic. He thinks it may be a good place for the white man to live, but of doubtful value to an Eskimo.

Not all Eskimos of the Pond Inlet area go in to the settlement to meet the ship. Some camps are too far away and the people lack large boats in which to make the trip. Other camps are close enough, but lack room in the small boats for all to go. Then usually only the hunters go in, leaving the women and children behind. Of the two hundred and fifty inhabitants of the area about one hundred usually manage to get to Pond at shiptime. There are many who would like to go, but cannot. There are others who have no desire to see the showy wealth of the white man.

A few of the Eskimos go to the settlement by dog sled before the breakup of the sea ice. These people camp on the sandy beach in front of the settlement, hunting for seals in the none-too-productive waters close by, and scrounging what food they can from the Eskimos in the employ of the various white establishments. A few are hired to do odd jobs prior to the arrival of the boat, for each establishment must be in tip-top shape for the inspection parties sent out from the various headquarters each summer. Gravel walks are raked, buildings painted, refuse cleared from the beach. When the ship arrives, the settlement is primped and shined as it has not been since the ship came one year before. One trader is so fussy that after he has had the brass door knobs shined, he covers them with small paper bags which are not removed until the first small boat from the newly arrived ship touches the shore.

Most of the Eskimos go in by small boat during the month of August, some arriving after the *C. D. Howe* has come and gone. There is no way for the Eskimos to know just when the boat will arrive. Living an isolated life far away from radio contact with the outside world, they go to the settlement in what they feel will be ample time to meet the ship. Shiptime in the Arctic means a great deal to the Eskimos. Due to the system of ordering used by the Hudson's Bay Company, the store invariably runs out of many items very early in the year. Without exception all posts I have known run out of many essential items. I have seen stores out of pablum in April, duffel cloth for parkas in March, drill cloth for covers in May, tobacco in June, biscuits in July. Until the boat comes again the Eskimo must do without. One would think that sufficient stock could be carried in the stores to take care of this, but running out of goods early seems to be the rule.

At Aulatseevik we had only a vague idea when the ship would be in. Idlouk decided to travel in to Pond Inlet on August 12th. We had just enough gasoline left to make the trip; Idlouk had been saving a few precious gallons for this purpose. Idlouk's family, Kadluk and myself would go from the camp. I was planning to board the ship at Pond Inlet and accompany it to the northern islands for ten days in order to observe the movement of Eskimos to new camping grounds, then drop off at Pond Inlet again when the boat headed back to the south.

Many others at the camp would have liked to go, but Idlouk said no. It would be very hard to feed a large group at the settlement. He and Kadluk would have to hunt very carefully as it was, for there would be seventy-five or a hundred other Eskimos all hunting around the post, in a small area not noted for its abundance of game. It would have been useless for him to take food with him, although we had plenty at the camp. The Eskimos would have soon eaten it all up, following the age-old custom of the land. No Eskimo goes hungry as long as there is food in another man's house.

This has often been cited as an act of charity on their part, but strictly speaking it is not so. Eskimos are the most individualistic people I know; they think of self and family only. They have little sense of community spirit or group action as we understand these terms in our modern society. Charity, the act of giving freely, of projecting one's thinking out from self to encompass all members of the group, is unknown to the Eskimo. What is mistaken for charity is the age-old custom of sharing food and hospitality with all who come your way. Every Eskimo knows that if he is hungry or starving he can go to the camp of his nearest neighbour and if the neighbour has food, he will get it. He can stay as long as he likes, eat as much as he wants, bring his family as well, sharing in the life of the camp in which he is a visitor. This has always been so in the lives of the Eskimos. Through necessity they have had to develop a set of customs that would give them some measure of security in the hard fight for survival in the high north lands.

But, although the hungry or starving Eskimo knows that he can always get food at his neighbour's camp, the neighbour would not think of taking food to the hungry man, except perhaps in the case of a near relative or extremely good friend. He would be more likely to shake his head and feel very badly for his neighbour and then on his next trip in to the settlement tell the policeman that he thinks his neighbour may be hungry, and that perhaps he could do with some food. The Eskimo feels a transient compassion toward his less fortunate fellow, but not such a deep and lasting compassion that he would instinctively go to his aid. Such thinking is foreign to his way of life.

Tied up with this is an almost complete lack of a sense of gratitude. Very few Eskimos feel in the slightest debt to a benefactor. The starving man, fed and housed, perhaps even clothed by his neighbour, feels under no obligation for such acts. He accepts them as his right, as having always been so, the pattern of life in his land. Some day he may be called upon to perform the same acts and he will not expect any thanks for what he may do. Such things are soon forgotten.

This lack of a sense of gratitude has alienated many an Eskimo and white. Many times white men have expected thanks for favours tendered and, not receiving them, have thought poorly of the Eskimo, not understanding that the Eskimo was acting according to the custom of the land. Any white man working with Eskimos must learn to accept this fact for some time to come. The attitude is changing gradually. Many Eskimos today, realizing that the white man expects thanks, are learning to give them. But it is a superficial gesture at best, and is often over profuse, due chiefly to a lack of understanding by the Eskimos of the part a sense of gratitude plays in our life.

Our trip to the settlement across the open sweep of lower Eclipse Sound was a smooth crossing. The sea lay calm as a millpond and the big boat ploughed steadily on, hour after hour, not travelling in a straight line, but always keeping a mile or two from the gently curving outlines of shore. The weather can change with remarkable suddenness in the Arctic and when travelling in an open boat it is not wise to stray far from shore.

At the half-way mark of the trip, we pulled into a small harbour near the tip of a large island. Here Idlouk had told me there were some very old Eskimo house ruins, relics of Eskimos who once lived in this land long ago. In particular he wanted to show me an old gambling ring used by these Eskimos before the coming of the white man to the Arctic.

The house ruins turned out to be old tent rings, large boulders placed in a circle about fifteen feet in diameter that had once held down the edges of a sealskin tent. The gambling ring was similar to the tent ring, but made of larger stones spaced about two feet apart. At one time a large flat rock had sat in the centre of the circle, but it had been re-moved by Eskimos who had recently used the site for their tent. The game was apparently a version of what we call spin the bottle. The Eskimos would all stand around the circle with one man in the centre. This man would spin a cylindrical or oval-shaped stone on the flat base, and when it stopped collect a forfeit from the Eskimo at whom the spinning stone pointed. Then that man would move in and the play was repeated. Idlouk said that Eskimos used to gamble a great deal in the old days and often for very high stakes, such things as kayaks, hunting gear, and often a wife being gambled away on the turn of the stone.

Our luck with the weather held and all day the big boat chugged steadily across the smooth waters of Eclipse Sound. Holding course was an easy matter, for the unmistakable pyramid-like bulk of Mount Herodier was clearly etched into the distant horizon. The settlement of Pond Inlet lay just eight miles from its base. As we approached from the south, the buildings of the settlement appeared as tiny white dots snuggled against the base of low hills reaching almost to the edge of the sea. Gradually the dots grew in size and assumed shape, the same clean white buildings that are to be found in almost every settlement in the Canadian Arctic.

Here and there across the vast sprawling mass of muskeg rock, water and ice that is Arctic Canada are these small groups of buildings, sometimes only one or two in a group, sometimes ten, less often more. A few years ago their names were relatively unknown: Pangnirtung, Igloolik, Baker Lake, Cambridge Bay, Aklavik, Eskimo Point, Povungnituc, Pond Inlet, and many more. Today, a new age is shaping for the far north posts, an age that owes its existence to the aircraft. Where once, only ten years ago and often less, the sight of an aircraft flying high overhead would have been talked about for weeks, aircraft now pass once or twice a month, and often many times a day. Airfields have sprung up where a few years ago only caribou roamed, transforming the face and the future of this far north land. Today these airfields are military, tomorrow who knows?

What is an Arctic settlement? It is many things to many different people. To most southern Canadians, the settlements are the last outposts of civilization in the vast wilderness of our northern frontier. To northern Canadians, the Eskimos, they represent civilization in its highest form. To most people in southern Canada, Churchill means the Arctic; to residents of the Arctic, Churchill is southern Canada. Viewed from the perspective of Montreal, Pond Inlet seems to be next door to the north pole; to the people at Pond Inlet the north pole is a remote geographic point fifteen hundred miles away, far off at the top of the world. On one point many Eskimos and whites seem to agree. The white man says, "How can people live in such a small settlement? What would they find to do? There would be nowhere to go, so few people to see." The Eskimo agrees, but he says, "How can people live at the settlement? There is too much hustle and bustle. There are too many houses and too many people. I cannot live at such a place. I will go back to my camp where I can breathe deeply again."

Most settlements are the centre for trade and administration in the land, the place where the Eskimos come to trade their fox skins and buy goods from the store; to collect Family Allowance issue; to go to church; to meet the ship. Pond Inlet has a Hudson's Bay Company post, a detachment of the Royal Canadian Mounted Police, an Anglican Mission and a Roman Catholic Mission. The buildings are well kept, painted white with roofs of red. Gravel walks, bordered by whitewashed stones, run between the houses, although these are visible only during the short summer months. On the beach stand the blubber sheds, small buildings made of sheets of tin, from which rises a rather obnoxious smell. In these blubber sheds is kept the store of seal and other meats for the dog teams of the Eskimos in the employ of the various establishments. On the steep hillside back of the buildings is the crest of the Royal Canadian Mounted Police and the words "Pond Inlet", each letter traced out in white-washed stones and almost twenty feet high.

Normally the settlement is a sleepy place. But at Christmas, Easter and shiptime, it is a hive of activity. It is then that many Eskimos come in from their outlying camps to visit and to trade, or to help unload the ship. For the brief eight hours or so that the ship rides at anchor off the shore, discharging her precious cargo of food and fuel and other goods for the long year ahead, all is hustle and bustle, confusion and noise. Barges scurry back and forth between ship and shore. Inspecting officers of the Royal Canadian Mounted Police and the Hudson's Bay Company pore over records and accounts. Government administrators check on matters that may have been saved up for many months past. On the ship long lines of Eskimos patiently wait their turn with doctor and dentist, who always have too much to do, and too little time in which to do it.

For the few brief hours at shiptime people from two

cultures mingle together. Here and there a single white man talks quietly with an Eskimo and his family. He may be a former policeman, or a trader, or a missionary renewing an acquaintance started many years ago. The two men talk quietly, now and again the woman joins in. At her legs a tiny tot clings stubbornly and gazes in awe at this white man his father seems to know so well. From deep inside the loose folds of the woman's parka hood a pair of dark shining eyes stare out, as the youngest member of the family rides cosily next to his mother's warm back, safe from the noise and confusion of the strange world outside.

Many of the whites on the ship are seeing Eskimos for the first time. They move from group to group taking pictures by the dozen, very friendly and jovial, handing out candy to the children, cigarettes to men and women. There is a bonhomie about shiptime that is hard to match; everyone works hard, talks and laughs. It is a case of "Eat and be merry for tomorrow we sail away." Differences in appearance, outlook and heritage are forgotten, Eskimo and white are human beings together, biologically alike as can be.

ON SEPTEMBER 15th we returned to the camp at Aulatseevik. The supply boat had come and gone, the excitement of shiptime was over for another year. Shelves in the store bent under their load of new merchandise, although by spring much of it would be gone and the season of annual shortages would begin again. Most of the Eskimos had obtained their Family Allowance issue, bought what they wanted with money obtained by working as stevedores unloading the ship, and were returning to their camps. Many of them would not go back to the settlement until Christmas.

Idlouk's big boat was piled high with goods. Family Allowance issue for five families, plus supplies of food purchased at the store, took up most of the room. On top of the load we had five huge buffalo hides. Each Eskimo family in the area had one; they were from the government herd near Wainwright, Alberta, the result of the annual kill. The hides were distributed to Eskimos throughout the Arctic where they were much valued as sleeping skins for the tents and small houses. As well, we had a small quantity of margarine that had been seized by the police in southern Canada for some infraction of the law, and then distributed to Eskimos throughout the Eastern Arctic. With its load, the boat was very low in the water, but we managed to reach camp without mishap, although a bad blow chased us into shelter half way across Eclipse Sound.

On our arrival, we had a little shiptime of our own. The same excitement that had accompanied the arrival of the supply boat at Pond Inlet was apparent with the return of our boat to camp. It was annual shiptime for all Aulatsee-vikmiut. Small children ran about the beach jumping up and down, shouting with joy as the boat appeared around the point of land to the east. People dashed from the houses and lined up on the beach, talking and laughing, shouting out greetings across the narrowing gap of water. The boat was run gently ashore on the sloping gravel beach and, after preliminary greetings, everyone set to work to carry the goods ashore. For an hour or two all hands trotted back and forth between the houses and the boat. Gradually piles of goods grew in front of each house as the food and materials for that house were carried up.

When everything had been properly sorted, all the goods were taken inside the houses. What excitement reigned! The camp had been out of tea, tobacco, sugar and flour for weeks past. Everyone smoked, ate bannock, drank tea, talked and laughed, visited back and forth among the homes, drinking more tea and smoking more tobacco than they could really afford. But who cared? This was holiday time at Aulatseevik. "Today we are happy, tomorrow is a long way away." Small boys and girls squirmed self-consciously in bright new plaid cotton shirts bought on Family Allowance; wives tried on new dresses or sweaters; daughters had slacks and kerchiefs and ribbons for their hair. There was candy for all; not much, and by night it would all be gone. Late in the evening I pulled my surprise from my kitbag, a big bag of oranges given to me by Father Danielo, the kindly little gnome-like Roman Catholic priest at Pond Inlet. I had intended the oranges to be a part of the celebration but my mother said, "Give them to me and I will put them away. We will eat them slowly. They are too precious to eat so fast tonight when we have much food. One a day would be better for such exquisite food, and everyone will share. We thank Kyukoluk* for his gift."

The festival was soon over. Next morning Idlouk made

* Eskimo name for Father Danielo.

plans for all hunters to start filling the caches with meat for the long winter.

Shiptime on north Baffin marks the beginning of autumn. On August 8th, the sun dipped below the northern horizon for the first time in three months. Each day afterwards it set a little earlier and farther to the west, and rose a little later, farther to the east. Soon there would be darkness on the land again.

Imperceptibly the land began to change. Slowly, almost reluctantly, it was getting ready for the long night to come when for three months the sun would not rise above the horizon to the south. Each night the small puddles of water froze over and, in the morning, the hummocks of soil were stiff with frost. The tops of the distant hills turned white with the first fall of new snow, then turned back to brown as the sun ate up the snow during the heat of the day. Small flowers froze in the cold night hours, but quickly came to life unharmed when the rising sun thawed their icy bonds. Plants in southern Canada would have passed on in the face of such treatment, but not their hardy cousins to the north.

By the first week in September, ice rimmed the shore of every inland lake and stream, each day creeping farther out from shore. By the end of the month all the small lakes were frozen hard, only the larger ones remained ice free far out from shore. It was a strange experience to walk on the newly frozen lake in the early fall with the ice two or three inches thick, smooth and clear as a sheet of glass. At that time the ice had not yet begun to heave and crack under the stress of expansion that would come as it thickened in the ever-increasing cold.

The first time I walked on such clear, flat ice was on a large lake near Wager Inlet, inland from the west coast of Hudson Bay. Itinua, an Eskimo from Chesterfield Inlet, and I had been hunting for caribou in the rocky hills back of the coast. All day we scoured the small valleys, but not a sign of the caribou did we see. Early in the evening we headed back for the boat, which was anchored in a small sheltered cove, undergoing engine repair. To save time we cut straight across

153

country keeping direction by the position of the setting sun. Coming down to the shore of the lake about two miles long and a mile wide, I was surprised to see Itinua make straight for the lake and walk confidently out onto the thin, clear ice. We had done this on a number of smaller lakes, but I did not think the larger ones would yet be safe. At first I thought he was going to skirt along the shore, but he headed straight for the centre and then started to walk down the length of the lake with me following in his wake.

To say that I was somewhat apprehensive of this move is to put it mildly. The ice on the lake was perfectly flat and so clear that when walking on it and looking down at it I could not see it. I had the impression I was walking on an invisible paper-thin lid on the lake, walking over the waters as it were. The water near the centre of the lake was about fifteen to twenty feet deep, and I could see the bottom quite clearly. At every step I expected to plunge through the ice, for it seemed impossible that it should hold my weight.

But the ice was three inches thick and perfectly safe. After my initial uneasiness wore off, I jumped up and down to test its strength and, although the ice shivered under my feet, it gave not a whit. Uneasiness gave way to exhilaration and both Itinua and I began alternately to run and slide down the lake, sometimes covering fifty or sixty feet in one long glide. I was a child again, sliding on bits of ice as I walked to school. Whooping and shouting, Itinua and I slid and ran, ran and slid, trying to knock each other's feet out from under until we arrived hot and panting at the far end of the lake. Once more we started the long hike over the rocky ground back to the boat.

As September wore on the dull brown of the hillsides showed spots of colour. Hillsides turned from brown to red and then to gold as all the tiny plants and shrubs took on the hues of late fall, the counterpart of forest colours in lands far to the south. The brilliant patches of colour from the full blooming flowers no longer startled the eye; vegetation halted its growth, slowly going to sleep for another year. Only the forlorn white heads of the Arctic cotton still bobbed bravely in the cold north wind. Drab and silent lay the land, waiting with patience for the long winter to come. Did I say silent? That is not quite true. Out of the north-west the chill winds blew, sometimes so softly that they merely rustled the stiff grass or whistled eerily through a crevice in the rocks; often they shrieked and howled like a thousand demons tearing at the stubborn land, howling down through canyons and valleys, probing and biting with new-found strength, bearing a forecast of the long cold night ahead.

But there was a silence to the land. It bothered me until I realized there were no longer any birds about. Through the long day of spring and summer my ear had become used to hearing a dozen tiny cheeps and chirps as I walked over the land. Now the birds had gone; all the migratory species that make this far north land their summer home and breeding ground had left for the south. Over the long sunlit hours of the Arctic spring and summer the birds had laid their eggs and raised their young. The young had grown to adulthood or had fallen prey to furred and feathered foe. From the hundreds of individual nests they had gradually drawn to-gether into flocks, circling and crying over meadow and sea. Day followed day and the sounds of the flocks in flight echoed over the land. One day the sounds were no longer there; the birds had left for the south.

A few birds stay behind; the north is their permanent home. The gyrfalcon, in its white phase, is totally white for the long winter months, but the raven scorns such subter-fuge. It stays as black as coal. The owl remains white or white flecked with brown. The ptarmigan changes from a dull mottled brown to snowy white touched by mere points of black over the eyes and the tips of the tail. Of all birds, the ptarmigan is the most practical for it grows feathers on its feet, snowy white spats that give it an air of impeccable dignity as it bobs about in search of food.

The land mammals change colour too. The dull brown of the Arctic hare becomes snowy white with only the tips of the ears showing a touch of black. The fox turns white and its mouldy summer coat begins to thicken and swell until the thin scrawny body is completely engulfed in a soft fluffy coat that makes it the most sought after pelt of all the land mammals in the Eastern Arctic. The caribou move inland away from the sea. In the deep valleys they gather together in herds and the bulls fight for their mates. October is the season of the rut on north Baffin, the time when the caribou are as tame as dogs and often can be called to your side. The thin coat of hollow-haired fur thickens daily in the ever increasing cold until by early winter the caribou is swathed in a blanket of fur, as near perfect an insulation against the severe Arctic cold as any mammal has been able to devise.

In the sea, the seals grow fat and float when shot. No longer are there any young seals about; the Eskimos say they have gone out into Baffin Bay to feed in the waters off the ice floe edge. No longer are there any schools of narwhals to be seen; they too have headed for the open sea, moving out of the bays well in advance of the formation of the ice cover on the sea. Sometimes narwhals are trapped in the bays by the sudden formation of heavy ice and cannot reach open water. When this happens they stay in one area all winter long and keep breathing holes open in much the same manner as the seals. I have never seen this, but the Eskimos assure me it is so.

Autumn is the most important season for the Eskimos on north Baffin, and in many other places in the Eastern Arctic. In the open water they can hunt by boat day after day, killing, killing, killing; filling the caches with meat and fat. Most seals float and few are lost. Day after day the small boats went out from the camp and each night the hunters returned to tell how many they had killed and where the meat was cached. Idlouk entered the figures in a little black book and each night added them up. Some days he was happy for the kill had been good. Other days he shook his head and murmured, "We need more. We have dogs and people to feed. We need food for the dogs on the long trap line trips if we are to have money this year. We need seals and more seals and more seals." Each day the hunters went off after more.

Not all Eskimos are this way. Many live completely for today, never a thought for tomorrow. If they feel like hunting, they hunt; if they don't, they stay at home. The catching of large quantities of food for the long period when they are patrolling trap lines and cannot hunt food for themselves and their dogs is a comparatively recent development in the long history of most Eskimo groups. Until they started trapping they had no need of large meat caches. They had only a few dogs and could spend all their time on the hunt.

While Kitchooalik, Oodleteetuk and the smaller boys continued to hunt in the sea around the camp, the rest of the hunters, myself included, and the older boys went off in the big boat to the lower end of Tay Sound. Here, we camped for three days and fished in a river near the place where it drained out of a large lake. It was the last week in September and the weather was quite cold. The hours of daylight equalled the hours of night, and all day the sun rode low on the southern horizon. Soon we would pay the price for the five months of continuous daylight we had enjoyed.

Each year in the fall the hunters from Aulatseevik make this long journey to the lower end of Tay Sound where a big river empties into the Sound, draining a large lake some eight miles inland from the sea. At many such places throughout the North, Arctic char run in the spring and the fall. The char is as fine a food fish as any I know. It closely resembles the Atlantic salmon both in appearance and in habits, ranging in size from five pounds to twenty-five and often more. It is a salt water fish, returning to the fresh water lakes each fall and running down to the sea in the spring. The timing of the migratory movements must be very exact, particularly in the fall when the run-off will diminish very rapidly once the ice cover on the source lake begins to dry up the water in the stream.

Near the mouth of the river where we camped, there was another Eskimo camp, that of the Ikalukmiut, the fish people, numbering four families, a total of fifteen people in all. For generations Eskimos have camped near this spot and there are three distinct areas in which the ruins of old Eskimo dwellings can be seen. The oldest site is on the river bank about half a mile from the present shore of the sea, although I imagine the site was on the edge of the sea when it was first inhabited. These houses, made of whalebone pieces, appear to be very old, grown over with a luxuriant growth of grass.

About a mile to the north of the river mouth and right on the sea shore is another group of old house ruins. These are of a more recent origin than the first, and have been occupied on and off almost continuously in the memory of living Eskimos in the area. At odd times one or two of the house ruins may be utilized today, but it has been thirty years or more since the houses have been used as semi-permanent dwellings of an Eskimo group. Each year the present-day Eskimos who camp at this spot build new houses with thick sod walls and roofs of sealskin and canvas. When we visited the camp at the end of September, the families were still living in tents although the men had started work on the sod walls of the new houses.

Inland, near the place where the river empties out of the lake, there is evidence of another campsite, a temporary one occupied only for a short time when the fish run in the river in the fall. Here can be seen tall piles of red stones set up in pairs, each one of a pair about fifteen feet from its companion. Across these piles of stone the Eskimos used to stretch lines of sealskin and on the lines hang fish to dry. There are a few dozen such rock piles and they are immediately opposite a place in the river where many rocks jut from the surface causing the river to run in small streams.

North of the area in which the stone pillars were set, a single pillar of large stones stood alone, whereas all the others were in pairs. It had been made in the same way as the other pillars, simply by piling stones one atop the other, but it was of a different shape, being wider at the base and much narrower at the top. At the base was a large flat rock about four feet by five feet on which the pile had been built.

158

The whole curved slightly so that from the south it appeared slightly concave. Looking at it from this direction I noticed another curious thing; the pillar was oriented almost due north and south, the concave side facing the low hanging sun. The temptation to call the pillar an altar was very strong.

Idlouk thought the pillar was just another rock pile on which the Eskimos put single fish to dry. Perhaps he is right. I think there is more meaning to it than that, but as yet I have been unable to find anyone who can throw any light on this matter.

Near the stone pillars were a few old graves. They were somewhat different from other Eskimo graves I had seen, having a small hollow on top, in which the person's implements were placed, instead of at the head of the grave. A much larger, and more recent graveyard is near the site of the present Eskimo camp; oblong piles of rocks that have at one time covered the bodies of those who died in this lonely spot dot the hillside facing the sea. Most of the graves have been broken open and the bones scattered far and wide. Here is buried the wife of one of the Eskimos who murdered the trader Janes in 1919. It was as a direct result of this murder that the present settlement of Pond Inlet came to be set up where it is. The son of one of the Eskimos who committed the murder is alive today and most of the Eskimos in the area still talk of the killing and the resulting trial.

Along the ridge of high land back of the campsite runs a well worn trail. It must have been used for a long time as it is clearly visible in the arid soil of the gravel ridge. It follows the ridge winding up from the south and disappearing off to the north. I believe the trail was followed by the old Eskimo groups on their annual migration movements to and from the camps on Eclipse Sound and on Baffin Bay. Many times these movements were made by sled and dogs on the sea ice, but often they must have been made by umiak and kayak after the ice had gone out in the summer. Then the umiaks would move along close to shore loaded with all the possessions of the group and paddled by the women, for the umiak was the women's boat. High on the rocky ridge the hunters walked, bows and arrows in their hands, eager for the sight of the caribou herds in the long valleys to the south.

With the Aulatseevikmiut I travelled in a much more prosaic manner. Idlouk's big boat chugged steadily along, past the towering rock walls of the upper Sound that gradually shelve back to become the gently sloping hills of the lower reaches of the Sound. Off the camp of the Ikaluk-miut we dropped anchor and ferried our small tent ashore to set up temporary camp with this group.

For two days we fished vigorously, getting over 600 fine Arctic char. Each morning we awoke at dawn and after breakfast of raw fish and tea walked the long eight miles to the head of the lake. We took with us three dogs and four pups, each dog with a sealskin pack strapped to its back. In the packs we put the smaller items such as the fish net and knives; on the return trip they would be loaded with fish. We each carried our fish spear and enamel mug while I took my camera and Kadluk the primus stove and a small tin of fuel.

The walk over the hills was very pleasant, early in the morning. Strung out in a long line, stopping now and again to pick and eat the berries that grow in profusion in the sandy soil of the hills, we wound our way up and down the hills, wading through shallow streams, crossing and re-crossing the large river in which we were to fish. Back of the mouth, the river was very shallow and swift. The pups were most reluctant to cross each time and the boys chased them into the water shouting and laughing as the pups howled in dismay.

About two hundred yards downstream from the lake, long rows of stones had been placed across the river to form weirs through which the fish could pass with difficulty. In the deeper channels below the weirs the char swam about by the hundreds searching for a way around the stone walls blocking their path to the lake. The weirs are of recent origin, useful only if the Eskimos have nets, as the fish tend to mill about in the larger pools out of reach of the spears. Idlouk said the Eskimos first built them in 1935. In one large pool about seventy-five yards long and fifty wide, the surface of the water was studded with the thin black fins of fish swimming restlessly about.

Immediately on reaching the river we all dashed into the shallows below the pools and for an hour speared fish as they darted upstream. The fish spear consists of a long wooden handle, usually about six feet long, on the end of which have been bound two curved and very flexible pieces of caribou antler. Each piece is tipped with a metal prong, running back towards the handle of the spear. Straight out from the end of the spear runs a third metal tip reaching about halfway to the ends of the caribou prongs. The spear is jabbed down over the back of the fish as it attempts to dash through the shallows. The caribou prongs open up as they slide over the back of the fish and, as it struggles to pull free, it is firmly hooked on the reversed metal tips. It is then swung inshore where, by simply bending the caribou prongs back and giving the spear a shake, the fish drops free on the ground.

The excitement of spearing fish was intense. The char were very wary, only the compelling urge of the migration movement forcing them to try to get past our spears. Many did get by, as they can move with amazing speed when alarmed. We laughed and shouted or let out cries of disappointment as one got away. But this type of fishing was not productive, it was merely good sport. We needed fish in quantity and caught in a short time. We were not true primitives hunting for our daily bread; we were businessmen hunting for a whole winter's supply. Away went the spear and out came the net.

Back and forth across the deeper pools we hauled the net. On each pass we hooked about thirty fish in the mesh and hauled them struggling ashore. Here they were pulled free and tossed up on the gravel bank where they flipped and flopped until hit on the head by one of the boys. The work was hard, for the net was heavy and the water ice cold. Our feet quickly became blocks of ice and lost all feeling, hands became numb from working in the ice cold water and from freeing fighting fish from the net. Every two hours or so we stopped to make a cup of tea and have a snack of raw fish cut fresh from the catch. By late afternoon almost three hundred fish lay dead on the banks and we had had enough for that day.

Then all the fish had to be cleaned. Stooped over from the waist, we worked our way through the mass, half of the group on one side of the river, half on the other. We worked with feverish speed for the light was fast failing and it was a long way back to the tent. At first I was awkward at this unfamiliar task, but after half an hour I could keep up with the rest. The movements got to be mechanical and I lost all track of time—grab fish by a gill, quick slit along belly from tail to head, grab guts back of head and pull, the mass stripping free of the fish to be tossed one way, the fish the other. Then the movements were repeated; fish after fish after fish after fish.

At last there were no more fish to be cleaned. Quickly we strung them on long sealskin lines, fifty to a line, and dumped the masses of bodies back into the river. Each took hold of a line and dragged the heavy load about two hundred yards down-stream to a place where rocks of all sizes lay about in abundance. Here were three empty cache sites among the rocks and we began the long task of carrying the fish to the caches and laying them neatly inside. By the time the last fish had been placed on the heap and the three caches covered over with rocks, it had long been dark and the moon rode high over the hills to the north east. Leaving the pups tethered beside the river with a pile of fresh fish close by, we turned our backs on the cache site and set out for the tent, eight miles away.

The walk back in the moonlight was beautiful and bad. In the shadows we stumbled over the uneven ground as everyone was tired out after the long day at the nets. We longed for hot food and rest. Instead of following the river as we had done on the way up in the morning, we took a short cut that led us straight up the side of the high mountain to the north. Up we climbed making for a narrow pass near the centre of the main rocky ridge. The pack dogs, each carrying three or four ten-pound Arctic char, had to be helped up the steeper slopes as they stumbled and fell under the sway of their heavy loads. In places we had to lift them bodily when their tired legs were not equal to the task.

At the top of the ridge we wound our way through the narrow pass to the far side and started down a long gentle slope to the shore. Inside the entrance to the pass I noticed the outline of a circle of rocks on the ground, the unmistakable sign of an old tent ring of rocks. But I was too tired and it was too dark to investigate further, and since then I have never visited that spot again. The old tent-site must have been used by Eskimos of long ago who waited on the high hills, hoping for signs of caribou in the valleys and plains to the south.

We reached the tent about midnight, wet through with sweat and tired out. Quickly we boiled up a big pot of fish and bolted it down. Then we clambered into the sleeping bags and were soon fast asleep. Silence settled over the little camp. Now and again a dog moaned as it sought to find a more comfortable berth. Under the bright moon, climbing higher and higher in the clear Arctic sky, the little camp lay silent and dark.

The second day was a repetition of the first, with about three hundred fish caught, cleaned and cached before we returned to the tent. On the third morning Idlouk, Kadluk and I left the four boys to fish at the river and went off in the boat to hunt seals, and to look for signs of caribou in the hills near the shores of the next sound to the east. The boys would fish for a few days longer until the caches were all filled (over a thousand fish in all) and then set out overland back to the camp at Aulatseevik. It would take them three days to walk the fifty miles, climbing over the high hills between our camp and that of the Ikalukmiut, sleeping out in the open in clefts in the rocks.* On the shore opposite Aulatseevik they would light a big fire and Kitchooalik would come across to pick them up in a small dory.

In one long day Idlouk, Kadluk and I reached the lower end of Paquet Bay, shooting six seals on the way. There we found the season much further advanced, heavy slush ice forming on the surface of the sea covering the entire lower end of the bay with an undulating layer of soft sea ice through which the boat had to force its way. On the second night after leaving the boys at the fish camp, snow fell, big flakes drifting slowly down out of a heavily overcast sky. In the morning the land was obliterated under a blanket of white, only the dark surface of the sea reflecting colour and giving perspective to the eye. This was in direct contrast to the spring season when the land rapidly becomes free of snow and the colour of the rocks breaks the unrelieved whiteness of the frozen surface of the sea.

For two days we hiked over the hills and valleys to the south of the bay, but caribou were nowhere to be seen. No tracks were visible in the new snow and Idlouk felt all the caribou were still inland in the rut. We could tarry no longer for each day the ice cover on the sea became thicker and firmer. The big boat ploughed through the soft ice with difficulty, long strips of wood peeling from the bow planks as the heavier pans crunched and broke under its weight. Halfway up the bay we broke clear of the ice and chugged along in clear waters. As darkness fell we turned into a small cove on the west side of the bay and dropped anchor in front of an Eskimo camp, a single house on the shore of the bay.

This camp was as unlike ours at Aulatseevik as a house in a slum is unlike a penthouse. It was nothing more than a hole dug into the side of a low gravel ridge and then roofed over with sealskins and sods, and the front closed up the same way. The back and side walls were the gravel walls of the pit covered with big flat rocks. Right and left of the

* For story of such a hike see my book *Sons of the Arctic* (Clarke Irwin, 1965).

door were small platforms also built of flat rocks on which the supplies of meat, fat and water were stored. Outside, the ground was littered with dog excreta and trash. Inside, the house was a dim dark hole, unspeakably filthy with dirt, fat and hair. Here lived the Eskimo Shituk, his wife, and family of four.

Shituk represents the bottom rung of the social ladder in the Pond Inlet area. Most of the time he lives alone with his family because few other Eskimos can stand the excessive dirtiness of him and his family at their camps. Of very low intelligence, Shituk is carefree and happy, as slovenly an Eskimo as I have ever met. His wife is an ogre, by far the ugliest woman on north Baffin Island. His two daughters, one six and one sixteen, are pretty but with the unmistakeable signs of the coarse features of the mother soon to come. In sharp contrast is the son, a boy of eighteen, whose father was a white man and who stands tall and slim. With light brown hair and fair freckled face he seems completely out of place in the dark hovel of a home. He is far more intelligent than his Eskimo father, and is the mainstay of the family. Every time I looked at him and then looked at his mother, I wondered how long the white man who was his father had spent in the land.

The fourth child in the family is an adopted daughter, a little over a year old. The child's mother had died the previous winter giving birth to the baby, and Shituk's wife had formally adopted her. The father remarried shortly afterwards and went to work for the Royal Canadian Mounted Police detachment as a special constable. He thought no more of the child.

Shituk's wife had no milk for the baby. She fed it powdered milk and pablum and the baby seemed to get along reasonably well. There was no regular bottle, so Shituk's wife had procured a whiskey flask from somewhere onto which she attached a rude nipple of soft sealskin through which the baby could suck the milk. She mixed pablum with powdered milk and fed this in the same way. The nipple was permanently attached to the bottle and was never washed. The bottle was heavily crusted with a mixture of stale milk and pablum, inside and out.

With the nipple sewn on tight, the method of filling the bottle was unique. First the milk or pablum was mixed in a small tin, itself so dirty that when I first saw it, I mistook it for the baby's pot. The mother would take a big mouthful of the mixture from the tin and, inserting the nipple of the baby's bottle between her lips, squirt the contents of her mouth into the bottle. About three such mouthfuls constituted a feeding.

Each time I visited this camp, which I did often over the winter which followed as it lay directly on the route along Idlouk's trap line, I saw the baby fed in this way. Each time she brought up a portion of the mixture onto the skins of the sleeping platform. The baby howled and cried and the parents bounced it up and down, passing it back and forth until it stopped, exhausted or asleep. Then all would be quiet for a while. The smell of the place was indescribable. Once it made me physically ill, the first time this ever happened to me in the Arctic, a land noted for strong unpleasant odours.

Never will I forget that little vermin-ridden hovel on the shores of Paquet Bay, with its filth and dirt, with its smells of urine and vomit and sweat, with its master sitting on the sleeping platform entirely oblivious of the squalor about him as he scratched his big body, or picked lice from his hair. I squirm as I write. Here was an Arctic slum.

13

OOKEEAKSHUK, October and November on our calendar, is the time when the ice forms on the sea and the sun is lost behind the horizon to the south. Freeze-up, like the break-up of two months before, is a much awaited event on north Baffin Island. In the fall strong gales rage out of the north, hunting becomes more difficult on the sea, and travel in the open boats is uncomfortably cold. The Eskimos grow impatient for the ice to form so that they can once again roam far and wide over the surface of the sea. In a land that depends on the sea for local transport in all seasons of the year, ice and open water each bring mobility where otherwise none would exist.

During the first week in October, ice rimmed the tidal zone along the edge of the sea. With each advance and recession of the tide, the ice thickened, reaching farther and farther out from shore. In a few days of calm weather the sea froze over a few hundred yards out from shore, slush ice two or three inches thick that would not support weight. Then a storm carried this ice away and the process started all over again. However, unlike Arctic areas farther to the south, where for weeks on end soft ice prevents travel by either boat or sled, the intense cold of the late fall days on north Baffin quickly froze over every sheltered bay. The still waters froze into large areas of thin rubbery ice that rippled and pulsated under the effect of small waves and swells. The frozen areas thickened and united; storms broke them up into hundreds of small ice pans which froze again after the winds subsided. The winds forced thin sheets of ice one atop the other, rafting as it is called, changing the outline and colour of the ice as each day went by. Under the combined effects of wind, frost and tide, the surface of the sea underwent constant change that would lessen in pace as the days wore on, but would never really stop until the ice went out next year.

On October 6th, Kitchooalik and Oodleteetuk loaded their sleds and dogs into the big boat and Idlouk ferried them to the lower end of the bay in front of the camp. There they were put ashore, the sleds loaded and dogs harnessed. The two men planned to travel overland to the south in search of caribou, keeping to the valleys in which enough snow had gathered to make possible travel by sled, or to the frozen surfaces of the rivers and streams. Somewhere to the south we knew there were herds of caribou and the hunters would not return until they had killed their quota, bringing back with them what meat they could, caching the remainder to be picked up later in the winter. If they were lucky they would be gone for only two weeks, if not they might be away over a month. By the time they did return the sea would be completely frozen over and they would travel over its surface back to camp.

On October 8th, the big boat was pulled out of the water. Everyone at the camp, men, women and children, took hold of the heavy rope and, with the aid of block and tackle, manhandled the boat high up on shore. Here it would rest until the following summer, its short travel season over for another year. "Now I can rest easy," said Idlouk, as he looked at the boat on the shore; "all summer while the boat is in the water I do not sleep properly. I lie awake listening to the sound of the wind and the waves, wondering if a storm is brewing and if so will the boat be safe at anchor on the bay. Storms come quickly and can blow a boat on the rocks. Last year the trader's boat was sunk in front of the settlement and the year before the police boat too. I think of this as I listen to the wind rattle the tent. Now I will sleep well. Let the storms rage if they will. My boat is safe on shore."

In the days that followed we hunted seals from the dory

and the canoe, or climbed the high hills back of the camp hunting the ubiquitous Arctic hare. October 12th marked the end of travel by boat. That morning Kadluk, Idlouk and I hunted seals from the big canoe. We shot six, but the ever encroaching ice cover on the sea kept forcing us to move the canoe closer and closer to shore. On a few of the larger ice floes we were able to pull the canoe up out of the water and stand on the ice itself while shooting at seals in the water around. By two o'clock in the afternoon we had to return to camp. Only with great difficulty were we able to pole the canoe the last hundred yards to shore through the heavy slush ice. As the sun settled toward the horizon to the south, I climbed the hill back of the camp and for an hour or so before the light failed, watched the final stages of the freeze-up of our bay. From shore to shore the bay was covered with big flat pans of shifting ice that grew visibly before my eyes. As the minutes passed I could see the new ice forming on the remaining patches of open water, creeping out in all directions, slowly but relentlessly clamping a lid on the restless surface of the sea.

The following morning we were up early. At the first sign of light in the sky to the south, all the hunters gathered on the shore, harpoons in one hand, rifles in the other. First Idlouk moved slowly out onto the frozen surface, at every step testing the ice ahead with the handle of his harpoon, probing for weak spots between the more solid floes. Following in his path went Kadluk, then myself, the others in single file behind. Slowly we moved away from the shore, our path twisting and turning as patches of soft ice forced us this way and that. Idlouk called me to his side and, as we moved along, told me how to watch for soft ice. The best guide was the colour; white ice was generally good, ice that was dark was likely to be thin and soft.

Clear of the shore area we scattered over the ice, each heading for one of the few remaining patches of open water or for areas that had only a very thin ice cover. The latter could be spotted from afar as the ice was black due to the closeness of the water beneath. The seals, rising up to breathe, easily broke through this thin soft ice. Shots began to echo across the bay; hunting seals from the ice had begun again.

We shot eight seals that day, a good day's hunt. It was impossible to retrieve them, the ice where they were shot was much too thin. They were left where they floated and two days later when the ice had thickened enough to support the sled and dogs, Paneeluk and Danielee toured the bay, chopped the frozen seals from the ice, and hauled them back to camp.

As the Eskimos of north Baffin must roam far and wide on the fall hunts, only rarely is meat and fat in excess of that required for two or three days' use brought back to camp at the time of the kill. Most of the Eskimo groups hunt in the same general area year after year, and they have cache sites scattered along the rocky shores. At the end of each day's hunt, the seals are put in the nearest cache, and left to freeze. During the winter, the older boys make frequent trips to these caches bringing the meat and fat back to the camp. The only meat never brought home is that in the caches along the route of the trap line, this being consumed by the dogs on the frequent winter trips. At the main camp the meat and fat brought in from the outlying caches must be kept safe from the dogs, no easy matter, for the Eskimo husky dog has a bottomless pit for a stomach, and a prodigious facility for scrounging food. I have known them to rip through half-inch planks with teeth and claws to reach meat inside a building. They are as crafty and cunning in the acquisition of food as in the avoidance of punishment for a misdeed.

At some camps the meat and fat is thrown on top of the small houses, along with all other gear that must be put out of the way of the dogs. This is messy as the fat soaks into the roof of the house and contaminates everything that comes in contact with it. At well run camps, the practice is to build an ice house on the beach in which all meat and fat not required for immediate use is put.

Our ice house was built on October 21st when the ice on

the bay was about six inches thick. Bad storms and high tides after freeze-up had broken the ice in the bay and large pieces had been up-ended by the pressure of wind and tide. All morning we walked over the ice in front of the camp searching for pieces of ice about six feet long and three feet wide, and trimming them into a rough rectangular shape. After a quick lunch of seal meat and tea, Kadluk and I, along with all the boys, took the sleds out onto the bay and began to bring in the selected pieces of ice. It was back-breaking work, for each piece weighed between two and three hundred pounds; three of them on the sled was all the dogs could pull over the rough ice. On shore Idlouk and his father cleared a small area above the high water mark and cut a shallow circular groove about ten feet in diameter in the frozen gravel. As each block was taken from the sled, it was tilted upright and slid into the groove. While the men held it in place, the boys packed loose snow and gravel at the base and wet this with sea water, tamping it down with their feet as it froze. Each succeeding block was slid into the groove, set against its neighbour to the left, and the join chinked up with snow and water that quickly froze in the below-zero temperature. Gradually a circular wall of ice, six feet high, grew up on the beach. In four hours the wall was within one block of coming together at the starting point to form a large open-topped igloo of ice. In the narrow gap remaining, a small wooden door and frame was inserted and firmly bedded into place. A half block of ice was set on top of the door, cemented into place, and our ice house was complete. High enough that the dogs could not jump over, the ice wall was thick enough to discourage any attempt to scrape through. We hoped to keep them well enough fed over the winter that they would not break down the door.

Into the ice house went all the meat and fat as it was brought in from the caches. Sometimes the house was stack-ed with seals, sometimes with frozen fish, or perhaps big slabs of muktuk and whale fat. At other times, usually when the men were away on the trap line or on hunting trips, it would get quite empty and the women would wish for the return of the men. When this occurred the arrival of a sled loaded down with meat from the hunt or from a distant cache was the signal for a banquet as everyone in camp rejoiced at the end of the temporary food shortage.

The Eskimos on north Baffin try to put up enough caches of meat and fat to last as dog food over the winter when the hunters spend a good deal of time on the trap line, hunting only to get fresh meat for the people at the camp. Not all succeed, and whether they are successful or not depends almost entirely on the personality of the individual Eskimo, or on that of the camp boss, if the camp has a boss. Some camps have little trouble securing enough food, Aulatseevik being the best of them all. Other camps get by, putting in caches of food though insufficient in number to carry them through until spring. These camps run short of food in mid-February and have about a month of short rations before the spring seal hunts bring the shortages to an end.

Still other camps have an annual period of starvation when they run completely out of food. In the spring of 1954 one such camp lost almost all its dogs through starvation and the people were reduced to eating the surviving dogs and the skins from the sleeping platform until help reached them in the form of an issue of relief and Family Allowance food brought to them by the Hudson's Bay Company clerk. In recent years few people have actually starved to death, but often death has lurked perilously close.

It is easy to condemn the Eskimos when this happens, for in many cases it is their own fault. Often they are the first to admit it. I once visited such a camp and talked with one of the men as he drank a cup of hot tea and munched biscuits from our grub box. For four weeks he and his group had been living on scraps of food and chewing old skins to keep alive; they had no heat in their little house and the damp cold penetrated to the bones. Their dogs were dead or dying and the camp had settled into a period of patient waiting; that was all they could do until the spring sun brought the seals out onto the ice. I asked the man why his group was starving, for this was a reasonably good hunting area. He replied, "We are starving because we have no food in our caches. We did not put up enough meat and fat in the fall."

"Why did you not put up enough meat and fat last fall?" I asked; "this is not the first time your camp has been this way."

He said simply, "I don't know."

That was the truth; he did not know. It would be easy to say that he and the other hunters were lazy, or incompetent, or of low intelligence, but this was not true. The man and his companions were not the best hunters in the area, but they were well up to the average. The answer was, I felt, that they, along with many of their fellows, had been unable to make the necessary adjustments that Eskimos of today must make in adapting their way of life to the changed conditions in the land. It is not easy for the great bulk of humanity, no matter of what race or group, to make such adjustments.

THROUGHOUT October the ice cover on the sea thickened daily but very little snow fell on north Baffin. Much of the land was blown clear and great stretches of sea ice were bare of snow. Huge areas of Eclipse Sound had frozen flat in the fall and our sleds bowled over the smooth surface at great speed with little effort on the part of dogs, covering many miles in one day. But close to our camp we had not been so lucky; fall storms had broken the ice badly when it was first forming and the bay was a mass of rough broken ice hummocks. Over these the sled moved swiftly for they were bare and shiny. As long as the dogs pulled well the long traces kept taut and rode over the obstructions, but if a dog slackened speed the trace dragged and immediately hooked under a jagged piece of ice. This was dangerous for both dog and man. Sometimes the dog would lunge forward and break the ice, thus freeing the trace. Then the passengers on the sled had to watch out, for the ice chunks flew back like bullets. One day I did not duck quickly enough and a large piece hit me square in the eye. Fortunately it hit flat and did not touch the eyeball, but I arrived at the camp that night with one eye swollen shut and frozen blood caking one side of my face.

If the dog was unable to break the ice then he was in trouble. The heavy sled kept moving forward under the pull of the remaining dogs, snatching the hooked dog backwards at great speed. Sometimes he would be jerked under the piece of ice and the trace would break with a crack like a pistol shot. But often he would not be so lucky and would be jerked back under the runners of the sled. Idlouk and I were fortunate in this regard. We had to haul many a howling dog from under the sled, but without serious injury to any. Kitchooalik was not so lucky. He ran over two dogs, breaking a leg of each.

The dogs knew their danger. It was an excellent season for showing up the slackers in the team, the ones who kept their traces reasonably taut but did little work. Often they let the trace sag slightly and in a twinkling it would hook an ice hummock. Howling in sudden fear the dog would be tumbled end over end back towards the onrushing sled. Idlouk and I kept constant watch for this when travelling in such ice. The moment a trace hooked, either he or I would be off the sled in a flash, running forward to try to free the trace before it broke, or maimed the dog. This was dangerous work and many an Eskimo has twisted and broken fingers as a result of a hand being nipped between the trace and the ice.

The lack of snow caused another inconvenience; it made water for tea hard to find when hunting out on the sea ice. Without snow the only way to get water was from a frozen-in iceberg and, if the hunt was in an area where there were none, it was necessary to carry a piece of fresh water ice on the sled. Often we forgot to do this and had to go for long periods without a hot drink. Later in the season we became more careful and chopped ice from each berg we passed.

The snow-free ice helped in one major way. It enabled us to locate the small volcano-shaped mounds of ice that mark the breathing holes of the seals—*aglos* as they are called by the Eskimos, the same name given to the openings over the holes but under the deep drifts of spring. In the fall when the ice is only three or four inches thick, the holes are about six inches across, covered by a dome of ice raised three to five inches above the surface of the sea. In the centre of the dome is a tiny opening to admit air. The seal comes up under the ice, sticks its head into the hole and breathes as it floats beneath. Some seals are cautious, coming up very quietly and breathing soft and slow. Others let out air like a whale with a noise that can be heard for half a mile. Idlouk and I usually hunted at the aglos together, although by this time I was becoming proficient enough to go off on trips with others from the camp, Paneeluk in particular being my companion on many a hunt. But I preferred to go with Idlouk; I learned more from him than from anyone else.

As a change from hunting seals on the ice, Paneeluk and I hunted rabbits in the high hills of our island. The rabbits were really not rabbits but hares, Arctic hares, but they are invariably called rabbits. They are big, twice the size of the cottontail of southern Canada, and they provide the Eskimos with a welcome diversionary dish from seal meat and fish. They are delicious when boiled although the small amount of fat on the meat is not sufficient to meet body require-ments. If they are eaten exclusively over a three or four day period, a craving for fat is set up and this must be relieved by eating chunks of seal fat or reverting to a diet of seal meat and fat. Rabbit is the only meat I have never seen an Eskimo eat raw.

On north Baffin the rabbits occur in small groups that inhabit certain sectors of the rocky hills. The most I have seen in a group was twenty-two. In the far-north islands, on Ellesmere in particular, the rabbits congregate in large bands, four or five hundred feeding together. When startled these groups move *en masse*, from a distance seeming to flow over the ground like a huge white blanket. They can move with remarkable speed and, if badly startled, individual rabbits will run over the ground upright on their hind legs. Wolves have been seen to separate a rabbit from a large group, run it to its death and devour it, while the remainder of the rabbits, once the victim has been singled out and separated, feed unconcerned nearby.

In summer the rabbits roam the lower slopes of the hills well camouflaged by their fluffy coats of mottled brown and grey. At this time the young are born, growing to maturity by the time the first snows of the winter have touched the rocky slopes. Very quickly then their coats turn to white, relieved only by the jet black of the tips of the ears. Once again the rabbit is almost perfectly camouflaged. On our island they took to the high hills in the fall and remained on or near the top of the island most of the winter. Occasionally they came down to feed on the gentle slopes near the shore, but only while the camp lay asleep. On these lower slopes they would feed quietly in the moonlight, muzzling down through the shallow snow cover to the mosses and grasses on the slopes or in the crevices among the rocks. With the first sound of life from the camp they would be gone again, hopping and running up the steep slopes, stopping motionless on a rock every so often before scuttling quickly on. Some mornings their tracks covered the lower hillsides but never once did we actually see a rabbit close by.

Away from the camp area the rabbits fed for long periods on the lower slopes of the steep hills. When we travelled by sled in the winter, the trail always ran along the shore, winding in and out with every indentation of the rugged coast, the sleds keeping just outside the area of rough broken ice of the narrow tidal zone. Travelling this way added many miles to the route, but it also added many a succulent rabbit to the grub box. On our trap line trips throughout the winter we lived on rabbits almost exclusively, feeding the dogs from the caches of seal meat set out along the way.

A rabbit feeding on the lower slopes will do either one of two things on hearing an approaching sled: it will take off immediately for the hill and be lost to your sight, or it will crouch down at the base of a big rock and remain perfectly still. To the untrained eye it is invisible. Each rock on a hillside has a small rounded hump of snow at its base, built there by the action of the wind whistling around the rock.

The crouching rabbit looks like a hump of snow. At first I could not see a rabbit crouched this way, even after Idlouk pointed it out to me. But after a week or two of watching I began to see that a rabbit crouched at the base of a rock was not, in fact, exactly like a hump of snow. There was something about it that made it a little different, although what the difference is, I do not know.

Hunting rabbits by moonlight was exciting. The full Arctic moon (it was also a full tropic moon although I did not think of that while looking at it through the haze of frost crystals on north Baffin Island) bathed the countryside in a blue white light. On a landscape that was almost totally white, the moon was as good a source of light as the sun except for two things: I could not see detail at any great distance and in the shadows I could not see at all. On the rocky slopes the hundreds of rocks threw a pattern of light and shadow that was confusing to the eye. In this maze of light and shadow the rabbits hopped about feeding the long night away.

I have shot many a rabbit in Arctic lands, but the one I shall never forget is the one that got away. I had gone hunting on the high hills back of the main camp at Aulatseevik shortly after freeze-up. All the rest of the men were off on the sea ice hunting seals but Kidlak had asked Paneeluk and me to get a rabbit or two as she was tired of seal meat day after day. Paneeluk went off the hills to the west while I climbed the hill behind the house. It took me about an hour to reach the upper slopes slowly working my way up the steep, broken hillsides to a place where rabbits might be feeding.

I found no rabbits but lots of tracks all leading farther up the slopes. One set was quite fresh and I set out on this trail. I climbed until I was nearly fifteen hundred feet above the ice of the bay. On a large rock I halted to rest. It was about noon and the sky, although overcast, was quite light. Far below I could see the tiny dots that were the sleds of the hunters moving over the ice. I chewed slowly on a

177

handful of snow to slake my thirst, and then started up again.

The trail took me right up to the highest point of the island, the last hundred yards leading almost straight up a steep snow-filled ravine that cut between high rock walls. The snow was packed very hard in the ravine and I had to cut steps in it with my small knife to reach the top. But I made it safely, and slowly worked my way over the brow of the uppermost rolling hills to the top of the island. Here I was met by stinging winds and light snow. The ice below was lost to my view. But the tracks led on and they were still fresh; the rabbit could not be far ahead.

For an hour I chased that rabbit all over the top of the island. I am sure it was not more than a quarter of a mile ahead at any time, but in the snow and fog I never did see it. The rabbit knew it was being followed for it doubled back now and again trying to escape and the distance between the sets of tracks meant it was running all the time. Knowing the habits of rabbits, I cut across the tops of small hills whenever I saw the tracks leading along one side for I knew the rabbit would double around the hill to come back in its own tracks. But always I was too late. More than once I came upon places where the rabbit had floundered in deep drifts and more than once I fell head over heels in the soft clinging snow in my haste.

Finally I had to give up; I could run no more and the light was rapidly fading from the sky. After a short rest I walked back to the steep slope up which I had climbed to reach the top of the island, and started back down. The new snow had made the steps cut in the slope very slippery but I managed to reach the base of the ravine without mishap and started the long climb down to the camp. The easiest way to reach the distant shore would have been to sit down on the hard packed snow of one of the many ravines that cut straight down the steep slopes almost to the shore. In this way I would have descended with the speed of a toboggan on an iced runway, but unfortunately without means of braking to a slow stop at the base.

Idlouk had often cautioned me to avoid such places when walking in the hills in the fall. Once started sliding, I would be unable to stop and would stand an excellent chance of being killed, dashed on the rocks far below. When Idlouk was a young man he had such an experience. Luckily for him the slide had not been long and he had not been killed; but he lay among the rocks at the bottom of the slide unconscious for over an hour and only with the greatest difficulty did he manage to return to the sled and drive back to his camp. He had been laid up for a month, his body battered and bruised from smashing into the rocks. Idlouk is adamant on one main point about walking in the hills after rabbits: you must not wear sealskin or caribou skin trousers. They act like sled runners giving new impetus to any slide.

Because of Idlouk's warnings I had always been very careful when crossing hard packed snow slopes. But on the night of the rabbit hunt I was tired, hot, hungry, and in a hurry to get back to camp. High up on the hillside I came upon a steep bank of hard packed snow cutting across my path as I angled down the slope. The snow bank was the start of a long slide that dropped off into the gathering darkness below. Although it was only fifteen yards across, opposite where I stood, I should have climbed up about fifty feet and gone around it. But I was too tired for this and elected to try to run quickly across to the far side, trusting to my momentum to carry me over.

It didn't. Halfway across my feet slipped out from under me and I fell heavily to the snow. The next thing I knew I was starting a downward slide, picking up speed swiftly on the steep slope. I rolled over on my stomach and tried to dig in with rifle butt and knees, but could make no impression on the cement-hard snow. Fifty feet down, my foot touched a small rock outcropping in the middle of the slide. Automatically my leg muscles tensed and I gripped hard with the flat of my foot. I rolled over, body swinging in a wide arc, foot clinging desperately to the rock. As I rolled my leg twisted sharply and I felt something give

179

in my knee. But my foot clung to the rock and I was brought to a sharp halt, lying head down the slope.

Pain immediately shot up and down my leg from the twisted knee. I must have passed out for I am still hazy about how long I lay on the slope. For about five minutes I remember lying still while the pain abated and I gathered strength. Then, ever so slowly, I worked my body up the slope, using hands and feet until I was able to grasp the rock and pull myself to a sitting position in the snow. Another rest and I threw myself hard to the right, rolling over and over until I hit the rocks at the far side of the slide and pulled myself clear of the treacherous snow. Here I lay down again for the intense pain from my knee sent fresh waves of nausea over my body.

When the pain subsided, I sat up and looked about. It was almost dark and there would be no moon that night. I had no desire to spend a night on the mountain, and I decided to get down as best I could. I shall not forget the descent as long as I live.

My knee was badly swollen and any attempt to bend it or put weight on it sent fresh waves of pain up and down the leg. Moving carefully from rock to rock I half crawled, half slid down the first rocky slope. Twice I hit the knee on rocks and had to lie still while the pain subsided. My rate of progress was so slow I thought it would take me all night to get down to the camp and that would never do. Turning right across the face of the slope, I managed to reach a small snow-filled ravine and decided to risk sliding down the ravines whenever I could. If I kept to the edge where I could govern speed by hanging on to the rocks I would probably be able to control the descent.

The first slide was a short one and I let myself go. Despite my bad leg, I felt quite exhilarated as I zipped down the smooth snow slope and plunked into a soft drift at the bottom. Angling to the left this time I came to another small ravine and again sat down for the short slide to the bottom. Once again I flashed down the slope into soft snow. I became quite cocky. At the next ravine I was not sure that I could see the end of the slide, but recklessly I pushed off from the top. This was a mistake. The slide was steep and long, and there was no soft snow at the bottom. I must have been going about forty miles an hour when I hit the end of the slide and slammed into a jumbled mass of small rocks. Head over heels I tumbled down the slope before I brought up short against a large boulder, the breath knocked from my body.

For about ten minutes I lay where I was, not caring particularly whether I ever moved again or not. Then I felt the the cold creeping in and got up. I did not seem to have broken anything although my shoulder felt bruised and a few new aches had appeared. I scrambled back up the slope to the base of the slide and picked up the rifle which I had lost in the tumble among the rocks. Again I made my way to a snow-filled ravine and started down. My tumble on the rocks had made me cautious and I slid down very carefully keeping close to the rocks and never letting my body slide free.

It took me three hours to reach the lower slopes of the hills about half a mile to the left of the campsite, sliding down the edges of the snow-filled ravines where I dared risk it, scrambling awkwardly over the rocks where the slopes were too steep to chance a slide. By the time I reached the bottom I felt much better, although completely tuckered out. My leg was stiff at the knee but the pain had subsided into a dull ache that flared up only if the leg was knocked on the rocks. On the gentler, lower slopes I hobbled over the ground.

No one saw me approach the camp as it was very dark and the hunters had not yet returned from the sea ice. I entered our house, found it empty and managed to get out of my wet clothes and into the sleeping bag without anyone seeing my plight. A few minutes later Kidlak came in after a visit with Kadluk's wife and was surprised to find me back and abed. She was disappointed when I said I had not been able to get a rabbit, and paid little attention when I told her I had twisted my knee. A pot of seal meat was bubbling gently over the seal-oil lamp and she dished out a large portion onto an enamel plate. I ate this with relish for my appetite had not been affected at all. After two mugs of steaming tea I rolled over and fell quickly asleep.

It was three weeks before my leg returned to normal and I could take an active part in the hunts again. For three days I was unable to leave the camp, three of the most trying days I spent during my time with Idlouk. My leg stiffened so that it could not be bent and I ached all over. Sleep came in fits and starts; every time I moved fresh pain brought me awake. How I longed for cool clean sheets and a dark, quiet room to myself. But life could not stop because I was laid up. In the little house, children dashed about, or cried if thwarted in play, women talked and sewed or chopped ice by my head. Idlouk listened to my tale and shook his head.

"You will have to be more careful," he said; "you are much like an Eskimo now and get along in my land quite well. But don't forget you are my son, and I am responsible for you while you are here. If anything happened to you while you were here think how badly I would feel. And what would I tell your wife, Amouleegah*, after I have promised her to see that you came to no harm in my land? For my sake, be very careful every minute you are in my land."

What better psychology could he have used?

* My wife's Eskimo name, meaning, "The Snow Bunting".

CHAPTER
14

NOVEMBER 1st brought a fundamental change in the nature of our existence; on that date the trapping season began. Throughout November, December, January, February and March, our activities would, to a large extent, centre around the pursuit of the white fox, a small creature that at one time was of very limited value in the Eskimo way of life. For the next five months the talk would be of foxes, or lack of them. No longer would we be hunters, but trapper-hunters, business men out to earn money for the year ahead.

The basic economy for the indigenous hunting population of the Eastern Arctic centres on the export of a single commodity, the pelt of the white fox. Although sale of handicrafts, wage employment, and a few other forms of endeavour are slowly broadening the economy of the region, trapping for fur remains the vocation of the majority of the Eskimos. Sale of the pelts, or skins as they are called, to the Hudson's Bay Company, provides the bulk of the funds used for purchase of goods at the store. Small numbers of seal, polar bear, cross and blue fox, weasel, wolf and wolverine skins are sold, but only the white fox occurs in sufficient numbers throughout the entire area to be considered a staple, although not a stable, product of the land.

The white fox is found almost everywhere throughout the Canadian Arctic. It lives in burrows dug in the sandy soil of the grassy meadows, in the coastal areas not far from the edge of the sea. The burrows are not hard to find as the underground passages in which the foxes raise the young honeycomb the area. For some distance around, a luxuriant growth of grass springs up, fertilized by the droppings of the animals. In summer the foxes range far and wide over the land in search of food: mice, lemmings, birds' eggs, and young birds. The summer coat is thin, mottled brown and white in colour, but as the cold weather approaches the fur changes to a solid white, becoming thicker and thicker as the weeks go by until the thin, scrawny body is completely engulfed in a luxuriant cover of downy white fur. The foxes take to the sea ice, walking along the shore in search of carcasses of sea mammals, raiding the meat caches of the Eskimos, or following the trail of a polar bear and feeding on the remnants of its kill. Often the Eskimos leave the carcasses of seals and whales exposed in the area of their trap lines so as to attract foxes into the region.

In the spring when the young seals are born under the snow cover on the sea ice, foxes search out their aglos by sense of smell. They listen for sounds of young seal beneath and, if they hear one, dig down through the thick snow trying to reach the young seal before it becomes alarmed. The foxes dig with amazing speed, snow flying up from the rapidly scraping paws like a stream of snow from the rotors of a miniature snow blower. In 1953, near the settlement of Pond Inlet, a fox killed an adult seal in this way and the smell of the dead seal attracted other foxes from far and wide. The carcass lay in the aglo beneath the snow. The drift above was honeycombed with holes dug by the foxes to reach the body and over an area about one hundred yards square the snow was packed as flat as the surface of a paved parking lot by the imprint of the feet of many foxes coming and going from the kill.

Before the coming of the white man into the Arctic, the Eskimos caught a few foxes in stone traps. This type of trap was made by piling stones so as to enclose a small rectangular-shaped hole, leaving only a narrow opening at one end. Above this opening a single flat stone, just big enough to block the entrance, was balanced. A piece of decayed meat or fat was placed at the back of the enclosed space and when the fox entered to reach the meat, the flat stone was jarred and fell across the opening to be held in place by other stones set for this purpose. These traps were used by the Eskimos to get foxes during the early stages of trading operations with the whalers, but it was not long before the steel trap was introduced to raise the numbers of the catch.

The white fox is a stupid creature, very easy to catch. On north Baffin Island most traps are set along the sea shore, although in a few places trap lines run inland following the beds of frozen rivers. They rarely extend more than a few miles from the sea. Where the land rises sheer out of the sea, traps are set at the mouths of the narrow valleys that cut back into the rock walls so as to catch foxes coming down from the interior. Usually such valleys have enormous piles of water-washed boulders pushed out from their entrances to form points of land jutting into the sea. Foxes, walking along the shore in search of food, often cut across deeply indented bays but they will always investigate the points of land. It is near such places that spring caches of meat and fat are placed and the traps set.

The fox trap is set in a slight depression in the snow, or in the gravel of the beach if there is not enough snow, usually at the base of a good-sized rock. Any prominent upright object will attract a fox for the usual reason and if no such object can be found at a likely looking place for a trap, the Eskimo will set a rock upright, or cut a snow block and stand it on end. The short anchor chain of the trap is firmly fastened beneath the rock, or bedded down under the hard snow. In the early fall when there is little snow on the ground the trap is left in the open; in the winter it is hidden beneath a snow block that has been trimmed to paper thinness so that it will break easily under the weight of a fox.

At times no bait is used at the trap, the Eskimo relying on the smell of the decayed meat in the cache nearby to attract the fox to the area, and on the natural curiosity of the fox to cause it to investigate the boulder or snow block beside which the trap is set. Usually a small piece of decayed meat or fat is placed under the rock beside the trap so that the fox will have difficulty getting at it and will have to manœuvre over the place where the trap is set. Different baits are good for different times in the season: rotten meat or fish is good in the late fall and winter; canned sardines are excellent during the month of March; and under certain conditions a heady perfume or shave lotion works well. Only rarely are traps set on the cache site itself, and then only after the cache has been opened and the meat and fat used as dog food.

Training in trapping comes early for the Eskimo boys, and for the girls as well. Although in their adult life the boy and girl will stay close to their own fields of endeavour —the man, the hunter and trapper, the woman, the wife and mother—as youngsters each takes part in the activities of the opposite sex. Boys help look after the children, donning their mothers' parkas and carrying the babies around on their backs. They learn to sew, repairing their own clothing and sealskin boots. Girls hunt rabbits and ptarmigan with .22 rifles; they assist their fathers to harness the dogs and hitch them to the sled; together boys and girls operate small trap lines in the vicinity of the camp, not for foxes but to catch weasels.

In certain sections of the Arctic, and in certain years, these little rodents are plentiful, inhabiting the rocky slopes in the vicinity of the campsites. In summer the coat is a dull brown, in winter it is white with a black tip to the tail and black marks on the feet. They are small, six to eight inches long, saucy, impudent creatures that can move with the speed of light when darting about among the rocks. The skins are purchased at the Hudson's Bay Company stores, the Eskimos receiving from fifty cents to a dollar for each skin.

In the Canadian Eastern Arctic the Eskimos do not register trap lines; as yet there seems to be little need for this measure because of the small number of Eskimos in the region and the dispersed nature of their camps. Each man sets an indeterminate number of traps, the trap lines running off in different directions from the camp. Traps are visited by any of the Eskimos from that camp who will pick up foxes and reset the traps, but the fox remains the property of the man who owns the trap. Trap lines sometimes run through an area hunted over by Eskimos from another camp; at times trap lines will even cross one another, but little interference arises. In the time I have spent in the Arctic, I know of only one case of alleged poaching on another man's traps.

At Aulasteevik Kitchooalik ran his trap line to the west and south in the direction of Milne Inlet; Oodleteetuk ran his northward on the south shore of Bylot Island; Elijah, operating the trap line for his grandfather, ran his to the south around the bay in front of the camp; Idlouk and Kadluk ran their trap line together far to the east and south, the longest trap line on north Baffin Island, extending over a hundred and fifty miles out from the camp. Together Idlouk and Kadluk had come very close to achieving a community trap line. Often their traps were set on opposite sides of the same rocky points: sometimes Idlouk favoured one location along the route, Kadluk another. When both liked the same spot, they set their traps side by side and joked as to who would get the fox. As with all the Eskimos their traps were left on the land the year round.

Each year at the close of the trapping season on March 31st, they make a last trip removing any foxes and springing the traps, but leaving them where they lie. In the fall when the season reopens, they journey over the route again, resetting the traps, repairing any that are broken, preparing the trap line for the long winter season ahead.

In November, 1953, I accompanied Idlouk and Kadluk on their first trip to the traps. Our journey was typical of all we were to make throughout the winter, the most uncomfortable season for work and travel. Winter on north Baffin, with its extreme cold and period of continuous darkness, is the only season of the year that the Eskimos do not enjoy. They do not complain, they simply live through it, and are thankful when all goes well. On our first trip to the traps all went reasonably well.

We left Aulasteevik at eleven o'clock on the morning of November 2nd. The sun had not risen over the hills to the south as we pulled away although the cloud-sprinkled sky was red with reflected light. Monday was a bad day to start a trip from an Anglican Eskimo camp as no one works on Sunday; therefore preparations for our journey could not be made in advance. Only a minimum of gear was taken but what a scramble it was to get it ready! Leah dashed about gathering up caribou skin clothing; Kidlak sat hunched over the sewing machine repairing Idlouk's trousers; the small tent was found frozen stiff with frost; one sled runner was discovered to be broken and hurriedly patched with a sealskin thong. Eventually we got away heading east and north through the narrow passage leading to Eclipse Sound. One by one the small boys, who always accompany a sled when it leaves camp, and who are always waiting on the sea ice when it returns, dropped off and waved goodbye.

Idlouk, Kadluk and I travelled together on one sled pulled by all Idlouk's dogs and half of Kadluk's team. The dogs were very unhappy about this, and fought one or two pitched battles before each team decided to ignore the existence of the rival group. The two sections of the combined team pulled well all day but left a wide gap between, across which dogs crossed at their peril.

By the time we turned eastward along the south shore of Eclipse Sound the sun had risen, but we could not see it. For the brief hour it shone on the land we travelled under the shadow of the high rock wall of the south coast while to the north the far-off mountains and ice caps of Bylot Island glowed red with fire. Our route closely paralleled that taken by Idlouk and me the previous spring when we had the hungry days and had to shoot the caribou to eat. This trip we would travel most of the time in the dark. Our gear was the same as that taken on the other trip. We would have preferred to have left the tent behind as it was in a bad state of repair and the temperature often dropped to thirty below during the night; but there had not been enough snow to form the hard packed drifts from which we could cut blocks for snow houses. Sleeping in the tent we were sure to be chilly before the trip was over.

Halfway along the shore of the Sound we came upon a tremendous island of old sea ice about two miles long and one mile wide. It must have been swept in by the fall storms from Lancaster Sound in the late summer and grounded on the steep rocky coast, freezing in before it could drift farther. Stefansson describes this type of ice as paleocrystic, sea ice that is trapped in a particular area for a long period (he suggests ten years or so) becoming thicker and heavier as each year goes by. Eventually it makes its way out of the region of its birth, and drifts south with the currents. Moving across the ice island on the sled I got the impression of travelling on land through an area of low rolling hills forty to fifty feet high. The valleys were filled with snow but the tops of the hills were bare with the smooth, pebbly surface that is so characteristic of old water-washed sea ice. On the hills the sled was almost impossible to control; going up it swung sideways dragging the dogs with it; on the short dash down the slopes it flew along with the speed of light, scattering dogs right and left. We had to be very quick on our feet to keep from being knocked down and run over. The ice island terminated in a sharp four foot drop which none of us saw until the lead dog jumped down, quickly followed by the rest of the team. Before we could stop the sled, it shot off the drop and landed with a terrific crash on the smooth ice below. The lashings gave way scattering the load for a hundred yards along the ice before we could bring the dogs to a halt. Fortunately nothing was damaged, even the cracked sled runner bearing up under the strain.

At the first of the meat caches made by Idlouk and me the previous spring we discovered that the cache had been broken open by a polar bear and the seal gone. Kadluk and I searched along the shore and found the remains of the partially devoured seal. There were no signs of fox tracks around the exposed carcass and this indicated that there were no foxes in the area. Of rabbit tracks there were hundreds, along the ledges of the rocky shore and well out on the sea ice. Idlouk said that rabbits sometimes migrated north across the sea ice in the fall and the tracks seemed to bear this out. Shortly after restoring the remains of the seal in the cache and leaving the site Kadluk and I each shot a rabbit and, at an aglo farther along the route, Idlouk harpooned a fine big seal which we cut up on the spot and fed to the dogs, keeping only a small piece of meat and fat for ourselves.

By late evening we reached the entrance to Paquet Bay. Idlouk decided to make a ten mile detour to the camp of the Ikalukmiut and spend the night there getting information on the foxes in the area. We dumped our gear on the ice to lighten the load and in a fast run along the coast arrived at the camp about midnight. The Eskimos were very glad to see us; they were always glad to see Idlouk as he invariably had fresh meat, tea and tobacco on his sled. At the Ikalukmiut camp we arrived with two rabbits, part of a seal, tea, tobacco and about half a dozen pilot biscuits. We were made very welcome as the people had been living on fish almost exclusively for the past two months, much of it decayed fish from caches that had been put up too early in the autumn.

The camp of the Ikalukmiut was quite different from Aulatseevik. Two months before, when we were there fishing for Arctic char, the Eskimos had started to build new houses of turf blocks but only one man had managed to finish his dwelling. The other two families had moved into the old Eskimo ruins nearby, roofing over two of the unused shelters with canvas and sealskin. The houses were dark, the stone and sod walls covered with wrapping paper that was soggy from damp and frost. The earthen floor was dirty with old seal fat and hair. A few days before, Idlouk had shown me the test applied by Eskimos to determine whether a camp they have visited was excessively dirty or not. After staying for a night one sits on the sled as it leaves in the morning dragging both feet along the snow. If the soles of the boots leave a dark stain that disappears after a short distance, the camp has been fairly clean. If the stain persists even though the feet are dragged for some time, the campsite and houses have become very dirty with old fat and oil. If no marks appear on the snow, the camp has been recently set up for no Eskimo camp could be that clean.

We slept in the house of Agnateeak which, although dark and dirty, was far more comfortable than our little tent would have been. On our first day we had set eleven traps without a sign of a single fox track. Idlouk was not too worried as this section of the trap line was not usually as productive as the lower end. But I hoped we would start seeing fox tracks soon; two bad years in a row would be very discouraging.

We left the Ikalukmiut camp about nine the next morning as the first light of the long dawn touched the land. The day was overcast with a light wind out of the south-east. During the morning we saw three seals on the ice but Idlouk could not get near enough for a shot as the ice crunched badly underfoot. Kadluk and I again shot a rabbit apiece—our supper for the day as we had used all our food at the Ikalukmiut camp the night before, together with too much of our meagre supply of tea and kerosene.

By two in the afternoon all light was gone. Travelling in the dark under the heavily overcast sky was a strange experience. The darkness had a woolly character that I find hard to define; the white landscape made the darkness grey so that nearby objects were silhouetted slightly without visible light. The sled seemed to glide over the smooth ice pulled by phantom dogs that floated in and out of my range of vision like ghosts on invisible strings. There was a curious sense of movement without motion; I knew I was moving by the feel of the sled beneath and the touch of wind on my face but there was nothing to give perspective to the forward motion over the snow. Only when I jumped from the sled to run alongside was I conscious that the sled was moving swiftly, covering many miles through the dark.

191

Darkness did not stop the setting of traps for Idlouk and Kadluk had on uncanny knowledge of where each trap lay. While I drove the dogs they rode behind, continually peering out into the night and at the snow beneath. At intervals they conferred shortly then dropped off to disappear into the blackness each with his snow knife and a small piece of rotten meat. I brought the dogs to a halt and, while waiting, untangled traces, adjusted harness, or just sat on the sled listening. Sometimes Idlouk and Kadluk shouted to each other as they worked; at other times there was no sound and I sat alone in a cold, empty world. Suddenly a whistle sounded up ahead. The dogs jumped to their feet, and set off at a gallop, the sled thumping over the small cracks in the ice. In a few moments their speed diminished and out of the darkness ahead loomed the forms of Idlouk and Kadluk to jump aboard as the sled moved slowly by. Travelling down the coast this way we set twelve more traps before deciding to pitch camp. Still there were no signs of fox tracks. Idlouk began to worry and expressed the opinion that this year would be as bad as the last.

"We shall have no money for extras over the winter to come," he said, "but it cannot be helped. This is the way in my land."

It took us two hours to make camp on a small gravel beach. The tent was so stiff with frost that it had to be pried open and we discovered that it had a long tear at the peak. Working by the light of our small kerosene lantern, Kadluk sewed up the tent with caribou sinew thread. Then we found that all the guy ropes had been removed and makeshift ones had to be devised from dog traces. The tent, when finally erected, provided only a minimum of shelter, good for calm weather alone; in a storm it would come down around our ears. But we hoped to find enough good snow for a snow house before bad weather came along; sleeping in the open in a gale with the temperature at thirty below would not be pleasant.

For supper Kadluk cut up the rabbits and put them on the primus stove to boil. In a few minutes the tent was full of steam from the pot and we lay in our sleeping bags enveloped in a clinging damp cloud that cut off all vision. Kadluk was so close I could feel his shoulder touch mine but I could not see him. A spot of light flared up briefly as the pot was taken from the stove and the heat of the roaring burner cleared the air, then the cloud settled down again as the pot was put back on to boil. My mouth watered as the smell of the rabbit filled the air for we had had nothing to eat all day.

The following day we set eight traps without seeing a track; Idlouk was now sure it would be a year similar to the last. In disgust he asked if I wanted his trap line; after the bad season of the year before, and the prospect of another one, he said that he felt like giving all his traps away. During the morning a strong wind out of the west sent the snow swirling into our faces and by noon it was blowing a gale. As we were in the vicinity of Shituk's camp and could not find snow for a snow house we cut across the bay to his house, arriving at the same time as Shituk himself, who had been out hunting ptarmigan in the hills back of the coast. The house had become grubbier than ever since my last visit in the early fall but with the icy wind howling out of the west it promised warm shelter for the night.

We were well fed at Shituk's, frozen caribou meat eaten raw, the meat thawed just enough to be crunchy. It was delicious. We supplied the tea and tobacco, for Shituk had none; he had not been in to the settlement for the past six months. His old clock was going and was only one hour out, but he did not know what day of the week it was. Kadluk told him it was Friday when it actually was Wednesday. Apparently this was a standard joke the Eskimos played on Shituk as he was always losing track of the proper day of the week. Not that it mattered in his existence.

While I ate the caribou meat with the men, Shituk's two young daughters sat on my left eating a raw ptarmigan apiece. The women and young girls consider raw ptarmigan a delicacy and the girls ate with gusto indicating their satisfaction with burps and much crunching of bones. At the end, nothing was left but feathers. Shituk sat on my right telling a long rambling story of his caribou hunts in the fall. His big body hunched over as he spoke, elbows resting on knees except when he waved his arms through the air to indicate a direction taken or the movements of the hunt. Every so often he reached under his parka to scratch. Beside him crouched his wife. She listened, nodding her head in agreement with the tale, gently bobbing up and down as she hummed a song, the baby asleep on her back. Every so often she leaned over and ran her fingers through her husband's hair, picked out a louse, cracked it between her nails and popped it into her mouth.

We awoke in the morning to find the wind had dropped considerably. After a breakfast of raw caribou meat, we set off along the trap line again. During the morning we set six more traps and for the first time on the trip saw fox tracks on the snow. They were those of a single fox that had passed through the area at least a week before. Shortly after noon as we left the sea ice and started the long climb over the height of land to the east arm of lower Paquet Bay, the wind rose again and quickly reached gale force. We found the large lake on the height of land without difficulty but were forced to pitch camp to await the end of the storm. By a stroke of extreme good fortune we found a small drift of snow hard and deep enough to provide material for blocks for a snow house, not a complete house but a circular wall of snow about five feet high over which we stretched the tent and weighed it down with blocks of snow and some of the heavier gear from the sled.

The snow house* has often been cited as an almost perfect example of good use of local materials and techniques in the construction of a dwelling. Out of this has grown the idea that it is the best type of dwelling for Eskimos in the Arctic lands. This is nonsense. The snow house is the best type of shelter one can have when travelling in midwinter

* The word *igloo* means house or dwelling, not necessarily a house made of snow; a snow house on north Baffin Island is called *iglooviuk.*

and early spring, for it provides excellent protection against wind and cold and does away with the need of taking a bulky, and often heavy, tent on the sled. But as a semi-permanent dwelling for the Eskimos of today it has limited value. A snow house quickly becomes iced up inside and this makes the atmosphere very damp. Sudden mild spells, which occur in the Arctic as well as in other parts of Canada, cause the roof to settle and the icy walls to drip. There is very little storage space and what there is usually is wet. The damp atmosphere makes it difficult to dry clothes properly. Worse than all this, however, is the fact that in many years it is impossible to build a snow house until very late in the fall or early winter; there is not sufficient snow. At such times the Eskimos shiver in their draughty tents in twenty below zero weather hoping for a snow and wind storm to come, bringing good snow for house construction. Eskimos on north Baffin have always preferred the small turf and whalebone or wood houses roofed over with sealskin, or canvas and brush, for their semi-permanent homes, using the snow house for temporary housing while hunting on the sea ice or travelling to the traps.

A snow house is built of blocks of snow cut from the hard, wind-packed drifts with a big knife or an ordinary saw. If the snow is deep enough the blocks are cut vertically, each one about four feet by three feet by four inches thick. If the snow is not deep, the blocks must be cut horizontally which spreads the work over a wide area necessitating longer and longer carries from the cutting to the building sites. But with the blocks cut vertically an overnight snow house can be built in forty minutes using only the snow from within the circle of the rising snow wall. The Eskimo literally builds himself into his home and must cut a door so that he can get out when he is finished. The first row of blocks is set up in a circle on the snow. All blocks slope inward slightly and each block is fitted to the snow beneath and to the previous one. The diameter of the circle governs the size of the completed dwelling, six feet for a small snow house, twelve to fifteen feet for a large one. I have seen a few snow houses twenty feet across, large enough to hold one hundred people.

When the first tier is completed a diagonal cut back is made through two or three blocks and the snow removed to form a large notch in the wall, thus creating a sloping ramp from the level of the snow floor to the top of the first tier. The first block of the second tier is set onto the sloping lower end of this notch, so that it, and all succeeding blocks, follow upward in a continuously rising spiral. Each block is slanted inward a little more and a little more until the upper ones are almost parallel to the ground, resting on the blocks of the lower row and on the side of the one preceding. The last block is inserted like the keystone of an arch and, with it in place, the snow house assumes its structural strength. After one night's occupancy the heat inside and the intense cold out hardens the entire structure into a tough shell. Then a person can stand on a snow house without fear of breaking it in, although a sharp blow of the fist could punch a hole in the thin snow wall. Inside, a platform of snow about two feet above the level of the floor is built to cover the rear two thirds of the snow house providing the sleeping platform on which the caribou sleeping skins and robes are placed. The door is a snow block cut to fit a small opening low down on the wall and is cemented into place with loose snow when all retire for the night. The more permanent snow houses have wooden doors set in frames in the snow wall. Ventilation comes from a small hole above the door and another in the roof.

Good snow for snow house construction is not easy to find. The best snow is usually found in a fairly hard drift that has been packed tight by the steady wind of one storm. Successive storms will build up drifts that are layered by streaks of soft snow that cause blocks to break when handled. If too hard the snow is almost impossible to cut with the knife or saw and the blocks, if cut, are very heavy to handle. Too soft snow causes the blocks to crumble when lifted into place.

In 1951, while travelling from Chesterfield to Baker Lake with Singeetuk as my guide, we built a snow house one night using blocks that were hard enough to handle but soft enough to wield together at the joint, leaving no "breathing space" between the blocks. We had two primus stoves going, one cooking our meat and the other melting ice to water for tea; light came from a small kerosene lantern on one wall and a candle stuck into the opposite side.

About an hour after the stoves were lit, the candle suddenly went out. Neither Singeetuk nor I paid any attention to this, thinking a draught had blown it out. A few moments later the kerosene lantern dimmed and Singeetuk, thinking it had run low on oil, reached out, took it from the peg stuck into the snow wall, and leaned over to set it on the floor in order to refill it with kerosene. As he bent over, he toppled from the sleeping platform, on which he had been kneeling and lay face down on the floor. For a few seconds I stared at him stupidly, unable to comprehend that something was wrong, for I felt nothing. Suddenly I realized that the house was flooded with poisonous fumes from the stove. We had had no warning other than the candle going out and the lantern dimming, both of which should have warned us but didn't, until Singeetuk collapsed on the floor.

Before I could move, Singeetuk reached forward and weakly punched a hole in the snow wall with his fist. Fresh air flowed in through the opening. Immediately I took a breath, I fell back on the sleeping platform, gagging. Both of us retched; my head and eyes ached; my body felt absolutely fagged out; I could hardly lift an arm let alone rise up from the skins. Singeetuk recovered enough to clamber slowly up onto the sleeping platform and we both lay quietly, too sick and tired to move. In a half hour we were well enough to sit up and unroll the sleeping bags. All night we tossed and turned as fever and chill chased one another through our bodies. In the morning we were still sick but well enough to travel and for a week afterwards my lips cracked and peeled as if to remind me of our close contact with death.

197

Idlouk, Kadluk and I worked as a team building our little half snow house as the storm howled through the night about us. With insufficient snow of poor quality, the house took shape slowly. The high wind ate through the weaker spots of the snow wall and we had to patch up the holes as fast as they appeared. A high wind will eat through a snow wall at an alarming rate. Actually it is not the wind itself that causes the damage but the abrasive effect of the snow particles carried along on the wind. These will wear through three or four inches of snow very quickly; you can actually see the holes appear. Twice in the evening the tent roof on our shelter whirled away into the darkness on the wings of exceptionally vicious blasts and each time we had to spend a half hour searching for it in the dark. By the time it was anchored in place again, everything inside the shelter was covered with snow. Fortunately there was no fear of its melting; it was far too cold for that.

The storm blew itself out during the night and we awoke to a calm, overcast day. Inside the shelter we were almost buried in deep drifts of snow blown in through holes in the snow wall and also from an opening in the roof where the tent had blown partially free. We had heard it flapping in the night but no one wanted to go outside to fix it; we snuggled deeper in the sleeping bags and ignored the sound and the snow. The previous night we had eaten what we thought to be the last of our food, a piece of raw frozen caribou given us by Shituk as we left his house in the morning, but while cleaning the snow from the bait box Idlouk found half of a frozen fish. The boiled fish breakfast was insufficient, but two mugs of tea helped fill the emptiness inside.

Leaving our gear in the shelter we took sled and dogs across the height of land and down onto the ice of the east arm of Paquet Bay where the trap line continued, running right around the bay. The sled went down the east slope of the ridge like a bobsleigh. We managed to miss most of the large boulders that dotted the hillside but ran over a good many smaller ones in the thousand yard dash down the hill.

Most of the time the sled pulled the dogs who howled their fright at this unorthodox juxtaposition. At the bottom of the hill we shot off a twenty foot drop onto the sea ice with an awful crash ending up in a heap on the ice. How the sled stood up under this treatment I do not know but even the cracked runner held firm. Except for minor bruises, so did we.

We made a complete circuit of the bay, resetting traps along the shore. High tides had caused water to flow onto the sea ice all along the shallow shore and in one or two places it was impossible to get from the ice to the shore. This occurred even in the coldest months of the winter and early spring. It was necessary for Idlouk to walk along the shore resetting the traps while Kadluk and I took the sled along farther out on the ice.

Just before dark Kadluk shot a rabbit which we boiled for supper at our snow house on the lake. During the afternoon the sky had cleared and the stars came out, but no moon. The temperature dropped sharply and as I lay in the sleeping bag after supper writing in my diary I could feel the cold creeping in—not blowing in, but creeping in—sending shivers up my back. In the increasing cold the ice on the lake boomed and cracked as it expanded under the pressures created by the frost. Our shelter was right on the lake ice which was approximately one foot thick and at each crack the ice seemed ready to break apart under our sleeping bags. A camp on the lake has definite advantages though; we had a small hole chopped through the ice outside the snow block door and could get water for tea without laboriously melting ice or snow. Getting water from ice is not too bad but melting snow is an awful job as it takes buckets of snow to get a cupful of water.

To date on the trip we had set sixty-one traps and had seen only the tracks of a single fox. Idlouk was definitely resigned to another poor year in fur. I suspected that he might be worried about how I would go through the long winter living on meat alone, with none of the extras such as hard-tack biscuits, sugar and tea, that we had been having at intervals through the summer and fall. I wondered about that myself.

All night long the ice on the lake boomed and cracked as the temperature continued to drop. In the morning it must have been forty-five below, but if Idlouk's predictions proved correct it should get much warmer as we travelled northward and got out onto the open expanse of Eclipse Sound.* We set ten traps at the lower end of the bay and then started on the return trip. We did not travel on the extreme lower end of the trap line where it extended inland from the sea as Shituk had said there were no tracks of fox down there and Idlouk decided to leave that portion until the next trip. As we returned up the coast we visited the traps set on the way down and to our intense surprise and delight found foxes in two of them, one each for Idlouk and Kadluk. Alleani! What pleasure! Then Idlouk spotted a fox burrow on a hillside. We climbed up to it and could hear foxes moving around inside. All this improved our spirits considerably. The two skins added to the load of the sled symbolized our hope for the future.

It was very cold travelling. Several times I froze my nose and chin, particularly after dark when it was impossible for the others to warn me when the tell-tale white spots appeared, and often I did not feel anything until too late. Each time I thawed the frozen part by covering it with my warm hand for a few moments. My clothes were damp from perspiration and this added to the difficulty of keeping warm; my feet were cold much of the time as the caribou skin socks were damp and there was no way to dry them completely at night; even taking them inside the sleeping bag did not dry them enough.

Until late in the afternoon the stars shone out of a clear sky, then clouds obscured the stars and a high wind blew up out of the south-east. By the time we decided to stop and build a snow house it was blowing a gale. Kadluk wanted to stop at Shituk's house for the night as we were not far from it when the storm hit but neither Idlouk nor I were very

* Idlouk was right. It got much warmer.

happy about this. The following day was Sunday and we would not travel; a week-end in that vermin-ridden hovel would not be pleasant. We stopped at Shituk's only long enough to give him half a seal we had picked up from one of our caches, keeping enough to feed our dogs for one night and ourselves for two. At a valley mouth a few miles north of Shituk's house we found enough snow to build a snow house, although it was necessary to cut the blocks horizontally. By the time the house was completed, we were quite worn out.

Our supper of seal meat was delicious. The meat was not fresh but I wanted seal meat and fat very much and the others felt the same. We had been having too much rabbit with too little fat and even the caribou did not have sufficient to satisfy our bodily needs.

For thirty-six hours we lay in the little snow house, never stirring from the sleeping bags, listening to the sound of the storm howl over the snow outside. About nine o'clock Sunday evening Kadluk and Idlouk conducted an abbreviated church service and then resumed talking fox prospects for the coming winter. We could not travel for two reasons: a storm was blowing and it was Sunday. Eat, sleep, talk; eat, sleep, talk; that was the pattern of our day. I cannot see that it brought us much closer to God but the missionary had apparently convinced the Eskimos that to hibernate on Sunday was a prerequisite for admittance to heaven.

Once again the storm blew out during the night leaving cold clear weather in its wake. We left our snow house at seven o'clock Monday morning, well before first light. Overhead the stars twinkled frostily and a single shaft of northern lights stabbed across the sky. Stopping only to visit the traps set on the outward trip, we travelled swiftly northward along the east shore of Paquet Bay. We again found foxes in some of the traps, three for Idlouk and two for Kadluk, making a total of seven fox skins for the trip.

With only a small breakfast of seal meat and tea, and after a week on short rations while travelling, we became cold and hungry as the day wore on. We saw no rabbits, but came upon a flock of about twenty ptarmigan feeding on the slopes near the shore. Kadluk tried to shoot a few but the .22 jammed in the cold and the birds flew off. About four in the afternoon Idlouk said that he had placed three hardtack biscuits under a rock on the outward trip without letting Kadluk and me know. From then on we all thought of the three biscuits under the rock up ahead. By the time we reached the place where they were hidden, I had transformed the hard dry biscuits into an enormous raisin-filled bannock that would chase my hunger away and fill my stomach as full as it was possible for it to be. The single biscuit apiece did not come up to expectations but, topped with our last mug of tea, it did make us feel warmer than we had been all day.

By two o'clock, the midday light was gone. As we were without food and fuel Idlouk decided to return nonstop to Aulatseevik some sixty sled miles away. Through the dark of the afternoon and early evening we moved steadily along the shore, leaving Paquet Bay, heading across the entrance to Tay Sound and through the narrow channel at Frechette Island out onto the smooth ice of Eclipse Sound. In the rough ice of the narrow channel we ran into trouble as we could not see far enough ahead to pick a good route. Fighting the wildly tossing sled through rough sea ice was like riding a bucking horse. The sled moved forward relentlessly, up and down over the ice hummocks, dogs urged on by voice and whip, for if the sled should stop against a hummock it would take a good bit of juggling to get it going again. Idlouk lay partially over one side of the sled, Kadluk and I the other. Half running, half walking we rode with the sled as it bucked and tossed over the ice, swinging this way and that, fighting it through the narrow gaps between the hummocks. Perfect team work was required to steer the sled by pushing sideways with our feet against pieces of ice as we passed. We had to keep our wits about us, watching continuously for pieces of upright ice looming out of the darkness ahead, ready to swing immediately to the opposite side of the sled before we were crushed between the ice and the side of the load.

All night we moved steadily over the ice of Eclipse Sound. The dogs kept up a steady trot hour after hour, stopping only when we checked the traps along the shore. We found no more foxes. The dogs were hungry and tired but it is under such conditions that the Eskimo husky is at his best. As a rule the Eskimo husky is not a top-notch sled dog. He can easily be beaten for speed and pulling power by better trained and better bred dogs. But when the going gets tough, when rations are short or non-existent, then he is without peer. For sheer dogged endurance he cannot be matched. He will pull until he drops; pulling is the only life he knows.

As we approached the familiar coast line near the camp, after some twenty hours of continuous travel, the dogs sensed that the end of the trail was near; food and rest lay just ahead. Tired heads swung into the air and woofs of pleasure broke from parched throats. Soon the dogs were running with tails held high, howling their pleasure into the sky as they dashed over the snow, the sled thumping and bumping in their wake. In a moment we heard answering howls from up ahead. Around the point of land we dashed and there in front lay Aulatseevik, four little pinpricks of yellow light that spelled warmth and comfort. With a last burst of speed the sled ran through the rough shore ice and swung to a halt on the snow-covered beach. The dogs from the other teams immediately jumped among ours and a battle royal was on. Into the fight we dashed, kicking dogs right and left, trying to break up the brawl before any of the dogs got hurt. The fight was soon over; we were home again.

CHAPTER
15

IN HIS great book, *The Friendly Arctic*, Stefansson notes that the Eskimos with whom he lived paid little attention to the disappearance of the sun in the late fall. I found this to be in contrast with the reaction of the Eskimos at Aulatseevik. While it is true none complained about the sun being gone, that no one became morose over the thought of getting along in a world of almost perpetual darkness for the next three months, the Eskimos missed the sun. On November 11th, the day its rays last touched our land, all work stopped for a few moments as we watched it peer over the saddle in the hills to the south. For a few brief moments our campsite was bathed in its light, before the sun slid from view. Behind the camp the rocky hills glowed red until this too darkened as the long shadow thrown by the mountains to the south chased all colour up the steep slopes into the sky overhead.

The Eskimos spoke about the missing sun wistfully, noting how much easier life was in their land when they had the sun to guide and warm them. As the period of light at mid-day grew shorter, this talk slowly petered out. Our lives became adapted to the new conditions; our allegiance shifted from the sun to the shiny white disc of the moon, as it rose from behind the hills to the north-west, bathing the land in ghostly white light. During the period of the month when the moon was lost to us, or was hidden behind clouds, we missed it as one misses a friend in time of need. We looked on the moon with new affection and no longer thought of the sun.

North Baffin differs from the high Arctic islands to the

north in that it is possible to go through the winter without ever having the full twenty-four hours of any one day completely dark. After the sun sets for the last time, the short daylight hours grow even shorter. By the first week in December, noon is similar to the hour of first light in more southerly parts of Canada, as the sun approaches but never reaches the southern horizon. First light comes about ten-thirty in the morning and all light is gone by half past one or two. By mid-December even this light has faded considerably and for the month to follow mid-day is neither dark nor light. About eleven o'clock in the morning, the horizon to the south lightens and a greyness disperses the dark of the night. This greyness becomes lighter as noon approaches until it seems that day is about to dawn on the land again. But the greyness fades and in an hour it is night again. This is the pattern when the sky overhead is clear, or at least clear along the horizon to the south. If it is overcast in mid-winter, there is no light at noon; the twenty-four hours round the clock are each as dark as the midnight hour. Then night is as long as a day or a week and, in extreme cases, as long as a month.

On north Baffin, when the skies are clear and the full moon rides high in the tremendous star-sprinkled vault overhead, night has a cold, hard beauty that stirs one's soul. The long wavering beams of the northern lights chase across the sky, shooting out from the tops of the distant hills to the south, growing out of the vast mass of the unknown universe, weaving and dancing as they shift in pattern and outline before disappearing into the empty void that is their home. A star topples lazily from its lofty perch and disappears without a sound; across the sky sweeps the fiery mass of a hurtling meteor, blazing earthward for a few brief seconds of glory before it is consumed by the forces created in its impetuous mad dash.

The long night did not change the basic pattern of our life; we still made the long trips to the traps, we still hunted over the sea ice. But considerable adaptation and minor change did result. Travel became more difficult, trips took longer to complete, and we did not roam as far afield on the hunting trips. Telescopes and binoculars were put away until spring, only the .22 rifles were kept handy for hunting rabbits by moonlight. The seal harpoon became our principal weapon and the seal net our biggest producer of food. The diet was more restricted and patterns of eating changed somewhat. Whereas in the spring and summer we had a variety of meats and alternated from day to day, now we had only a few meats, seal and fish the staples with smaller amounts of caribou and muktuk. For a week or more we ate seal meat every day. Then a sled would make a trip to our caches near the camp of the Ikalukmiut and for the next five or six days fish would be our only food, after which we would return to the diet of seal. The dogs were fed on seals brought in from the caches scattered over the land, but Idlouk liked to have fresh meat for the people at the camp. Often we ate spoiled meat and fish as a change from fresh, for many tainted meats were considered as delicacies. If there was flour, we had bannock for a treat, but always the basic diet was meat; meat eaten raw, raw frozen, or boiled, whichever we preferred or could have at the time. Tea was the standard drink, Eskimo tea, boiled black as the midnight sky.

All during the winter months, the ice on the bays and sounds of north Baffin grew thicker and thicker. Maximum thickness which sea ice will reach depends on many things: the degree of cold in the area, the length of the cold spells, the depth of the snow cover on the sea ice, the strength of the currents beneath the ice, the time of the year the snow cover becomes thick enough to act as insulation, plus the interaction of these and other factors. Heavy snow soon after the initial freeze-up of the sea prevents the ice from thickening and for a long period it will be thin. Water seeps up through this ice as it is depressed by the weight of the snow until it is impossible to travel by sled; the dogs bog down in the heavy slush. If little more snow falls, this slush ice freezes causing the ice to build up both from above and below so that what started out as thin ice becomes very

Twice a month, during the periods of the highest tides on the sea, the ice cover shifts under the pressures created by the tides. Long cracks appear, often running for miles through the ice cover. The cracks are as little as a few inches wide and as much as a few feet. Without fail they appear in the same locations year after year. The open water in the cracks quickly freezes over in the extreme cold but not before seals in the vicinity discover this water and the new source of access to open air. Many seals leave their regular breathing holes and start a new series of aglos in the ice forming along the cracks. This situation is made to order for the Eskimo hunters.

Immediately after a period of high tides, a hunting party of four or five men and boys went out from Aulatseevik to the places where, according to past experience, the best cracks should have formed. Two to a sled, each man with only his seal harpoon and snow knife, and perhaps one rifle among the group, we travelled along the shore to a place where a crack began, running off seaward through the ice. The new ice on the crack was about one inch thick and new aglos were clearly visible, even in the dark, as we walked beside the crack. We left the sleds at the shore and, as a group, started to run along the edge of the crack. Every time an aglo was reached, Idlouk made a quick inspection and, if he thought it was a good one, a hunter immediately took up position beside it and readied his harpoon while the others ran on into the darkness. In about fifteen minutes we were strung out in a long line over the ice, each waiting patiently and silently beside an aglo, alone in the blackness of the night. The last hunter did not stop, but ran on down the crack for a half mile or so breaking in any aglos he found before turning at right angles to run off over the

207

sea ice searching for other minor cracks in the area in which seals might have started new aglos. When he found them he broke them in and continued his wide circle around the crack along which the hunters waited.

Often we were fortunate, and even before the last hunter had started his run over the ice a shout from the darkness would indicate that a seal had risen in an aglo and had been harpooned by the waiting hunter. Then we all walked over to where the seal lay, guided through the dark by the sound of the shout and by the outline of the crack in the ice. Sometimes we waited beside the aglos for over an hour but no shout came, and nothing happened at the aglo over which we stood. In such cases, one of the Eskimos would whistle and soon the sleds would appear out of the darkness pulled by the willing dogs who, driverless, followed the crack out to where we stood. The search for a new and more productive crack began.

We hunted seals this way immediately after every change of the moon throughout the winter. The men and older boys at the camp were roughly divided into two groups; one group hunted seals at the aglos and cracks, the other, split up into sub-groups, patrolled the trap lines. During the period of the next high tide the groups reversed roles so that everyone alternated between hunting and trapping throughout the winter. On the hunting trips we would be gone for two days or up to seven and eight, depending on the success of the hunt, travelling over the ice of Eclipse Sound searching out the best cracks in the ice. Often from the time we left camp until the time we returned, we lived and hunted in complete darkness. If fortunate, we had the light of the moon to guide us; if not, we got along as best we could without. We were rarely warm and never comfortable. Temperatures stayed at forty to fifty below and strong winds swept across the open sweep of the Sound from the ice caps of the far north isles. Our little overnight snow houses were barely big enough to sleep three men side by side, and were without light and heat. Our food was the meat of our kills, eaten raw at the time of the killing or raw frozen in the snow house at night. For the first two or three days of each trip we had mugs of tea. Then the kerosene for the primus stove gave out and we went for two or three or four days with only snow to chew or the blood of the seals to drink. All too often we waited over aglo after aglo and had nothing appear. Then we went hungry, one day, two days, three days, before making a kill again or heading back to camp. When the storms struck we lay in our sleeping bags in the little snow houses listening to the wind howl, hoping it would stop so that we could resume the hunt again.

Despite the discomfort I liked the winter hunts. For the first time since coming to the Arctic I was hunting in exactly the same manner as the old Eskimos must have hunted before the coming of the white man. Our little group had almost no help from twentieth century technology. True, our harpoon heads and handles were made of steel but the principle of operation was identical to that of the harpoons of long ago when the heads and handles were carved from the ivory of narwhal tusks. Fresh meat from my harpoon had a flavour it otherwise could not have. At least I thought so, but I was probably being romantic. The Eskimos found no difference at all.

Although hunting by harpoon provided meat and adventure, the seal net was the real producer of food in the dark winter months. The seal net, similar to a fish net, but with heavier twine and larger mesh, was set under the ice of the new cracks that developed off the rocky points of land. It was set near the shore, just beyond the area of rough ice in the tidal zone. Setting the net in the crack was a simple operation. It was laid out on the ice beside the new crack, small boulders were attached to the slings on the bottom, and the net was let down into the water. It was left fairly loose with the top strand about three or four feet below the under-surface of the ice. At each end and at one place in the centre of the net, short guy ropes ran up to the ice surface terminating in loops through which were threaded the long handles of harpoons or fish spears laid across the narrow crack to hold the net in place.

Thereafter the net was visited daily. As the crack froze over and the ice grew thicker, the guy ropes had to be chopped out each time the net was hauled out of the water through one hole chopped large enough for this purpose. A long line, usually the trace of the lead dog, was attached to an end guy rope, and the net pulled out onto the ice by the opposite guy rope so that the line threaded under the ice following the net. The line was used to pull the net back into place when the seal or seals had been removed. Ice in the holes thus chopped out never became very thick providing the net was visited every day, but if two or three days went by and the holes were not chopped clear, twelve to eighteen inches of ice would form and the job of clearing the guy ropes was laborious.

The net was left set in the water for as long as it caught seals. This period varied from two days to two weeks. At the end of two weeks it had to be removed for high tides again caused the ice to shift. If left set the net could easily be torn badly or lost altogether. The power of ice under movement by tidal pressure in mid-winter equals that of ice under pressure from wind and current in the summer. It is tremendous; four- and five-foot-thick ice will be lifted and crushed, or torn apart under the press of the rising waters. At such times, the net was not put in the water until the new pattern of cracks in the ice had developed. Always the net was set in the immediate vicinity of the camp or in the area in which a hunting party was operating so that it could be visited every day if possible, at least every other day. A net with dead seals in it was as useless as no net at all, as the struggle of the seals to free themselves soon wound the entire mesh tightly about the bodies.

The first time Idlouk, Paneeluk and I set the net we did not put it in a new crack but in an old one covered by two feet of ice. We chopped a series of small holes along the crack, one every six feet or so, for a distance equal to the length of the net. Then a dog trace was fastened to one end of the handle of an ice chisel and the handle pushed down the end hole under the ice. With my arms up to the elbows in the icy water, I pushed the handle towards the second hole where Paneeluk lay on his stomach peering down into the dark water. When the handle slid into his view, he immediately pushed it towards the next hole while I ran to peer down. The handle was manœuvred from hole to hole under the ice until pulled out at the last one, bringing the trace with it. The net was attached to the trace, pulled under the ice, and set in the usual fashion.

All three of us worked together chopping the holes, for it was hard work. After this was finished and the line threaded through, Paneeluk and Idlouk set the net, while I returned to the sled to make a pot of tea. When the tea boiled I called to the others and we had a mug of hot tea with raw meat from a seal I had harpooned an hour before. We then returned to the net to make last minute adjustments before continuing our hunt. As Idlouk hefted one end of the net to make sure it was not snagged on the ice, he paused for a moment and tugged it again. "I think we have a seal," he said.

Sure enough, there was a seal in the net. It was a big one and fought madly as the three of us pulled it out through the hole onto the ice where a blow on the head ended its life. We were so overjoyed at our good fortune that we immediately started up the primus stove and had another mug of tea with a meal of seal liver fresh from our catch.

The celebration turned out to be premature for we did not get another seal at that spot. In addition we had no further luck hunting at the aglos in the area. For the next three days we roamed over the ice in the vicinity of the net, stopping to hunt at the aglos we located, sleeping out in the little snow houses, returning to check the net once every twenty-four hours. But at the end of three days we had no food of any sort; we had not eaten in thirty-six hours; we were all very cold, tired and hungry. We saved enough kerosene in the primus stove for one mug of tea at the

seal net as we took it out of the water before setting out
for camp some twenty-five miles away.

At the crack we worked to get the net out of the water.
It is a disagreeable job, working with bare hands in ice cold
water for long periods with the temperature about forty
below. But it is surprising how long you can work this way
once you get used to it. As we tried to pull the net clear it
stuck, and Idlouk was forced to remove his outer parka in
the bitter cold and wind, lie flat on the ice over the hole,
and fish around with his arm up to the shoulder in the water
before he could free the net. At the time I could not understand how he could do this, but later on I had to do the
same thing and discovered that, as with many things, it
is surprising what you can do when necessity forces you to.

After the net was brought onto the ice, Paneeluk started
the primus and melted ice for tea. While the water came
to a boil he left the stove to help Idlouk and me fold the
frozen net and load it on the sled. He returned to the primus
every few moments to check the pot of water and at the
right time threw in the handful of tea. Just as he did, the
primus ran out of fuel; we had just made our last mug of
tea. In the dark we sat side by side on the sled, dropping
little lumps of snow in the tea to cool it. I lifted my mug
and took a small sip as it was still very hot. It tasted a little
odd but this was not surprising as most tea made on the
trail does. I added another piece of snow and then took a
real swallow.

I very nearly gagged; the mouthful of tea came right
back out onto the snow as I tried to clear my mouth of the
awful taste. Idlouk, sitting next to me in the dark, said,
"What is the matter, Kingmik, are you ill?"

"What is the matter with the tea?" I gasped, "It tastes
worse than gasoline or garbage."

Idlouk took a small sip and immediately spat the tea on
the snow. He dumped out his mug and started to chuckle.

"Don't you know what is the matter, Kingmik? I thought
you were a real Eskimo. While the water was coming to the
boil on the primus and Paneeluk was helping us with the

net, a dog has lifted its leg to the pot. They are sharpshooters; they seldom miss."

Eskimos of north Baffin have a wealth of such tales about minor mishaps that occur during the time of the long night. Often when visiting at another camp, they will press the host into telling his story of an incident that had happened while he was hunting or travelling in the dark. Or when Idlouk and I were lying in a little snow house listening to the storm rage outside, he would recount episodes affecting himself and others at the camp. The tales are usually short and undramatically told, but the Eskimos remember them. They bring quiet humour, where humour could very easily not exist.

Here are some of these tales:

A Story by Idlouk

I was hunting seals on the ice of Eclipse Sound while on a trip to the settlement. In two days Paneeluk and I harpooned three seals in the aglos. We cached the meat under the snow intending to pick it up on the return trip to camp and set out for the settlement about thirty miles away. The sky was clear, full of stars. An hour after we started for the settlement the moon rose over the distant hills and the land around stood out almost as clear as when under the rays of the sun. It was the kind of weather we hope for on our winter travels for under such conditions very little can go wrong. But sometimes little things do go wrong.

As we moved over the ice, we came upon a new crack leading off across the Sound. We had enough seals but the crack was such a good one, it enticed me. I said to Paneeluk, "We will follow the crack for a little way to see if there are any more aglos. But we will not go far as I want to reach the settlement soon." We left the sled and started out along the crack carrying our harpoons. We walked for about a mile but did not see any aglos so we returned to the place where we had left the sled. But the sled was not there, nor were the dogs. New tracks in the snow led off to the north-west; the dogs had gone off with the sled. By the look of the tracks I knew they were running and thought they must have caught the scent of an aglo close by. Paneeluk and I started out after them, running along the tracks in the moonlight.

But we could not catch them and they did not stop. On and on we followed the tracks until we could go no further. I said to Paneeluk, "We will walk to the settlement, for I think the dogs will run a long way. They may have smelled a camp farther up the coast, or they may run until they reach the next camp."

We walked into the settlement. It took us a long time and we were very tired. As we drew near, the lights from the houses seemed to taunt us with their nearness but we walked and walked and we did not seem to get any closer. I was very angry with my dogs. If I could have found them then I would have shot them all.

We finally arrived. How the other Eskimos and the white men laughed when they saw Idlouk, the hunter and traveller, arriving without his sled and dogs and his boots worn through at the soles. I laughed too for it was very funny, but I was worried about my dogs. I stayed at the settlement for three days. On the third day Akpaleeapik arrived and he had my sled and dogs with him. They had run into his camp and he thought I would be at the settlement so he brought them in to me. I was very happy to see them. A hunter is useless without his dogs.

A Story by Kitchooalik

My camp was then on the shore of Bylot Island directly across the Sound from the settlement. Many times I had gone in to trade and returned to camp the same day, for it was an easy trip over the smooth ice. But once it took me three days just to reach Michimatelik*. It was in the middle of winter and the air was clear and cold. Stars twinkled in the sky although no moon shone on the land. The moon was gone for a while. As I travelled along I was happy for my camp had food, I had foxes, and the weather was

* Pond Inlet settlement.

good. Far off on the distant horizon I could see two or three "stars" very low down and I knew these were the lights of the white men's houses. Coming in from the sea I could see the tiny pinpricks of light for many miles and it seemed to take hours and hours before I got close to them. But this is always the way with these lights.

Eventually I came to the lights. About one mile out from the buildings I stopped my dogs. I took the half seal I had on the sled and chopped it up to feed them for I intended staying at the settlement over Sunday, which was the next day, so that I could go to church. We always feed our dogs out on the ice before arriving at the settlement as there are too many dogs running loose there to be able to feed your own team alone. I hummed a song as I chopped the frozen seal; I was happy for in an hour I would be sitting in the kitchen of the trader's warm house, smoking his cigarettes and drinking a mug of his tea which has sugar and milk in it. My mouth watered at the thought for I was hungry and I chewed on the small chips of frozen meat that flew up from the axe.

While approaching the land I had felt a wind on my face, not a bad one, just the usual breeze that blows off the land in winter along the coast. Small spirals of snow whirled into the air and by the time I had stopped to feed the dogs the light wind was causing the snow to drift. Ahead I could see the lights of the buildings quite clearly and so I paid no attention to the wind. But the wind grew stronger and stronger; the lights of the houses were blotted from my view. Quickly I finished chopping the meat and loosed the dogs to feed. In a few minutes the meat was all gone and the dogs hitched up again. Immediately I set out to cover the last mile to the settlement.

An hour later I still had not arrived; something was wrong. I had not bothered to steer the dogs as I thought the scent would take them straight in. In the swirling snow I could see nothing. I stopped to search the ice but could find no indication of where I was. The wind had now risen to a gale and was howling over the snow. It had been blowing off the land when I started out after feeding the dogs and although I was still heading into it we had not come to the land. The wind must have changed and the dogs changed course with it. I turned the dogs to the right and went on again but there was still no sign of land. I turned to the left but still no land rose up out of the swirling snow. I knew the settlement was not far away but I did not know just where. I decided the only thing to do was camp.

I built a small snow house out of the ice; just big enough for one person to lie in. As I had not brought my sleeping bag I was very cold in the little house lying on the snow with only a small bear skin from the sled to protect me. For two days I lay in my shelter while the wind howled over the snow outside and I became hungrier and hungrier, and colder and colder. After two days the storm blew out and once more the stars appeared in the sky overhead. As the wind died and the snow swirls lessened I crawled outside to see where I was camped. And there, about one mile ahead, the lights of the buildings twinkled merrily, just as they had done two long days before. I had spent two days lying in my cold little house, without food, almost within shouting distance of food and warmth in plenty. Iyonamut, such is the life of an Eskimo.

A Story by Kingmik

I was sitting with Idlouk on the sleeping platform of the house of Nashuk at the camp of the Kownukmiut on the west coast of Eclipse Sound. The house was large and it was very hot for all the hunters were gathered talking about the seals they had harpooned during the day. The soft yellow light of the flickering seal-oil lamps reflected from the brown faces as beads of sweat gathered, running down from forehead to chin before being wiped away. Through a small slit in the parchment-like skin window over the door I could see a segment of the clear sky. Stars twinkled and the full moon rode high.

Suddenly there was a commotion outside the door. All the men looked up as three women from the neighbouring

216

houses dashed inside and stood cowering inside the door. Their faces were pale, their breath came in short gasps; they did not say a word, just stood together by the door.

One of the men asked, "What is the matter?"

The youngest of the women whispered, "Look outside. Something is happening to the moon. I think it is about to fall on the land."

The man laughed and got up from his seat. Going over to the window he peered out through the slit. He uttered an exclamation and peered intently out into the night. "What is it?" we cried.

He turned and said, "A shadow has come over the moon, slowly it is being put out." We all dashed outside.

It was the beginning of a total eclipse. Already the leading edge of the shadow of the earth had cut deeply into the moon. Deeper and deeper it cut until the moon was completely hidden from view; only a bright halo of light radiated out from top of the space where the moon rode, hidden behind the massive shadow of our earth.

Total darkness lay on the land; we could not see from one house to the next fifteen yards away. The three women still huddled in the corner of Nashuk's house, afraid to return to their own homes, although the quiet laughter of the men had lessened their terror somewhat. Not until the shadow of the earth slowly passed across the face of the moon and the gleaming white orb once more bathed the land with its light did they venture forth into the night and return to their homes.

I watched the eclipse of the moon standing on the ice-bound shore of the Sound. As I watched I wondered which of the early explorers in this far north land had also stood on this shore and watched a similar eclipse of the moon on a clear cold night long ago, and thereby named the body of water that lay beneath the layer of thick ice at his feet, Eclipse Sound.

CHAPTER
16

SLOWLY the long night retreated from north Baffin. Day after day throughout the month of January, first light came a little earlier in the morning and lingered on longer beyond noon, touching the sky to the south at ten-thirty, moving up to ten, to nine-thirty and on to nine, until by the end of the month there was light on the land from eight in the morning until well after four in the afternoon. The greyness of the mid-winter mid-day gave way to clear brightness as the sky overhead reflected light from the invisible sun. By the end of the month, mid-day brought pale colour to tint the land; delicate mauves and pinks painted the high clouds and sky, reflecting downwards to touch every pinnacle of ice and rock of the snow-shrouded land, casting long dark blue shadows over the pink of the snow. For a few brief moments at noon the golden rays of the invisible sun shone briefly out of the southern sky, while to the north the brighter stars rode in a sky of deep blue, twinkling brightly in the vast shadow cast into space by our earth.

The gradual return of hours of light to each day altered our daily pattern of life. We rose well in advance of first light and were away on the trips by the time darkness had begun to fade from the sky, taking full advantage of every moment of the fast returning light. Hours of sleeping began to conform to hours of light and dark, and in so doing conformed more and more to the hours of day and night recorded by the clock. Hunting trips became longer, not in time spent away, but in the distance we were able to travel out from camp. The trap line trips took a shorter time as light enabled us to go faster and farther each day. No longer did we struggle through areas of rough broken ice; we climbed to vantage points on the hills and searched out the best routes ahead. But if the return of light brought many blessings to our life, it made no difference at all to the numbers of fox we found in our traps.

"Where are the foxes," said Idlouk sadly, "they must have left this land for good."

Slowly he straightened up and looked down at the smooth patch of snow beneath which the trap lay hidden. No tracks marred the clean surface of snow; the nearby cache, opened to feed the dogs on a previous trip that way, bore no evidence that foxes had picked up the strong scent. Only the tracks of rabbits stitching across the hillsides gave silent evidence of wild life close by. For three months we had been visiting the traps, alternating with Kadluk and Paneeluk so that each trap was visited twice a month. This was the count: November, six foxes; December, four foxes; January, seven foxes; and the last day of the month was close at hand. Seventeen foxes for three months of hard toil in the dark, three months of fighting wind, cold and hunger on the long journeys to the traps; one hundred and nineteen dollars toward the annual budget of our family for the year, and already half the short earning season had slipped away. For the second year in a row, north Baffin was having a bad year in fur.

Nineteen fifty-one and fifty-two had been a peak year for fox. On Idlouk's first trip in the fall he had returned with twenty-five foxes and this pattern had kept up all winter long. But 1952-53 had been the reverse and his traps had yielded a total of only eighteen foxes for the entire five months of the trapping season. The foxes had disappeared. He, and other Eskimos of the area, told me of their long journeys through the winter when time after time they returned to camp without a single fox, without having seen any tracks on the land. They had no money to buy kerosene for the primus stoves, therefore no way to make tea on the trail. For long periods they lived on frozen meat alone.

Over a month at Aulatseevik the people had no extras at all, not even tea; they lived on meat, drinking the water in which it was boiled, when it could be boiled, over the seal-oil lamp at camp. Travelling in the extreme cold mid-winter, without hot food and drink now and again, made life very miserable indeed.

"Pooyoujangneelungah," said Idlouk, "I will never forget it." Then he added, "Iyonamut. It can't be helped; these things have to be."

Money was scarce at Aulatseevik during the winter of 1953-54. Pilot biscuits and bannock were luxury items in our diet, tea the only staple we bought at the store. Now and then we had rolled oats, and once a small jar of jam for a treat. But the caches, put up in the fall, fed the dogs well and winter hunts at the aglos brought good supplies of fresh seal meat and fat. By the end of January the last of the fish and the muktuk had been brought back to camp and eaten; only the few remaining caribou in the distant inland caches made by Oodleteetuk and Kitchooalik on their hunt the previous fall provided a welcome change from the staple diet of seal. Now and again, usually when out on the trail, we had a rabbit. On the hunting trips we managed to eat fairly well, but on the long journeys to the traps we regularly ran short of food.

Over the long months I had become used to the diet of meat. On trading trips to the settlement I enjoyed having meals of vegetables, roast meat, pie for dessert and cups of coffee with sugar and cream. Pete Murdock insisted on stuffing me every time I came in, and at Christmas, through a series of unforeseen developments, Idlouk and I spent three weeks at the settlement, enjoying the varied diet for a change. But I did not hanker after white man's food, and I switched from straight meat to vegetables and cereals with relative ease. Certain dishes from both diets had become my favourite foods, and I looked forward to a meal of raw frozen caribou meat or seal heart with the same anticipation I previously had applied only to the thought of fine steak fried in wine.

220

In the beginning of my life as an Eskimo, there was a two- or three-week period when I could not eat enough meat at one time to satisfy my hunger. I ate meat until I could not eat any more, but I was still hungry, for anything but meat. I solved this by eating small quantities every two hours or so. Gradually the amounts eaten grew larger and larger until, in about one month's time, my capactiy for downing meat at a single sitting was equal to that of Idlouk and Kadluk, prodigious eaters both. I was unable to eat as fast as they, for I liked to chew the meat, taste it well before letting it slide down. Not so Idlouk; his satisfaction came from a stomach that was full; the sooner the food reached his stomach the faster came his delight.

I have been told by doctors that, with a meat diet, this is by far the best way. Certain elements are extracted from meat far along the digestive tract and for the body to get the maximum amount of good from meat, it should be digested slowly. The less it is broken up by chewing in the mouth, the slower the digestion process will be. Certainly the eating method of Eskimos bears this out. They often swallow huge pieces of meat, getting them down with difficulty, ending up gasping, eyes watering from the effort involved. I never reached this stage, but as time wore on I chewed less and less. This was a practical measure, for if I did not, I had no hope of getting the better pieces from the pot.

Many people are still astounded that Eskimos, and myself when I am living with them, have no vegetables or fresh greens of any sort. It seems impossible for them to believe that the body can remain healthy on a diet of meat alone. I assure them it is so. I have lived on a diet of meat for varying periods of time and have felt no ill effects at all.

If I were to compile a list of my favourite Arctic dishes, it would run like this:

1. Raw frozen caribou meat eaten with chunks of back fat; meat thawed just enough to be crunchy.
2. Boiled muktuk and whale heart, done together in the same pot.

3. Raw frozen square flipper seal intestine, contents squeezed out at time of kill.
4. Raw frozen Arctic char, fish cut in sections, section next to tail most delicious part.
5. Boiled caribou, char, rabbit, ptarmigan, with drink of soup of water used for boiling in each case.
6. Boiled seal meat, the flippers the choice part, with ribs close behind.
7. Raw unfrozen meat from young seal in the spring, heart and liver the choice tidbits. Liver has onion taste.
8. Dried strips of whale meat or Arctic char.

This list presupposes that boiling is the only means of cooking. If it were possible to fry meats well, then fried seal liver and caribou steak would rank high, and fried char is a tasty dish. If the meat could be roasted, stuffed baby seal would probably head the list.

The list is prepared in retrospect and is extremely arbitrary, for many local factors change the order of precedence considerably. There are a number of dishes that I have not eaten often enough as yet to develop a taste for them. Often the term "favourite dish" is affected by the unavailability of different meats at certain seasons of the year, which brings about a repetition of the same meat day after day. Although I have listed raw frozen caribou meat with back fat as my first choice, I have eaten caribou meat until I became so sick of it I thought I would never want to see it again. If asked for an opinion at such a time I would probably have said that boiled seal meat was my favourite dish and this would be doubly so if my body craved fat. Although seal meat has almost no fat in the meat, parts of the heavy surrounding layer are always left attached to the meat as it is cut up. This applies to muktuk from the narwhal and white whale as well. Walrus and bear meat have fat in the meat, but I do not care for either of these, the first being too strong and the latter too stringy for my taste.

I have not included any of the rotten or tainted meats on the list. I did become fond of one or two, but I would not term them favourites.

Of all the different foods eaten by Eskimos in the Arctic, I was unable to stomach only one; the meat of the old male seals, called by the Eskimos *teeguk*. Many of the seals that remained under the ice and sounds during the winter were big old males weighing up to four and five hundred pounds. During the early part of the winter a change of some sort came over their bodies; literally they started to stink. By the time February came round, the body odour of the old teeguk seals was so potent that it hung in the air for some distance about the breathing holes under the snow. It was a chemical smell and very strong, as obnoxious as anything I have encountered. Whenever I smelled it my stomach did flip-flops and I felt as though I was going to be ill. The air inside the breathing holes was putrid from their breath and every part of the seal smelled this way. If I brushed my fingers lightly along the hair, the smell lingered on my fingers for some time. If the fat from one was used in a seal-oil lamp, the entire house took on the odour and did not clear for days after its use in the lamp was discontinued. If the meat from a teeguk seal was put in the box in the corner of the house, all meat for the next week or two was contaminated if put in the same box, long after the teeguk meat had gone.

At times I had to eat seal meat that had been in contact with teeguk, and afterwards was unable to get the taste out of my mouth for days. If I was in a house in which teeguk fat was being used in the kudlik, I had to go outside every few hours for fresh air in order to keep from being ill. In the early spring when we hunted the young seals in the aglos under the snow, I often broke into an aglo expecting to grab a young seal, only to be greeted by the overpowering stench of an old teeguk seal.

At Aulatseevik the Eskimos were overjoyed at the first teeguk seal harpooned. Everyone had a big feed of the meat while I ate frozen fish. But that was the first and last time they ate it that year. Afterwards, everyone looked on teeguk meat with disgust, fit only for the dogs. Idlouk said that this was the way with teeguk meat; after the first meal he ate it only when there was no other food. Why he liked it the first time and not again, and why this pattern was repeated year after year, he did not know. It was just so.

Of all the foods eaten at Aulatseevik none aroused the enthusiasm of the Eskimos more than a dish called *aluk*. This word is used to describe a spoon and it also indicates any dish that is eaten with a spoon, even though the dish may have another name which refers to content rather than to the manner in which the dish is eaten. Rolled oats for instance, of which the Eskimos eat a lot when they have the money to buy them at the store, are called *akeetooyak* in their uncooked state. This name is also used after they have been cooked, but then they also become aluk, the dish you eat with a spoon.

On certain occasions aluk means one specific food, an ancient dish of the land made by the old women at the camp in a way handed down from mother to daughter for generations. To some groups of Eskimos it is a commonplace dish, but to the Eskimos of north Baffin it is a rare delicacy, for the basic ingredient is caribou fat which is hard to get at a seal culture camp. It is never eaten as ordinary food; it is made part of a feast in which all members of the camp take part, young and old jammed together in one of the small houses, laughing and talking, eating and eating until stomachs distend so that the participants in the feast can hardly stoop to get out of the door.

As I have related previously, early in the fall Kitchooalik and Oodleteetuk had been taken by boat to the land across the bay from the camp and there put ashore with their sleds and dogs. We saw no more of them until three weeks later when, late in the evening of a very dark night, all the dogs started to howl and we knew a sled was approaching over the ice. We dashed outside into the cold to see the sleds of Kitchooalik and Oodleteetuk pull to a halt on the beach. Each sled had a load of two frozen caribou carcasses, four in all, and sixteen fine new skins covered the loads of meat. While the two weary hunters greeted their wives and children, willing hands unharnessed the dogs and dragged the frozen meat and skins into the ice house on the beach. This done, everyone gathered in Idlouk's house to drink tea, listening while Kitchooalik told of the adventures on the hunt.

The heat inside our little house, plus the effect of three cups of hot tea in their stomachs, made the returned hunters' heads droop as the story was being told. Oodleteetuk went to sleep sitting up while Kitchooalik talked, and then finally they both staggered off to their house to sleep. We did not see them again for twenty-four hours.

Late that night our house was quiet; seven people dozed and dreamed, each in a world of his own. Idlouk and the three boys slept; Kidlak sewed; Leah made a small sealskin doll; I made the daily entry in my diary. Of physical privacy in our little house there was none, but occasionally it was possible to achieve a certain privacy within the mind.

Suddenly the outer door was flung violently open and the voice of a small boy floated in from the dark of the outer snow porch, "Aluk, aluk, aluk. Kigeechee, kigeechee." "Aluk, aluk, aluk. Come along, come along."

In a moment our house was a bedlam. Idlouk was awake in an instant, shouting to Leah to bring his sealskin boots. Kidlak frantically searched the cluttered shelf for spoons. Everyone dashed out of the door into the crisp night air, each with a spoon clutched tightly in one hand. The night was pitch black. After coming from the light of the houses, we could see nothing and stumbled, laughing, over dogs sleeping on the snow. Across the beach we made our way all heading for the next house but one, the home of Akomalik and Agnowyah, Idlouk's parents. Others joined us, laughing and talking about the aluk to come.

In a few minutes everyone except Oodleteetuk and Kitchooalik was gathered in the tiny house. On the sleeping platform the women and children sat, bare feet tucked underneath; men and boys crowded the tiny patch of floor. In each hand was clutched a grubby spoon, on each face an excited glow. Behind the seal-oil lamp, patiently building up its flame, Agnowyah sat. In front of her, below the rim of the lamp, was a rectangular roast pan filled to the brim with a dirty white substance that looked like a cake mix, stirred up but unbaked. This was the aluk, the dish we would eat with a spoon, the very special aluk made of the back fat of the fall-killed caribou, as succulent a dish as can be found in any snow house across the top of the world.

For three hours prior to our coming, Agnowyah had been busy. Into the deep tray she had first put a quantity of caribou fat and heated it slightly over the gentle flame of the seal-oil lamp. With the tray on the sleeping platform at her knees, she then began to stir the mass of fat with her fingers, grubby unwashed fingers, but this apparently added zest to the dish. Slowly she stirred alternating from one hand to the other as fingers became stiff and muscles tired under the ceaseless movement. Every ten minutes or so she spoke softly to her husband who sat close by. He rose and, taking a small tin from the food tray beside the door, poured a quantity of rancid seal oil into the tray as the fingers stirred on. A half cupful of water was added and mixed with the mass. Half hour passed into an hour, still there was no cessation of the movement of the hands.

Under the continuous mixing, the fat fluffed up and spread over the tin. Higher and higher it rose, bubbling up slowly as if charged with baking powder or gas. The process went on for three hours—stir, stir, stir, add rancid seal oil and water, stir, stir, stir—.

Not until the mixture rose to the edge of the pan did Agnowyah sit back with a sigh. She dipped a finger into the mass and put a small amount on her tongue, rolling it around in her mouth. Then she relaxed and murmured, "It is ready, call the others in."

Immediately her grandson, Danielee, who had been sitting watching beside the door, jumped to his feet and dashed from the house. From house to house he ran, pausing at each one only long enough to open the outer door and shout for the occupants to come. In a few minutes everyone at the camp was gathered in Agnowyah's house, talking and laughing, spoons held poised for the attack.

When everyone was ready, Agnowyah passed the tray to the man closest to her. He took a spoonful of the mixture and passed the tray to his neighbour. From hand to hand went the tray and at each a spoon dug deep and transferred a liberal quantity of aluk to its owner's mouth. Only at the small boys did the tray come to a momentary halt to allow them full chance of getting their share. Across to the women and children on the sleeping platform it went, each one taking her share and helping the small ones get theirs. When it came back to Agnowyah, she took a spoonful and started the tray around the circle of men again.

Round and round the house went the tray, and after each passing it held less and less. Few words were spoken for the mixture was gummy and not easy to get out of the mouth. Everyone chewed and chewed trying to be ready for the pan the next time it passed by. Five times the pan circled the house before ending up at Agnowyah with not a single trace of aluk inside. Only then did the excited talk resume. Months had passed since aluk had been tasted in the camp, and how the Aulatseevikmiut had looked forward to this day. Akomalik spoke a sharp word to his two grandsons who dashed out of the door into the darkness of the porch. A moment later they backed inside dragging with them a whole carcass of frozen caribou. As they placed it on the floor of the house, Kadluk picked up a small hand axe. With a mighty chop he split a huge chunk of frozen meat from the shoulder and handed it to the women on the sleeping platform. More blows from the axe, and more meat flew free. Soon everyone in the house was eating raw frozen caribou meat from the carcass lying on the floor.

Again a silence settled over the house. For ten or fifteen minutes everyone ate, stuffing the meat into their mouths as if they expected never to have any more. The axe scarcely stopped chopping and small knives carved busily. Splinters of frozen meat cluttered the already littered floor. Slowly talk resumed as stomachs began to fill and people dawdled over tidbits exclaiming their delight at such exquisite food. Everyone ate until they could physically eat no more.

One by one they closed their pocket knives or put on their shoes and disappeared out through the door. An hour after the aluk had started a silence had settled over the camp. Under the dark skies the camp lay quiet and still; the Aulatseevikmiut slept, stomachs distended, content with their lot.

The first aluk I attended was an unsatisfactory affair. I knew only that a very special Eskimo dish was in the offing and had decided to take still pictures of the Eskimos as they ate. When the call came and the others grabbed for the spoons, I stuffed my camera into its insulated bag and dashed over to Agnowyah's house, ready to record the event. As the tray passed from hand to hand, I manœuvred in the tiny house trying to get good pictures. But when I finished and exchanged the camera for a spoon I found that I was too late, the aluk pan had been picked as clean as a boiled bone. For many days afterwards this provided humour for all at the camp.

The next time I heard that an aluk was in the offing I resolved to be in the front line. When the invitation came, I grabbed a large tablespoon from the shelf and ran with the rest to Agnowyah's house once again. The tray passed under my nose and I dug the spoon in deep. Up came a tremendous spoonful of the gooey mass which I popped into my mouth and began to chew. The taste was unusual, with a strong tang of tainted meat and fat. I chewed and chewed, and chewed some more, but there was little I could do with it. When the tray passed again I had to watch it go by, my spoon at my side, for my mouth was still full of aluk, a gummy ball of fat too big to swallow and impossible to break up. Twice I had to let the tray go by, while I struggled to do something with the mouthful I had. The Eskimos noticed my predicament and all began to laugh. They pointed at me and laughed until tears ran down their cheeks. Still I struggled with the mass in my mouth. Finally I could stand it no longer and dashed outside to get rid of the ball. Returning I joined in the mirth and meekly asked for some more.

Such dishes as aluk meant a great deal to the Aulatseevikmiut. It provided them with a favourite food, but, more than that, it somehow symbolized much of what was fine in their life. For the aluk was a dish that brought memories of a life that has almost passed; memories of great events that took place long before the white man entered the land— the caribou hunts on the inland plains in the fall; the gathering of the camps at the floe edge in the spring and at the fish rivers in the fall. These are memories that raise nostalgia for the days of long ago, for they were good things in the life and they happen no more. These events brought the Eskimos together, even if for only a short time, in the same way that the Aulatseevikmiut came together to eat the aluk in the small house of Agnowyah.

Community gatherings occur less and less in the Eskimos' changing world and the coming of the white man has been responsible for the change. We brought new concepts of private property and individual freedom into their lives. The operation of a trap line introduced the element of competition, and competition is opposed to the concept of all things for the common good. Less and less the Eskimos fished and hunted as a group, or a community of groups. More and more they travelled their individual trap lines, hunting food for themselves. They looked upon the fox pelts as their own; the element of private property attained new stature in their lives.

This development has been inevitable in the face of past and present events. To a great extent it is necessary, for it is on such bases that our economy functions. It provides much of the motivation for advancement of members of a group, although in so doing it can bring grief as well. Although the Eskimos never developed a stabilized community, the harsh environment often forced them to work together in their land. A rebirth of this "working together" might help them develop it more fully into a new way of life.

CHAPTER
17

THROUGHOUT January light appeared a little earlier each morning and farther to the south-east, while the pale light of the dusk hung longer in the afternoon sky and daily crept farther to the south-west. February dawned with light slowly growing out of the eastern sky and dying out behind the high rock hills due west. Still no sun shone on the land although the mid-day sky overhead often reflected shafts of light from the sun as it hung, invisible, below the horizon to the south. During the first week in February we could see the faint blue outline of our shadows against the pinky whiteness of the snow. On February 6th Idlouk said, "To-morrow the sun will return to our land."

In the small hours of the following morning the white shrouded land lay deep in shadow, only the craggy outlines of the distant rocky hills faintly etched the blue of the sky. Overhead myriads of stars twinkled in the clear frosty air; long shafts of ghostly white light wavered across the sky as the mysterious northern lights danced ghost-like among the stars, but in puny display compared to those of the sub-Arctic lands to the south. Not a breath of wind stirred the frost-bitten air; the only sound was the occasional muted thump of heavy sea ice dropping on a falling tide. Fifty below zero, and the land lay deep in sleep.

Slowly, almost imperceptibly at first, the darkness became less intense. Far off in the sky to the east stars began to pale and the colour of the sky changed from midnight blue to dull grey. The shadows lightened, the land assumed shape and form; the snow, the rocks the ice. The grey of the snow turned to pale blue as stars were rapidly swallowed up by the encroaching light. High in the heavens, the shadow cast by the tremendous mass of our earth could be seen rushing through space, retreating northward and westward under the press of the whirling sun. Star after star was snuffed out until only the brightest of them still shone out of the sky in the north.

High cirrus clouds built up a thin veil to the east. Slowly they shifted in pattern. Suddenly a tiny shaft of pink shot straight up into the sky. Another followed and another until the entire sky to the south-east was aglow with a shifting pink veil that gradually deepened to mauve then changed to red. Over the top of the hills to the south a bright halo of yellow light came into view chasing all colour from the sky, and the land stood out clearly in the pale, ever-whitening light.

The high rock walls of the tallest hills first caught the rays of the slowly rising sun. Their dark surfaces and snow-filled crevices took on a deep reddish hue that grew brighter and brighter until the top of every hill glowed red with fire. Down the hillside raced this red light, chasing a dark shadow in headlong flight, until in a last mad dash all shade disappeared as if swallowed up whole. Over the horizon to the south the red, red rim of the sun peered out on the frozen surface of the sea. For a few minutes the land lay bathed in its light before the sun slid slowly from view below the distant hills. The sun had returned to north Baffin again.

In the days to follow I often watched repeat performances of this magnificent dawn of each new day; and I was moved deeply by them. Here was release from the world of physical things. I stood facing something much bigger than my life on earth, something that stirred forces deep within about which I was only vaguely conscious. Standing thus with face upturned to the morning sky, I felt detached from the earth. Wave afer wave of emotion swept through my soul at the majesty and grandeur of the display. How easy to understand the worship of sun, moon and star. How easy to establish a heaven in the sky, for no earthly being could produce such beauty and colour. I stood in the presence of God, and I felt the touch of His hand on my throat.

Here was the essence of the deficiencies I found in my Eskimo life. For alone of the Aulatseevikmiut I stood under the changing sky. My friends still slept or hurried about gathering up the dogs, preparing for the day's hunt. Theirs was the physical world of yesterday and today, a world they could see and feel with eye and hand. Their emotions were intense and narrow for they lived largely within themselves; fear of the unknown burned strong in their breast. They avoided the new and unknown and stayed close to the world they knew, a world almost untouched by beauty. No Eskimo I have met has ever been moved by the delicate curve of a piece of wind-sculptured snow, by the fragile beauty of crystals of water-washed sea ice, by the music of the wind on the sea, by the sight of a magnificent sunset in a sky of glacial blue. Even their ivory and soapstone carvings reflect their preoccupation with the world of physical things.

Many people have asked me if I found it difficult to eat raw meat as a staple food, to endure the intense cold, to go for long periods without bathing. To this I must answer that physically one can do almost anything one desires within the capacity of the individual body. I have little trouble with wind and cold, or eating raw meat. Indeed, I prefer some types of meat to be eaten raw and I often feel exhilarated in a storm.

But if I have no trouble with physical things, I am bothered by matters less well defined. Let me quote from my diary an entry I made on October 12th, 1953, after I had lived at Idlouk's camp for five months. I had just come through the best part of the Eskimo year, the long dark winter still lay ahead. It was early evening as I made the entry and all the hunters were gathered in the house talking, smoking and drinking tea.

Slowly I am learning how restricted the world of the Eskimo can be. Endlessly we talk of the hunt, of the weather, of the dogs, of the condition of the surface of the sea. We talk of yesterday and today, perhaps even tomorrow, but rarely of next week, next month or next year. We talk of the concrete things we can see and feel and hear. Rarely do we talk in the abstract and when we do, it is only for a very short time, for the effort involved seems to exhaust the Eskimo mind. My friends belong to an age long since past. Their lives are bound up in snow and ice, wind and water, seals and whales. When they become restless their only outlet lies in physical release of energy. They go off hunting and trapping, travelling for miles over the sea until they feel calm again. If they cannot travel or hunt, then they eat and eat until they can eat no more, then sleep the restlessness away.

I am a product of the twentieth century, a civilized man trying to live the life of a primitive hunter. I am enjoying the life I live, for it presents a challenge, and I must answer that challenge. But to attempt to live this way for a lifetime with only the mental and spiritual horizons of the Eskimo would be sheer murder for me. Decry civilization with its disease and war if you must, but do not sell it short for the ephemeral glories of the simple life of primitive man. I am fond of my adopted land and of the people with whom I am living and working, But I am beginning to get pictures into my head that seem to express the endlessness of this way of life: Kidlak scraping a sealskin as the women have done for longer than anyone can remember; Idlouk skinning a seal after the fashion that must have been evolved in ages now long since dead; Kadluk patiently carving a harpoon head that was designed six hundred years ago and that has changed not a bit since that time; little Mosesee growing up into a carbon copy of his father, everything he does an almost exact imitation of practices laid down in the misty days of a far distant past. Why are we alive when our race has been doing the same things for the past hundred years, perhaps the past thousand years, perhaps even the past ten thousand? Never is there a sign of expression of hope for a better life in the future; the future is merely a continuation of the past. Rarely do the Eskimos think of comfort, they are so inured to hardship that to search for a better life simply never occurs to them. Hardship is their heritage, transient happiness their only hope.

Physically I had no trouble becoming *inoongwah,* one living in the likeness of an Eskimo; mentally I could not do so. I live for the future, always striving to make it better than the past. Thought of the future is behind almost every move I make; I accept the past only in so much as it enables me to understand better what may lie ahead. My concept of hardship in the Arctic lies not in the physical aspects of the land and of the life, but in the restrictions that are placed on my intellectual, cultural and spiritual activities by the very nature of the people with whom I live and work. Deprive me of access to philosophical talk, cut me off from music and poetry, from contemporary sculpture and fine art, from the accumulated wisdom and knowledge of our libraries, take away my contact with men of science, of religion, of commerce, of art, and all meaning goes out of my life; I stand condemned to die a slow death.

THE RETURN of the sun seemed to inject new energy into the hunters of Aulatseevik. Although we were never a group to spend much time in the houses at the camp, through February and March wives saw husbands and sons less and less as they roamed far and wide over the ice, hunting for food or journeying on the long trips to the traps. Temperatures were still in the low forties, storms still swept out of the north, travel was anything but comfortable on the slow-moving sled, but this did not matter any more; we had the light from the sun to guide us over the snow. By the first of March, we could face the sun at mid-day and feel the warmth of its rays on our cheek, even though our parka hoods were rimmed round with a white collar of thick frost and ice.

Certainly I felt the release from the long period of dark. During December, January and early February, I had been too busy to have the darkness get on my nerves. I found that I did not think about the land being any other way and went about my business, making the necessary adaptations to a life without light. But without noticing it, my attitude toward life had undergone a slow change. Rather than take an active interest in all that went on, I had simply been doing the job that was required, without zest, thinking only that the job had to be done. In so doing some of the joy of living went out of my life, but so slowly that it did not make itself actively felt. Not until the daylight hours began to lengthen again as the sun crept closer and closer to the southern horizon each day at noon did something stir deep inside me. I became increasingly restless as the days wore on. By the time the sun peered over the horizon to the south, I wanted no part of life at the camp. I wanted to go and go and go, to travel far and wide over the ice.

That this feeling was universal among the hunters was plain to see. "It is this way each year," said Idlouk. "When the light returns to the land I cannot stay at the camp longer than a day. In the winter I do not mind spending three or four days at my house, but with light on the land again, I cannot sit still. Our camp has meat in plenty, but still I must hunt and hunt, travelling miles over the sea ice. Most of the Eskimos are this way. It is as if something had burst and scattered us far and wide. You notice when we visit the other camps now, how seldom there are any men around? They are like ourselves, good hunters and bad; they are out hunting, always on the move."

As the sun climbed higher in the sky each day, we began to wear sun glasses to protect our eyes from the fierce glare. The smooth white surface of the sea reflected the rays of the sun as from a giant mirror, burning our faces to a deep brown, bringing on attacks of snowblindness whenever we forgot to wear sun glasses while hunting on the ice. In the days before the coming of the white man, the Eskimos made their sun glasses from strips of bone or ivory in which a number of narrow slits or holes had been drilled. Today they buy them from the store. Both the old and new type of glasses fulfilled the purpose of protecting eyes from the sun. The old style goggles were superior to the new in that they were virtually unbreakable; but they were inferior because they limited the line of vision one could take in without movement of the head. Wearing the old slit bone goggles, it was impossible to see the ground near your feet without looking down, which was bothersome while hunting seals on the ice.

The days when the sun beats down on the snow from a cloudless sky are very hard on the eyes, but they are not the days when one has to be most afraid of contracting snow-blindness. On heavily overcast days all perspective is lost, the land becomes largely a misty white blur in which detail is hard to find. On such days one always strains to see things which under other conditions would be perfectly visible. Eyes that are wide open throughout the day, continually peering into the vague whiteness of snow and ice ahead, are almost sure to become snowblind unless dark glasses are worn at all times. The discomforts of snowblindness can easily be avoided by always taking proper precautions to protect the eyes. I class snowblindness with frostbite, for both are the result of carelessness on the part of the individual. Accidents can always happen but, under normal circumstances, when a person suffers excessive frostbite or snowblindness it is usually his own fault.

By the first of March the hours of daylight in each twenty-four hour period equalled the hours of dark. The early spring months brought the clearest weather north Baffin Island enjoyed during the year. Day after day the sun shone down out of cloudless skies. Temperatures remained low, ranging down to forty below, but the high rising sun offset this, bringing a warmth nothing else seemed able to impart. Only when storms blew out of the north did the cold bite of the frosty air make us take shelter. No longer did we gulp down our tea at mug-up time on the trail; we sat on the snow, backs to the sled, faces to the warmth of the sun, sipping and talking, revelling in the comfort of the heat we felt on our faces. We still wore our caribou skin clothing and had to keep our caribou mitts on while holding the enamel mug or eating the frozen meat, but this did not detract from the sense of warmth we got from the rays of the ever-climbing spring sun.

As we had been doing throughout the winter, we alternated hunting at the aglos for seals with making trips along the trap lines. As the end of the trapping season approached, interest in the trap line declined, for rarely did we find foxes. It was not unusual for us to return to camp, after being gone for ten days visiting over one hundred and fifty traps, and have only two or three fox skins on the sled. When the trapping season ended on March 31st, Idlouk had caught only thirty-four foxes for the winter, a total earning for him of two hundred and fifty dollars for five months' work. This was barely enough money to provide the necessities from the store during the winter months and left no money for the summer needs, none for replacing equipment such as clothing, rifles, boats and other items that were continuously wearing out. But he did not complain; after ten years of such ups and downs, he and his group were used to doing without. Not once did he suggest that he would like to use some of the money that was mounting to his credit at the store for acting as my parent, although I often was tempted to suggest that some of it be used. I did not do so for two reasons: the success of my entire trip depended on having nothing interfere with the normal life of the camp; and I knew that Idlouk, realizing this better than anyone else, would not agree to use the money until after I had left his camp.

The month of March brought an air of expectancy to the camps on north Baffin. In that month the baby seals, *netiaks* as the Eskimos call them, were born in the aglos under the snow on the sea ice. Each day the sun shone through the tiny window of our house to cast a square of bright light on the wall at the rear. "The day on which the rays of the sun shining through the windows of our house creep down to touch the sleeping platform at noon, will mark the beginning of the time when the young seals start to be born," said Idlouk, "and we shall hunt them out from their aglos under the snow." On March 14th we captured our first baby seal.

During most of the year seals roam as individuals, but in August they mate and often appear in pairs swimming along in the open water near the rocky shores. By the middle to the end of September the mothers are carrying the young, usually only one but occasionally twins. Except for the hair, the seals are perfectly formed very shortly after conception, and often we would cut the tiny red body from the womb of a mother we had shot or harpooned and take it back to camp for the young children to use as a doll. There was no easy way to distinguish the male from the female seal when it was swimming in the water.

Throughout the winter the unborn seal grows bigger, from a bare six inches in length to about eighteen inches at birth. By mid-February, the body is covered with a downy white fur and it is in this garb that the small seal first sees the light of day. As the time of birth draws near, the mother seal chooses a breathing hole above which a drift of snow has formed. She enlarges the hole, climbs out onto the ice, and proceeds to make a large cavern, or a series of tunnels, in the drift, all of which have access to the hole in the ice leading to the sea. In the caverns or tunnels the baby seals are born and here they spend the first weeks of their lives until the downy white baby fur moults and is replaced by the dark mottled grey fur of the adult seal. The netiak then becomes a *netiavenik*, "that which was a baby seal before." Until mid-May the young seals stay close to their mother, but by June they usually are on their own, self-sufficient in every way.

I have always been fascinated by the correlation of various natural events in our world and the example of the reproduction of the seals seems to be an excellent illustration of this. The seals mate when there is open water in which they can swim about together; the mother carries the unborn seal during the season when the ice covers the sea and forces one of her most rapacious enemies, the killer whale, to leave the area for the open sea, freeing the seal from fear of death at its jaws; the young seals are born during the first month of winter in which there are sure to be deep drifts of snow on the ice in which the caverns can be dug; and the baby seal quickly reaches maturity in the caverns with a good degree of protection from marauding mammals above, such as polar bears, foxes, wolves and man.

For the first month of its life the baby seal lives almost entirely in the cavern, diving into the sea only if forced to do so by the mother when she senses that danger is near. Except for appearance, the baby seal is much like the human child; it suckles at its mother's breast, its cries are identical to those of a month-old child. The big brown eyes staring out of the winsome, fur-covered face make its head not unlike that of some monkeys I have seen at the zoo. Even the thought that I was killing for food and clothing could never dispel my regrets whenever we caught a baby seal. The Eskimos hunt it chiefly for its skin; the soft white fur is much valued for use as insert material in fancy sealskin boots, as well as in rugs and slippers made for sale to the store. The skins are also purchased by the store for seventy-five cents apiece, not a high price, but enough to give them value especially in a year that has been poor in fox fur. The meat of baby seals under two weeks old has no fat and is considered unfit as human food. But the meat from a three-week-old seal, simmered slowly over the gentle flame of the seal-oil lamp, is as tender and delicious as any spring chicken could be.

After the fourteenth of March our seal hunting tactics changed considerably. No longer did we drive the sled over the ice waiting for the dogs to smell out the aglos and lead us to the places where the seal lay hidden under the snow. No longer did we search out the new cracks after the periods of high tides looking for aglos in the thin new ice. Now our eyes scanned the surface of the sea ahead, looking for areas in which hummocks of ice had caused deep drifts of wind-blown snow to form, for it was under such drifts that the young and their mothers lived. When in an area in which many such drifts had grown up, we left the dogs to sleep on the snow and, taking our seal harpoons and lines, walked for miles over the ice searching out the aglos under the snow.

At first I was useless on this type of hunt for I could not tell which were the most likely drifts. But as the days wore on, and I followed Idlouk on the hunts, I began to see the drifts as they appeared to him. Superficially they were all alike, but a careful study revealed that a few significantly differed from the rest. When a seal hollows out an aglo under a drift, the heat from its body, and the body of the young, causes the snow above the aglo to settle slightly. On the surface this produces an almost unnoticeable concave depression in the snow. The snow surface is covered by such depressions formed by the winter winds, but there is something about a depression over an aglo that is different. The difference is one I cannot describe. I recognize it more by feeling than by sight. Some people, and this includes both Eskimos and whites, attain a high degree of perfection at spotting the depressions that signify aglos beneath, while others never are able to tell. Fortunately I am among those who can tell, and although I have yet to reach a high standard of efficiency, I did become proficient enough that I could take an active part in the hunts.

When searching out the drifts that have aglos beneath, the hunter walks quietly, skirting the large ice hummocks by a distance of fifty feet or more, trying to keep the main drifts between himself and the sun. This backlights the snow and causes any slight depression to stand out. If he circles an ice hummock and sees nothing that leads him to believe there might be an aglo beneath, he walks up to it and, with the steel shaft of the harpoon, probes down into the snow along the full length of all the drifts. If there is no aglo, the harpoon shaft slides down with equal pressure. But if there is one, the harpoon will move evenly through the layer of snow above and then break free into the opening beneath and drop to the ice surface or perhaps even into the water of the hole in the ice. When this happens the hunter jumps into the air and breaks in the snow cover, hoping to find a baby seal in the aglo and get to it before it can be shepherded into the sea by the mother. He does not usually get a seal as both the baby and the mother will have heard the footsteps above and at the first sign of danger have disappeared into the hole. But by breaking in the snow cover, the hunter drives the baby and the mother to other aglos in the vicinity that he hopes to find by sighting the depression on the snow.

Idlouk caught three young seals before I made my first capture. We were searching out aglos on the ice of Eclipse Sound about five miles north of the island of Aulatseevik. We had left the dogs and sled, and were walking along parallel to one another but about half a mile apart, checking all the ice hummocks we passed. Although the temperature was thirty below, I was very hot; warm air rising up from my body escaped around the neck of my parka and coated my eyebrows, hair, and parka hood with a thick crust of frost. After walking for about two miles and not seeing anything that I felt was an aglo, I caught sight of a shallow depression in the snow beside a single upright piece of ice about fifty yards ahead.

Immediately I stopped and looked all about. I moved carefully around the spot letting the shadows thrown by the low-lying sun outline the extent of the depression. As I circled I became more and more convinced that an aglo lay beneath. Slowly I walked in towards the depression, my feet in their caribou skin boots slipping noiselessly into the deep soft snow. Twenty-five yards away I halted and transferred my harpoon and line to my left hand. Across the ice I could see Idlouk still walking over the ice; otherwise nothing else moved, no sound broke the stillness of the late afternoon. Twenty-five yards away I felt sure a baby seal and its mother lay on the ice under the snow. I could see nothing of them, of course, and could not be sure they were there except for that one shallow depression that somehow I felt to be not quite like the other depressions that dotted the snow. I took a deep breath and suddenly started to sprint over the snow.

Up to the drift I dashed as fast as I could go. In seconds I reached the depression. Quickly I shuffled about, thumping on the hard snow of the drift with my heels. At once I felt the hollowness of the cavern beneath. I jumped high in the air and, with knees stiff and heels pointed down, came down hard onto the snow. The weight of my body on outstretched legs sent me crashing through the hard snow roof to sprawl awkwardly in a wide cavern beneath. One foot slipped into the water of the hole leading into the sea wetting my leg to the knee. Quickly I scrambled upright and ducked down into the cave, looking about for some sign of a young seal. I was fortunate in that I had broken into the aglo right above the hole and thus cut off all escape to the sea.

The aglo was a series of low caves that radiated out from the breathing hole in the ice. Two ran off to the left for about six feet and I could see they contained no seal. But a third took a jog about five feet along its length, and I could not see to its end. Placing a chunk of snow over the entrance to this cave, I climbed out of the hole, ran along the snow above the cave, and by tapping the snow with my heel found the cavern beneath. Once again I jumped in the air and came down hard on the snow, breaking in the roof over the canyon back of the bend. Lying full length on the snow, I let my head and shoulders down into the hole and peered all about. There, not three feet from my head I looked into the big brown eyes of a baby seal, crouched against the snow at the end of the cave. I reached in with my mitted hand and, catching it by a front flipper, pulled it out onto the snow.

By this time Idlouk had come up for he had seen me jump in the air and break into the aglo. While I held the baby seal in my arms, he quickly readied his harpoon and then, taking the seal from me, tied a short length of stout cord to one hind flipper and let the baby seal loose on the ice. The cord had a large knot about two feet above the point where it was tied to the seal. We then worked together clearing the blocks of loose snow away from the hole into the sea. Taking his harpoon, Idlouk jumped down into the cavern and stood over the water in the hole. He rested the harpoon across the edges of the broken snow, harpoon by his right hand and the line by his left. Around one leg he securely tied the end of the harpoon line. I retrieved the baby seal and gave it to him. Holding the end of the cord tied to its flipper in his left hand he dropped the seal into the water where it promptly disappeared under the ice.

We were using the baby as bait to try also to get its mother. The mother seal would not be far away and we hoped the cries of the baby would make her risk coming back to see if she could help her young.

Back and forth the little one swam, crying for its mother. In a few minutes its white head appeared above the surface of the water in the hole, and it bobbed gently about, breathing on the surface. After allowing it to replenish its breath, Idlouk tapped it on the head with the harpoon handle and immediately it dived into the sea and commenced swimming about. For a minute or two nothing happened, then suddenly I saw Idlouk's body tense. Slowly he reached for the harpoon and raised it above his head. Turning to me he whispered, "The mother is down there. She has a hold of her baby. I can feel her trying to tug it away."

Slowly he drew in the baby seal by the cord, taking care not to jerk it free of its mother. By the tautness of the cord I knew the mother held her young in her front flippers, trying to draw it away from the hole. Up and up it came until the knot in the cord broke the surface. Idlouk raised the harpoon high, but before he could bring it down, there was a tremendous splash in the water of the hole and the baby seal bobbed to the surface alone. The mother had taken fright, let go of her young, and dived deep into the sea.

243

Once more the baby seal bobbed in the hole breathing until Idlouk tapped it again. Down it went and we waited in silence once more. Minutes passed; there was no sign of the mother. I thought she had gone until once again Idlouk tensed and reached for the harpoon. "She has come back again," he whispered, "this time I will get her."

Slowly and carefully he drew the cord in. Foot by foot it rose above the surface, weaving tautly back and forth as the invisible seal waged a tug of war for her young. The knot broke the suface and Idlouk's arm went up high, paused, then came down with a flash. As his right arm came down, his left, holding the cord attached to the baby seal, jerked up, pulling the baby out of its mother's flippers and onto the ice nearby. Immediately there was a tremendous commotion in the water below. The water slopped up and down, the harpoon was jerked from sight beneath the surface, and the harpoon line ran out free as the seal, with the harpoon head buried deep in her back, took off for the deep. Idlouk and I grabbed the line and hung on. The seal reached the limit of the line and tried to pull free, but the harpoon head held firm and so did we. The seal was safely hooked. Back and forth it swam under the ice while we hung on above. In about five minutes the line suddenly went slack and Idlouk picked up the handle of his harpoon which was close by in the snow. Handle raised above his head he waited. In a moment the large head of the seal broke the surface and down came Idlouk's arm. The steel shaft sank through the skull with scarcely a sound. The seal relaxed in death while blood flowed freely into the water and slush of the hole.

We were not always successful in attracting the mother back to her young. In fact it was the exception when this happened. Time after time we waited over the broken-in aglo while the baby swam about below crying for help, but no mother appeared to retrieve the young. "Itah," said Idlouk when this happened. "Too bad. The mother seal must have no feeling at all for her young. Imagine her going away and leaving it crying on the end of a string, refusing me the chance to make an easy kill."

Nor were we always successful in capturing baby seals. Often we broke into aglos to find the mother and young had escaped into the sea before we could get through. Once I broke into an aglo right over the escape hole just in time to see the baby seal slide into a second escape hole about six feet farther along. Sometimes we saw two depressions on the snow, about ten feet apart. Then the question arose, were there two escape holes or only one, and if only one, under which of the depressions did it lie? If we chose the wrong one, which we often did, the seals invariably escaped into the sea. All too often we broke into teeguk aglos by mistake, and came up coughing and gagging from the stench. At Aulatseevik we managed to catch only thirty-two baby seals, roughly one for each member of the camp. Only six mothers fell to our harpoons. In this type of hunting, the odds were all with the seals.

BABY SEALS were not the only things arriving on the wings of spring. Ever since Christmas, Kidlak's slight figure had been noticeably thickening at the waist. By March her swollen body made it difficult for her to move about in the cramped confines of our little house, but still she carried on with her normal duties, melting snow for water, sewing clothes, taking care of the children throughout the day. She was helped by Leah, but as the wife and mother she took the brunt of the work. An air of expectancy settled over our house, everyone looking forward to the arrival of Kidlak's tenth child.

When I first arrived at the camp in the spring of 1953, Idlouk and his wife both told me they wanted no more children. But as the small daughter Ruthee gradually began to get around by herself, and as Leah's young body showed the unmistakable signs of budding womanhood, which meant that she would soon marry and leave her parents' home, they reconsidered their decision and decided to have just one more.

"We have decided to have one more child," said Idlouk to me one day, as we paddled side by side in our kayaks hunting seals, "for my wife will be unhappy without a baby girl around the house. Normally we prefer to have boys, but in my family we have too many boys; there is a limit to the number of hunters one needs in a single family. My wife will have life easier as she grows old if we have a young girl around the house to help with the chores, and so we are hoping the new child will be a girl. We do not want a boy. If, when the child is born, it turns out to be a boy we plan to give it away to Merkoshak who has only girls and whose wife can have children no more. Merkoshak is very unhappy that he has no sons. It will be very funny as the time of birth grows near, for my wife and I will be wishing for a girl, and Merkoshak and his wife will be wishing just as hard that it be a boy."

During the winter two children had been born at the camp; a son to Ishoogituk and Oodleteetuk, their first child; and a daughter to Rebecca and Kitchooalik. Each child was born with the mother in the care of the older women of the camp. To the last day, indeed to the last hour, they had gone about their normal duties as best they could, until the pains told them that the time was near. Then they retired to the house of Kadluk to await the coming of the child. All the men, as well as the boys and girls, were excluded from the house, only the older married women who had children of their own were allowed in. Kneeling on the sleeping platform of the dark little house, the expectant mother waited patiently as her baby moved restlessly inside. Beneath her was an old caribou skin on which the baby would be born and which would be used to remove the afterbirth and clean the body of the newly arrived child. Over the seal-oil lamp the kettle bubbled merrily, for when the waiting was all over and the baby cuddled safely to its mother's breast, then all would want a cup of tea while relaxing from the strain.

I have been present at a number of births in the high Arctic lands. Contrary to the popular belief that women of primitive groups generally have babies with relative ease, it is my opinion that Eskimo women are not too unlike women in the rest of Canada. Some present their husbands with babies with the greatest of ease, while others go for long agonizing hours before bringing the child into the world. Ishoogituk had eight hours of labour when giving birth to her son, and the next morning when I visited her I noticed that her lips were badly bitten and she looked pale and wan. But I also know of cases where birth came while the woman was on the trail and the husband barely had time to erect a shelter of snow before the baby was born. Usually the husband tries to be away at the time the baby is expected to arrive, but often he finds himself in the role of midwife for the birth.

With no heat or light other than that supplied by the seal-oil lamps, the Eskimo baby arrives in this world. The little red body steams in the cold as the midwives wipe it dry before one puts it to her breast until the mother is ready to take over. Word spreads through the camp that the baby has arrived, that it is a boy or a girl, that the mother had trouble or the baby came easily. In twos and threes the people gradually gather in the house where the mother lies on her side, her new baby snuggled tight to her breast. Proudly she shows her child, and the others lean over to touch the tiny wrinkled hand and listen to the lusty cry. Everyone drinks mug after mug of steaming tea, and talks about life and death, and about the new child.

It may well be that the child has already been promised in marriage even before birth. Good friends often offer the hand of the unborn child of one of the wives to the little offspring of the other, providing it proves to be of the right sex. The boy and girl grow up knowing they will marry one day, even though they may see little of one another in their adolescent life. This practice of parents promising the hand of young children has often been decried as violating the fundamental freedom of the individual to make a free choice. I have no doubt that the practice is subject to abuse, but in my experience in the Canadian Eastern Arctic it seems to work very well. The parent is usually motivated by only one thought when he seeks a mate for his child; he is trying to find someone who will be a good wife or husband; if a girl, a good sewer and cook; if a boy, a good trapper and hunter. Then the parent knows that his child's marriage will have the best chance of success. If a son is born, the father immediately casts about among his immediate friends for one whose wife is an excellent sewer and a good cook, and not a gossiper likely to be a troublemaker within a group. If he finds such a person and that person has a young daughter who has not been promised, he will ask that his son be permitted to marry the daughter when the two little ones grow up. Or if the friend has no daughter, but his wife is expecting a child, he will ask for the hand of the unborn child if it should turn out to be a daughter.

Immediately after birth the child is given a name. Formerly the grandparents named the young child, and if it was the first-born, the grandparents often took the child and raised it as their own, although today this practice is dying out. Names were often those of deceased relatives who had been good men and women in their day and whose spirit was thought to live in the body of the child so named. With this rose the belief that to chastise a child was wrong, for you were really chastising the deceased grandparent which was not a good thing to do. Other factors have a bearing on the attitude prevalent among most Eskimo groups that to chastise a young child is wrong. One of these is that in the Eskimo society the child, as it matures and comes of age, will look after the parents as they grow old, and parents, knowing this, do not want a child to grow up thinking ill of them, for their lives will one day be in the child's hands. Today some Eskimo parents do spank their children; it is a part of the changing attitudes of the group. Idlouk and his wife, who chastise their sons and daughters for doing wrong, have been criticized by other Eskimos who do not think this is right. Idlouk retaliated by quoting six different references in the New Testament to show that spanking of children is a good thing.

Today Eskimos are passing through the stage of naming their children after Biblical characters, a trend encouraged by the Anglican missionaries. In my own family there were children with the names Leah, Noahkudluk, Mosesee. The odd endings are the result of the names being taken from the Testaments, printed in syllabic characters. This system, in which sounds are represented by syllables, is the only form of writing the Eskimos of the Eastern Arctic understand. It is a phonetic system of writing first devised by the Reverend James Evans for use with the Cree Indians in northern Manitoba and later introduced by the Anglican and Roman Catholic missionaries into the Eastern Arctic. Syllabic writing is unknown in the Western Arctic where the Eskimos write Eskimo using the English alphabet. Syllabic character writing, while an excellent means of teaching illiterate groups to read and write an unwritten language in a short space of time, has outlived its usefulness in the Canadian Arctic. It is too inexact to convey clearly words and meanings to any but those with an intimate knowledge of the Eskimo language. For instance, my Eskimo name is Kingmik, and this is written in syllabic character writing as

The former is the symbol representing the sound KEE, the latter is the symbol representing the sound MEE. Read literally it would be KEEMEE. Only by a complete understanding of the total text in which the symbols would appear could one read them as KINGMIK. Syllabic writing has undoubtedly been responsible for the mispronunciation of many Eskimo names by the whites reading them. KADLUK is written in syllabic characters so as to become KADLOO and is often so pronounced by white people.

The chief drawback to the continued use of syllabic writing is that it is impossible to print any volume of books in it. This means that the Eskimo of the Eastern Arctic is cut off completely from all the great wealth of literature printed in English, or any language using the twenty-six letter alphabet. Newspapers, magazines, books, instruction manuals are useless to him.

Usually, the Eskimos have only one name, or at least use only one name at any one time, although, among some groups, a man will have two or three names and be known by different ones at different times in his life. The single name for each Eskimo led to a great deal of confusion when the issue of Family Allowance was introduced into the country as there are usually many Eskimos of the same name in each area. In order to simplify the identification, the government issued each man, woman and child with a numbered dog-tag to be worn about the neck like a soldier's identification tag. This has kept the records of vital statistics clear although it has not solved the problem of Eskimo names.

Idlouk and Kidlak's child was a girl, born on the night of April 17th. They named the tiny baby Susan. They were both very happy although Idlouk spoke of his regret that his happiness should bring unhappiness to Merkoshak and his wife. As we sat on the sleeping platform sipping tea, the new baby snuggled close to her mother's breast, Idlouk and I talked about the baby, about my young daughter whom I had not seen for over a year, about the sex life of his group. Much has been written about this phase of Eskimo life and usually it stresses the morals of the Eskimos which differ from our own. Certainly their concept of sex and the role it plays in life is quite different from ours. With them sex is not something to be kept in the dark; it is as much a part of everyday life as any other physical act. Their humour is often coarse and earthy, centred on sex life, and among some groups primitive forms of prostitution seem to exist. But with them, as with us, a moral code does exist. It is far more flexible and realistic than ours will ever be. I had known this for a long time, but it was never more strongly brought home than by something Idlouk said to me just before I left his land to return to my home in the south.

"I am very angry with some of the other Eskimos," said Idlouk, "for they are saying that my daughter is your child.

I would not mind if this were so, for you are my friend. Your wife is a friend of me and my wife. As we have often told you over the past year, it is not good for a man to be away from his wife for too long a time. Man needs woman, and woman needs man. Because you are my friend, my wife would have been glad to accommodate you at any time as we have already told you. You did not ask and perhaps this has been best. But now I am angry that some Eskimos should say that my baby is yours when this is not true.

"I will remember you for a long time, Kingmik. I will remember you for many things. But mostly I will remember that you did not ask for my wife, or for any other woman at the camp while you were here. My wife has asked me to tell you that she has always been a little afraid of white men, for many reasons. Now she does not think she will be afraid any more."

18

"ATATAVOOT Kilangmeetooteet, ateneevoot ateereet . . ."
"Our Father who art in Heaven, hallowed be Thy name
. . ."

The low rumble of voices filled our little house at Aulatseevik. It was eleven o'clock in the morning, Sunday April 14th, 1954, my last day as a member of the Aulatseevikmiut; my life as an Eskimo had come to an end. Two days before we had seen the first *ootook* of the year and I shot the seal as it lay on the ice by the breathing hole, basking in the warmth of the high-riding spring sun. For the past three weeks the hours of darkness in each night had grown less and less as the earth tilted on its axis, slowly presenting the north polar regions to the smiling face of the sun. In a few days there would be no night on north Baffin and the return of the long day would bring a repetition of the yearly cycle of life I had just completed.

The women and children were first to arrive for the morning church service. As they entered our house they removed their sealskin boots and sat on the sleeping platform, children at the back, women and girls to the front. The men drifted in, sitting on the low platforms on either side of the door, while the boys set upturned crates on the tiny patch of floor. Every face had been scrubbed until the dark skin shone in the soft light; all clothes were washed as clean as minimum water supplies allowed. The worshippers brought with them the strong smell of laundry soap, for water was far too precious to use for a thorough rinsing of the clothes. Washed once and rinsed once in an inch of water in a tub was all they could afford and if any soap remained it had to stay.

252

Sharp at eleven Idlouk, who sat on a crate near the door, started the service for the day. How different our church service at Aulatseevik from that in cathedrals far to the south; and yet how much the same. The service was read from the Anglican Book of Common Prayer, printed in syllabic character writing, and the sound of the Eskimo language gave the liturgy an unfamiliar ring. Here was no pageantry and pomp, no ostentatious display; here were men and women gathered together for the sole purpose of paying homage to their God. As I sat with the men, and my eyes roamed over these people who were my friends and whom after tomorrow I might never see again, I thought that perhaps the early Christians assembled thus in the caves and grottos of their far-off sun baked lands. Our little house had changed character as the people gathered and the service began. Less and less it became our home; more and more it became our place of worship. Physically it changed not a bit—the soft yellow light from the seal-oil lamps reflected back from damp, paper-covered walls—but subtly the atmosphere became that of a church.

Carefully Idlouk read out the prayers and led the singing of hymns. Until 1935 Idlouk had been a pagan Eskimo. Until that year, he did not believe, as he put it. What changed his mind I do not know but today he and his group are staunch Anglicans, firmly wedded to the Christian church. The Aulatseevikmiut believe firmly and simply. They have an extensive knowledge of the writings of the New Testament, for this book, printed in syllabic characters, is their only form of reading material, and they have come to know the contents well. They do not fully understand much of what they read. As Idlouk often said to me, "I must be very dense. I read what it says here, I know what I read, yet how often I cannot understand it. But no matter, I believe, and that is what is important."

Christian teaching is playing an important role in the re-shaping of the life of the Eskimos. For the first time in their long history they have an organized religion. For the first time they have a written document setting out the fundamental beliefs of that religion. In their old existence their spiritual life hinged on a set of beliefs in spirits, shadowy beings who lived in a world apart. Most of these spirits were evil, out to do harm to the Eskimos if they violated the taboos by not following patterns of conduct prescribed for the group. Some taboos were well founded, but others had little meaning except to give power and scope to the activities of the angakoks, who were neither medicine men nor witch doctors but something of both, people living on earth who could communicate with the spirits of the other world and who interpreted the world of the spirits to the people of the land.

In their pagan existence the Eskimos lived in great fear of the spirits and of the angakoks. Belief in Christianity has done much to dispel these fears and to lessen the power of the angakoks. Most adult Eskimos of today still retain some of the fears of former days but in the younger generation they are weaker. Here and there Eskimos still profess to be angakoks and to have magic power. Their neighbours have a lurking dread of such individuals but the fear is not deep-rooted, for belief in the validity of the angakok's claim to power has weakened considerably. In time it will disappear altogether.

Strange conflicting opinions arise out of the mixture of old and new beliefs. Eskimos, who to all intents seem to have completely accepted the teachings of the Christian church, still retain some belief in the world of the spirits they knew in their youth. Singeetuk is an Anglican Eskimo of the Chesterfield area on the west coast of Hudson Bay. He is forty years old and has lived all his life in the shadow of the white man's world. He speaks quite good English and for the past six years has worked for the medical officer at Chesterfield. In his little house the few Anglican Eskimos of this predominantly Roman Catholic community gather each Sunday to take part in the church service, often conducted by Singeetuk. One evening, as Singeetuk and I sat talking of the old days in his land, he told me of something that had happened in his youth.

254

"I was a boy at the time," he said, "and my family were living south of Iglooleeajuk* for the winter. There were four snow houses in our camp and one of the men was a powerful angakok. Many times he would speak to the spirits from the other worlds and always in a language none of the other men could understand. When anyone in the camp was ill, he treated them by driving out the evil spirits from their bodies, or he found out what taboo had been violated. He was a powerful man, more powerful than any white man I have seen. He understood magic. One night when all the people were gathered in my father's igloo, the angakok did strange things. Throughout the evening all the men danced to the sound of the drum, while I sat with the other children at the back of the sleeping platform and watched. The angakok danced and danced until he seemed to be no longer with us in our house. Suddenly he ran to the far end of the igloo and, with his fist, punched a small hole in the snow wall above the door. He ran back to the other side, turned, and ran quickly at the hole in the wall. He dived out through the wall, out through the small hole he had punched with his fist. We dashed outside through the door and there he was standing on the snow. I saw that and I have never forgotten." There was not the slightest doubt in Singeetuk's mind that the man actually did dive out through the small hole in the snow wall. The man was an angakok, quite capable of such things.

Living in the Pond Inlet area today there is an Eskimo who professes to be an angakok and many of the other Eskimos, including Idlouk, are a little afraid of him. This Eskimo is reputed to have murdered his father, shooting him with a .22 rifle as he lay asleep in a snow house not far from the campsite at Aulatseevik. He is reputed to have rendered another man's wife barren in response to a request of his own wife; to be able to commune with bears and have dominion over them when he meets them on the hunt. He is no longer able to exercise much control over the group through these supernatural powers but the Eskimos do not

* Chesterfield.

doubt that he has them, and they always try to keep on his good side, or to keep out of his way.

As time goes on these old beliefs will die out and be lost, to be replaced by new ones based on the teachings of the missionaries, Anglican and Roman Catholic. The little missions that form part of almost every northern settlement are playing a vital role in assisting the Eskimos to make the transition from a primitive to a modern existence. The part played by the individual missionary in conducting the work of the mission is often open to question, but of the importance of the work of the missions themselves there should be no doubt. From them the Eskimo should get his faith in his future. For "the missionary with understanding of the processes going on about him (will) find his opportunity to introduce religion and help create the constitution of a new cultural universe."*

SHORTLY after twelve noon, Idlouk brought the church service to a close. Everyone in our little house relaxed, cigarettes were rolled, and the kettle hung over the seal-oil lamp. Subdued conversation rose and fell, the same talk of the weather and the hunt that makes up so much of Eskimo conversation. One by one the Aulatseevikmiut rose and picked up their New Testaments and Books of Prayer. As they passed Idlouk on their way out, each shook his hand in exact imitation of the closing ritual practised by the missionary. I sat in the corner watching Idlouk as he played patriarch to his group.

Idlouk is unquestionably a leader among his group, not a chief or a boss, but a leader none the less. It has often been said that the Eskimo is a rugged individualist, perhaps the last remaining in the world today. He has no formal tribal society, no system of chiefs or medicine men. He can do very much as he pleases. His chief responsibilities are to his family alone; the family is the highest social unit.

In a loose sense this is true. The Eskimo is a rugged indi-

* *Human Problems in Technological Change*, a Case Book edited by Edward H. Spicer. Russell Sage, 1952.

vidualist. He comes and goes very much as he pleases, his movements governed more by the forces of nature than by any force of man. But often Eskimos do submit to nominal authority invested in one individual. Some Eskimo camps have leaders, usually an Eskimo who has shown himself to be extremely capable in the hunt and on the trap line, and whose camp is rarely without food. Other Eskimos come to depend on his judgement in hunting and trapping, simply because he is usually right. In return for the privilege of being a part of this man's camp, they surrender to him their right to come and go as they please on certain types of hunting trips. When these hunts take place, all hunters at the camp follow the directions of the leader. They can disagree with the leader; they are not forced to do as he says, but if the disagreement reaches the point where the hunter goes his own way and completely disregards the wishes of the leader, then the hunter will be asked to pack his gear and find another place to stay.

I have been unable to find any pattern in the development of such people. The leadership is never handed down from father to son. Indeed it seems to be the rare case when a son of a leader is himself responsible enough to assume such a role on attaining manhood. In my experience the reverse seems to be true; that the sons of a leader are held down so much by their father that they often develop into mediocre hunters and trappers and, in a few instances, into the ne'er-do-wells of the group. Sometimes a leader starts out by holding control over his sons as they grow to manhood. He will form a camp composed entirely of members of his own family, over whom he retains the control a father always has over his children. As time progresses, other Eskimos may drift into this orbit and become part of the camp, attracted by the prosperity of the families living there. Often they will not like submitting a portion of their freedom to the control of the leader, and in time move on to form a loose alliance with another group of Eskimos who are not as well fed or clothed, but who have a greater measure of

257

individual freedom to come and go as they please at all times of the year.

On north Baffin Island Idlouk is the outstanding example of such a leader. In a country where few men, Eskimo or white, have achieved economic success, Idlouk has achieved a degree of prosperity unmatched in his area. His success as a hunter and trapper is matched by no other Eskimo; his camp is never without food, his income is usually double or triple that of his nearest rival. Just why Idlouk is this way I am not quite sure. White people who knew him when he was a young man say that he displayed no great qualities as a hunter and trapper. But it is interesting to note that when Idlouk was a young man his father went to work for the missionary at Pond Inlet, leaving Idlouk and his brother to get along on their own. Shortly after this, Idlouk's brother died, as I have related earlier, leaving Idlouk alone with his family. Completely removed from all the authority that usually binds the development of the Eskimo boy and young man, Idlouk was free to develop his own personality, free to become a self-reliant and driving personality. His own intelligence did the rest. In our world we would call him a self-made man.

Unfortunately Idlouk's success and prosperity have done little to improve his relationships with his own people or with many of the whites with whom he comes in contact. His material success has only served to endanger his standing within his group of people and has given no promise of anything better to come. The other Eskimos look askance at his worldly wealth. "Why should you have so many foxes and so much money when we have so little?" they ask. "You are more like a white man than an Eskimo." Many of the whites coming into the area also look askance at this Eskimo with his proud, domineering manner. Here is not the submissive savage gratefully accepting the bounty of the white master; here is a man capable of meeting all who come his way on terms of equality—socially, economically, culturally.

Within every group of Eskimos whom I have known,

there have been Idlouks, intelligent and enterprising, ready to soak up the great wealth of knowledge and experience brought by the contact with twentieth century civilization, ready and eager to adapt to the changing conditions in their land. Economically they have had little trouble achieving a fair degree of prosperity, but economic security alone has failed to better their lot.

Idlouk's problem is not an unusual one, nor it is peculiar to the Arctic lands. It symbolizes one of the basic problems faced by all members of minority groups everywhere as they search for a new way of life in the face of violent change in old patterns of living. Such groups need assistance, provided by people with an understanding of the processes that are going on about them. In Canada we have been both fortunate and unfortunate in our dealings with the Eskimos. We have been fortunate in having a small number of understanding persons who have done much to ease the shocks of transition. I know some of these people personally; others I know only by reputation and I have the highest regard for their capabilities. They are to be found in the ranks of all organizations, government and otherwise, working in the Canadian Eastern Arctic. We have been unfortunate in that we have had, and still have, so many people working with the Eskimos in the Eastern Arctic, well-meaning and well-intentioned, but uninformed as to the processes that are going on about them. These people cannot interpret what they see, hear and feel except in terms of their own western culture and all too often this works to the detriment of the Eskimos. They fail to realize that our contact with the Eskimo has largely destroyed his old concepts of life, his culture. For many Eskimo groups, life has lost much of its meaning, for the meaning was closely tied in with a system of beliefs which we have held to be largely untenable. This has been inevitable. I know of no way in which many of the old beliefs of the Eskimo can exist alongside the new ones he must inevitably pick up from the white. But we must be sure we recognize that if we destroy old beliefs we must do all we can to replace them with new ones, ideas the Eskimo can grasp and either weave into the framework of his quasi-primitive existence or build on top of it.

Take, for example, the question of hunting. Before going North, I had never been able to take up hunting as a sport. All too quickly I became bored with it. But hunting as a way of life was a different matter. Day after day, I hunted for my daily bread and never was I bored. The quarry was inevitably the same, the seal, but the procedure for getting into position for the shot varied from day to day, from season to season, and from seal to seal.

To the Eskimo hunting is something more than just providing the daily bread. It gives reason and meaning to his existence. How often I have seen Idlouk returning to the camp sitting atop a load of newly killed seals, head cocked jauntily to one side, faded blue beret on the back of his head, singing the ancient songs of his land. He was *inook, angoteealook,* a human being, a big man. Into his hunting he poured all the energy and emotion that a painter sets on his canvas, a musician brings from his instrument, a writer from his pen. He was an artist, as fine a craftsman as his land could produce, and he was happy in this knowledge.

We must remember this when we remove the Eskimo from his life as a hunter. It is relatively easy for an Eskimo to change his trade, to become a carpenter, a truck driver, an electrician, for his new vocation will soon give him the same emotional response that he formerly got from the hunt. He will look with nostalgia to the hunt and the way of life it implies, but he will get over this in time, as long as he can see himself progressing in his new way of life, and as long as we allow for certain differences in his emotional make-up. If an Eskimo feels like working, he works, and his energy is prodigious. If he does not feel like working he does not work, and no amount of forcing will make him do it well. It will be a generation or two before Eskimos become completely adapted to the idea of a full work day and a five-day week. The Eskimo does not work for riches, for personal gain, for possessions; he works to be happy, a happiness that comes from a feeling of satisfaction in being a human being, and a big man; not big as a boss, not big in wealth, but big as a fearless animal.

MOST OF my errors of judgement in my dealings with the Eskimos have been small, or at least I hope they have been, and some have had their comic side.

During 1950 while I was working in the Chesterfield area, I was appalled at the poor state of many Eskimos' teeth. Eating soft foods such as bannock, using sugar in tea, never cleaning the teeth, all had contributed to produce excessive decay. As it has been my policy never to put undue pressure on any Eskimos to do anything, no matter how beneficial I may think it may be for them, I did little but try to explain to them why their teeth were as bad as they were.

However at Idlouk's camp in the spring of 1951 I dropped hints now and again suggesting that, although most of his group had good teeth, it would be much better if they cleaned them as often as they could in order to prevent possible decay brought on by the introduction of the new foods into the diet. I was careful that whenever I cleaned my teeth, which I did almost every morning, Eskimos at the camp should see me do this.

After a few weeks I noticed that Idlouk's children were cleaning their teeth, not regularly, but they were all doing it, even little Noahkudluk who liked the taste of the toothpaste so much that he ate the greater part of a tube one day when no one was looking. I was pleased with this cleaning of teeth, for it proved a point: that it was not hard to make Eskimos understand these things if you went about it in a sensible way. As the days went by the habit of cleaning teeth spread to others in the camp, although old Akomalik and Agnowyah, Idlouk's parents, refused to have anything to do with this white man's fad.

About a month later I was sitting in Idlouk's house when Padluk, Kadluk's son, came in. He said, "I would like the toothbrush." Kidlak reached over to the shelf, took down a rather battered toothbrush, and handed it to Padluk who then scuttled out of the door. A horrible thought struck me. Turning to Idlouk, I asked, "Why does Padluk want the toothbrush? Hasn't he one of his own?"

"No," said Idlouk, "there is only one toothbrush in the camp and so we all have to take turns using it. This makes it wear out quickly, but there are many more in the store. I will get another one when I go in to the settlement next time."

To that I did not know what to say.

On another occasion in 1951, Idlouk, Kadluk and I were sitting in front of the tent talking over the day's hunt. Kidlak offered us each a cup of tea and a piece of bannock and then asked if we would like butter on the bannock. Idlouk and Kadluk both said yes, but I said no, I would rather have mine without butter. Normally I like butter on bannock, but just then I felt I would rather have it without. Kidlak brought out a tin and buttered two pieces of bannock. I noticed it was margarine she was using and not butter; the Hudson's Bay Company post at Pond Inlet had imported a small stock of tinned margarine to see if the Eskimos would like it as it was much cheaper than butter. I thought no more of this incident.

The next time I visited the settlement with Idlouk to trade at the store, he ordered two tins of butter and none of margarine. The trader asked him why he did not order margarine, and he said his wife did not like it as well. Again I thought no more of this. But one day in the early fall of 1953 we were all gathered in the house having a cup of tea. All the Eskimos at Pond had been given some margarine by the Royal Canadian Mounted Police and Kidlak was spreading pieces of bannock with margarine. When she came to my piece she passed it over dry. I refused it and asked her if I could have margarine on it like the others. She looked very surprised and did as I asked.

Idlouk, who had been watching what happened, turned to me and said, "You remember in 1951 when you were here, and Kadluk, you and I were sitting in front of the tent and you said you did not want butter on your bannock, and the butter was really margarine? Well, since that time, my wife has refused to eat margarine and has not let me buy any in the store although it is much cheaper than butter. She thought you refused the margarine because it was not fit for the white men to eat, good only for Eskimos. Until we got this margarine from the police, free, we have had no margarine in my camp. I tried to tell her that perhaps you just didn't like margarine, but she would not listen. Now I hope she understands and will let me buy margarine again."

One episode my wife and I started is still not over and I do not know what the end will be. It has to do with water, a very vital element in any community, in any part of Canada. In 1951, my wife and I had as part of our camp equipment a large galvanized wash tub and a copper wash boiler. The boiler was used to melt ice over the camp stove and the tub was used for the family washing and baths. When we came south on the boat in the summer, we gave both these items to Idlouk along with a good deal of our gear, as it would cost more than the original price to ship the goods outside.

When I returned to the camp in 1953, Kidlak still had the galvanized wash tub, but the copper boiler was nowhere to be seen. One day I asked Idlouk about it and he said that it was on the bottom of his big boat. A bad storm in the fall of 1952 had blown the boat ashore and punched a small hole in the bottom. The copper sheeting of the boiler had been used to repair the damage. He said his wife had not wanted to let him have it and she had cried when he said that he must, as there was nothing else with which to repair the big boat.

This loss of the copper boiler completely upset the balance of the two items—the wash tub and the boiler. For the wash tub was a fair size and required large amounts of water for washing clothes and bathing. Without the copper boiler in which to melt the ice necessary to produce this water, Kidlak had to use the much smaller pots that could be bought at the Hudson's Bay store. The store would quickly have ordered another copper boiler if Idlouk had asked, but this did not occur to him, such items not normally being a part of his life. Kidlak spent a great deal of her time shuffling ice and water back and forth between the various small pots trying to keep ahead of the insatiable demand for water, brought on largely by the continued use of the galvanized tub for washing clothes and taking baths. The washing of clothes was certainly a step in the right direction and the baths as well, but the house was not equipped to supply water for such chores on a large scale.

Our house was always running out of water. Our clothes were cleaner than anyone else's in the camp, and so were we, but at what a price! Kidlak had ice stacked everywhere melting it down. Often we had no water for tea after a big wash, and we would have to borrow water from the house next door. Once, after I had made such a trip to the house of Agnowyah, Idlouk's old mother, she looked at me and said in mock anger, "Out, out, all you come to my house for is to get water. What do you think I have in my house, a lake?"

When I left the camp in the spring of 1954, the wash tub was still eating up its weekly quota, and as long as it does Kidlak will never have a free moment in her life. I could send in another copper boiler to Idlouk, but I do not think this would provide an answer. Sooner or later the wash tub will start to leak seriously; the water shortage and drudging would start again. I can only hope that the remaining tub will either spring a bad leak or be lost and Kidlak can have some rest. Until she has a home in which she can produce the large quantities of water that are needed for washing clothes once a week and taking the weekly or bi-monthly bath, items like the wash tub and copper boiler will serve only to make her already hard life that much harder.

It is often difficult for people working with Eskimos to know beforehand the effect an action may have on an Eskimo group. At shiptime, 1953, Pete Murdock gave Idlouk a number of baby sealskins he had bought from the Eskimos of the area and asked Idlouk to have the women at the camp make the sealskins into rugs and slippers that could be sold in the Hudson's Bay Company stores in southern Canada. Each person would make the rugs and slippers to certain standard sizes, but they would use their own initiative as to shape and inset design work. Idlouk took the skins back to the camp, distributed them among the women and the older girls, and all during the early fall they utilized every leisure moment cutting and sewing rugs and slippers.

After freeze-up the completed articles were taken to Pond Inlet where Pete Murdock pronounced himself well satisfied and bought the lot. Each article was marked with the name of the girl or woman who had made it and also the number of skins used in the manufacture. Each of the women received a credit slip at the store for her work. They had all given Idlouk lists of things they wanted with the money they earned and these goods were purchased and brought back to the camp for them.

The women were overjoyed with the results of their efforts, for the payments had been substantial. It may not have been the first time they had money of their own, but it was the first time so many had had so much and all at the same time. But what of the men? For the first time in Idlouk's life he was placed in the position of not being the provider for his family. During the fall there had been no way for him to earn money and the trap line, started November 1st, had not yet yielded any return. His wife and daughters had been able to buy goods from the store while he, the hunter and provider, had been unable to buy anything, for he had no money.

It was a humiliating situation. For a few days the men were quite unhappy, and a little unsettled. They laughed about the incident and the women joked with them, but the humour of the men was wistful. Something had happened in the life of this small group of people that upset the traditional relationships between husband and wife, between father and daughter. Small wonder the men were unhappy; something was gone from their life.

If I seem to lay too much stress on such episodes and the effects they produce, I would ask you to remember that I have travelled extensively in the Canadian Eastern Arctic and all too often I have seen such incidents, and others with worse implications. Perhaps I should tell you of the time I saw Eskimos standing outside the door of a house while they called their Family Allowance requirements through the partially opened door to an interpreter inside who translated for the white man at the typewriter; or of the wife of a resident of an Arctic settlement who refused to let any Eskimo set foot in her house and would not let her children play with Eskimo children; or of the white man who, on his spring trips to the neighbouring settlements, had sugar and milk in his tea and who ate pre-cooked food while his Eskimo guide ate frozen seal meat and drank his tea black, and was not allowed to smoke in the snow house at night.

A better way to create a group of second-class citizens in Canada, I do not know.

This is a difficult and critical time for all Eskimos in Canada. Old beliefs are dead or dying while new ones are being formed slowly or not at all. Ambitions and energies are being blunted on the walls of indifference and misunderstanding, often thrown up by the people who are in the best position to help.

The Canadian Eskimo needs assistance from missionaries, scientists, administrators, educators, doctors, welfare workers, traders, policemen; all have a significant role to play in helping the Eskimos develop a new future, a future in which life has meaning and zest as well as economic security. Too often we are concerned with physical and spiritual well-being as separate things and ignore intellectual well-being altogether. None of these elements can be ignored if the Eskimo in Canada is to take his place in the mainstream of Canadian culture, to find his place in our changing world.

He has a place in that world. More and more attention is being focused on our Arctic regions, one of the last great frontier areas of the world. By and large, we have shown ourselves to be woefully incapable of living in the country and liking it but, to the Eskimo, this land is home. He understands it. He is our only true citizen in the Arctic regions. As a Canadian citizen the Eskimo helps immeasurably to maintain our sovereignity over this tremendous land mass to the north.

To those who have never been "down north", the Arctic is a frozen land of ice and snow, peopled by a primitive race, eking out a miserable existence in a land devoid of comfort and beauty. To those who have lived in the country, the Arctic is a land of many faces. I have known times when, caught on the trail by a blinding blizzard, I have wished to be anywhere but where I was. Then I have cursed the Arctic with its storms and snow, with its freezing cold and howling winds. But an hour later, settled comfortably inside almost sound-proof circular walls of snow, with a cup of hot tea and a piece of frozen fish already beginning to warm my cold and tired body, I have felt peaceful and relaxed, with a tranquility that comes only after prolonged hardship and struggle. Beside me, my Eskimo companion was already dozing over his steaming mug of tea. Slowly his eyes closed and his head nodded forward. A slight smile spread over his face. The storm and hardships were forgotten, and I knew what he was thinking.

He was thinking of this land and of his family. He was thinking of that day each year when, for the first time in three months, the sun peers over the southern horizon, announcing its triumphal return to a darkened land; and of the joyful warmth of the long spring days, when the geese wing high, and the seals bask on the ice in the hot sun. He was thinking of the day when he harpooned six whales and he knew that his family had food for a long time to come; of the day his first son was born and of how proud he had been.

His happiness and hardships are much the same as yours and mine. He has his share of both, just as we do. If he lives in a harsh land, he has the benefit of few complexities in life; no bills, no traffic problems, no land to buy or home to rent. He knows no wars, and he has no fear of death, for he lives with death at his elbow.

In the future development of the Canadian Eastern Arctic the Eskimo has a place, an important place. Who can say yet just what it will be? We do not know enough about him yet, what are his capabilities and his limitations. We must guide him forward to the day when he will be a full contributing member in the community of Canada. The Eskimos are proud, intelligent people. Canada is made up of a great diversity of proud, intelligent people. From this we gain our strength.

INDEX

269

Books in the Clarke Irwin Canadian Paperback series: